# MAKING A
# *Difference*

STREAMLINING PATIENT CARE AND
LIBERATING RESOURCES

ROSE HEATHCOTE

Published in 2016 by Heathcote & Associates
© 2016 Rose Heathcote

First published 2016
ISBN: 978-0-620-72895-9
Editor: Amalia Christoforou
Proofreader: Sean Heathcote
Book Design by: Samantha Rowles
Cover Design by: Samantha Rowles
Typesetting and Layout by: Samantha Rowles
Images sourced from: Adobe Stock, Dreamstime, Shutterstock and photographs taken by the author

**Acknowledgments**
The Publisher and Author would like to acknowledge and thank the Gauteng Department of Health for permission to use the photographs included.

Heathcote & Associates
Postnet Suite 749
Private Bag X153
Bryanston
Republic of South Africa
2021

# CONTENTS

# DETAILED CONTENTS

## PART I: CLEAR DIRECTION

## CHAPTER 4: DELIVERING COST-BENEFITS     78

## CHAPTER 5: LEADING THE CHANGE     89

# PART II: EXECUTION

## CHAPTER 9: THE DIFFERENCE     207

# PART III: EXAMPLES AND TEMPLATES

# FOREWORD

We need to ask our leaders in public healthcare, 'What will public healthcare provision be like in fifty years? In twenty? In five? In one? What is your vision, over what time horizon?' We, the people of this land, cannot have more of the same. We cannot continue with what has brought us here. We cannot repeatedly blame 'lack of' (be it budget, skills, resources...) for where we are. *Making a difference* to the future must start now. The journey, for that is what it is, must start from where we are and with what we have at our disposal.

It is often said that all improvement requires change, but that not all change brings with it improvement. Just so with '*making a difference.*' I need not point out the many political leaders who have '*made a difference*' and in doing so made the lives of millions miserable. It is likely that in at least some such cases, the leaders' intentions were indeed for the good of the many. But alas, intentions are not enough.

Rose Heathcote, in writing '*Making a Difference*', is providing us with a carefully considered and structured proposal for making a positive difference, for the specific benefit of those in healthcare, be they patients, staff or funders. We are well advised to take her proposal seriously. The insights to which she directs us have been hard won. There have been successes and less-than-successes in attempts to improve conditions, in healthcare and the many other industries in which Rose has worked over two decades. Her proposal draws on tested approaches arising from those twenty years of experience.

I have been an observer and sometime collaborator with Rose for some fifteen of those years. As I reflected in preparation for writing this foreword, I made a spontaneous list of the attributes I find so admirable in Rose Heathcote:

- o Brave
- o Professional
- o Personable
- o Perceptive
- o Persevering
- o Generous
- o Encouraging

I need to add one more now as I conclude the final edit of the foreword: Hard-working. This particular book is the product of hard work and a brave experiment. Rose Heathcote was among the lead researchers conducting the experiment. No laboratory mice were involved, only real people. The laboratories were actual public hospitals, four to be exact. Those hospitals swarmed with people: patients, nurses, porters, clerks, paramedics, doctors and of course managers. Not everyone knew an experiment was underway, but a core team was, and Rose was a key member. Each hospital conducted three specific experiments. Each experiment sought to understand the causes of slow and erratic service. And to find countermeasures for at least some of them.

From that experiment and her other experience, she sets out in this book her accumulated wisdom for when she works with those of us who want to *make a difference*. She knows that our good intentions are not enough. She is consequently making available to us a pathway she has found necessary, and effective, in reducing the risk of unintended negative effects from our improvement efforts.

If anything, she has been too exacting and precise in her advice. But that is necessary. Each of us in trying to *make a difference* will have our own unique set of circumstances with which to contend. Rose will not be there to sift through those circumstances and offer customised wisdom. And hence the diligence reflected in the detail of her book.

The content of the book is considered and intentional, by topic and the sequencing of topics: The North Star (be very deliberate and clear about your purpose); A Vision for Best Practice (an appeal for a broad perspective, and perseverance); The Lean Value Stream (we must respect the 'as is' or current condition of what we are trying to improve); Delivering Cost Benefits (there can be no shying away from this challenging issue for healthcare professionals); and Leading the Change (consider carefully - the Achilles heel of many an improvement initiative lies here).

With those initial chapters she helps us set the 'clear direction' for our efforts. Then she sets out the principles for effective execution. How important it is that we get beyond planning and strategizing! (Execution: such a strong expression; it has power over mere 'implementation.') She coaches us for getting rapid improvement, and the systems needed to sustain those gains, and for establishing improvement as part of everyday work.

In the final section of the book, Rose pours her treasure-chest of templates into our laps. These templates are tried and tested. She gives them to us as a rich starter-kit to our efforts, whether we are newcomers or veterans to the ambition of '*making a difference*' in public healthcare provision.

The hospital experiment Rose was involved in had its own precursor experiments, locally and world-wide. The application of operations management principles to healthcare is by no means new. The experimental application of a subset of operations technology, lean thinking, to healthcare began in Australia, the UK, the USA and elsewhere in the developed world during the 1990's, and in South Africa in the early 2000's. Lean thinking has many tools at its disposal. Yet Rose will affirm to you that, effective as the tools might be, it is crucially important to grasp that the tools are arranged in a particular toolbox, a philosophy. These are the elements of the philosophy: respect for people, thoughtfulness, humble enquiry, and clear direction. The term 'psychological safety' applied to the people in a lean system captures much of what the lean philosophy must achieve.

In practice, our commitment to the philosophy is tested when we make mistakes. Our mistakes will test our grasp and practice of respect for people, thoughtfulness, humble enquiry, and clarity of purpose. So, the test is in our making mistakes. Or, perhaps even more challenging, when others in the experiment make mistakes.

Rose will acknowledge that she will continue to make mistakes (as I will), and so will you, the reader. It is in the nature of experiments: we cannot guarantee the desired outcome. Experiments are about learning. The only failed experiment is the experiment from which we fail to learn. Our hospitals and clinics are our laboratories. They are where we experiment. When our best efforts 'fail' we need to extract the valuable lessons and move forward with renewed insight. The bridge between failure and progress is respect for the thoughtful (and sometimes stumbling) participation of those who are involved in the experiments. Ultimately, lean thinking involves a management system that constantly (hourly, daily, weekly...) tracks 'normal from abnormal' and equips and empowers the front-line caregivers and their managers to learn to make a positive difference, to move closer and closer to 'right first time, every time.' Is that a vision, a challenge, for the next twenty or fifty years? If so, read on.

**Norman Faull**
Chairman: Lean Institute Africa
September 2016

# ABOUT THE AUTHOR

Improvement specialist, author and advisor Rose Heathcote has, over the last 20-years, raised the performance of enterprises in varied industries throughout Africa, the Middle East, Indian subcontinent and the United Kingdom. More than one hundred organisations—from micro enterprises to large multinationals—have benefited from Rose's passion and expertise in strategy, execution methodologies and learning of Operational Excellence.

A proud South African, Rose's philosophy on improvement centres around 'keeping it simple'. She understands the complexity of problems faced by organisations and the need for tailor-made, streamlined, targeted solutions applicable particularly to the most challenging scenarios.

Rose has spent years testing a multitude of philosophies, methodologies, tools and techniques in a variety of environments. Her coalface research has resulted in a consolidated and proven approach that is particularly effective in uplifting enterprises in emerging, developing economies—such as those typical of the African continent.

Rose is the founder of *Thinking People South Africa*, a consultancy that specialises in delivering an integrated approach to Operational Excellence. With a background in Industrial Engineering and Business Management, Rose continues to research new ways of achieving excellence through first principles.

Rose adores her supportive husband and their beautiful daughter.

# WHO SHOULD READ THIS BOOK

This book will benefit anyone aiming to understand or execute structured change in the public sector. However, those who will derive the greatest gains from and have primarily motivated the writing of *Making a Difference* are:

o Leaders and Department Heads in the Public Health Sector
o Physicians, Medical Practitioners, Nursing Professionals and other Supporting Staff
o Business Improvement Specialists, Change Agents and Consultants
o Students from Health Science, Engineering and Business Management disciplines.

# ACKNOWLEDGMENTS

Four public healthcare facilities—Chris Hani Baragwanath Academic, Leratong, Sebokeng and Kopanong Hospitals—took part in the first Cohort's Service Delivery Improvement Initiative using Lean Management. Leaps in performance were seen across the board and praise for this progress falls squarely at the feet of dedicated members of staff, each of whom set out to learn about and apply Lean Management principles to their area of influence. Their hard work and dogged determination resulted in dynamic gains in performance. The Lean Institute Africa (LIA) facilitators remain grateful for their trust in our process, that led them from overwhelming challenge and opportunity, through uncertain territory and on to a new baseline of knowledge and performance.

**Gauteng Department of Health**: Ms. Q. Mahlangu (MEC Health); Ms R. Chigwedere (Lean Programme Manager); Mr E. Mathipa (Lean Apprentice); Ms M. Khutoane (Lean Apprentice)

**Chris Hani Baragwanath Academic Hospital**: Dr S. Mfenyana (CEO:2015); Dr K. Mustafa; Ms D. Ngidi; Mr S. Dikgang; Mr T. Mkhwanazi

**Leratong Hospital**: Mr G. Dube (CEO); Dr R. Phanzu; Mr G. Molefe; Ms N. Serunye; Ms F. Lahri

**Sebokeng Hospital**: Dr Z. Ngcwabe (CEO); Dr S. Lunda; Ms N. Mapunja; Ms M. Radebe; Ms T. Sejake

**Kopanong Hospital**: Dr M. Kgomojoo (Acting CEO); Ms G. Nkutha; Ms I. Ramsden; Ms R. Mohlapo

**Lean Institute Africa**: Prof. N. Faull (Learning Collaborator); Ms R. Heathcote (Master Facilitator); Mr T. Thobejane (Co-Facilitator)

**Provincial Support Staff**: Ms D. Mothopeng; Ms N. Bomela

# AUTHOR'S NOTE

## BEGIN YOUR JOURNEY AS AN OUT-PATIENT...

My journey as a public health patient is a complex and fascinating one. On better days I arrive in my own transport, and navigate the parking lot maze. But, most often, I am at the mercy of a heavily burdened public transport system. Either way, I wake up around 03h00 or 04h00 to arrive at the hospital as early as possible. With some luck, by 06h00 I have secured my position in the queue to registration.

I commence my wait. The line edges forward, slowly. At first I stand and later slide from chair to chair as I get closer to the first counter of many to come. It is unsettling to think that the long wait extends the amount of time for which I am exposed to infections harboured by sick patients all around me. Of course, none of us feel particularly well. A queue marshal directs patients until finally it is my turn to approach the counter and state my business. On days when I have been fortunate enough to get my file from the filing clerk and bring the right documentation along, my registration for the day's visit is relatively smooth and unhindered. Still, the glass barrier separating me from the clerk leads to a strained conversation. I lip-read much of the time and the clerk pre-empts much of what I try to say. Once my registration is complete and assuming I am a paying patient, I proceed to the payment counter where one's knowledge of the system and financial stability determine how quickly matters are finalised. With the administration complete I prepare myself for the next part of the journey and make my way to the clinic to which I am directed.

Once there, I see the faces of people who were with me in the registration queue. Strangers, we recognise in each other's faces the shadow of quiet resignation to the interminable wait ahead of us. I present myself and my file to the reception desk and then, again, find my place in line and begin polishing more seats as I shift slowly forward. It is after 08h00. I have been awake almost five hours. The waiting area is filling up quickly and the nurses move between the crowds of waiting patients, going about their business. No sign of any doctors yet. They are either still on their way in or performing ward rounds. The nurses call us up one-by-one to a consultation room where we get our vitals checked. It's now closer to 09h00. My file is updated and I am moved back to the line, to await my doctor's arrival. I read every pamphlet and information notice I see and make small talk with other patients—mostly about how long we wait for. If only I had brought something to read.

I am not aware of the fact that at an academic hospital, the principle of 'Continuity of Care' means I wait for the particular doctor who treated me in the ward as an in-patient—he will see me again today. But, the doctor does not arrive until after midday. Finally my doctor comes, grabs an armful of files and starts the consultation process. Patiently I wait my turn for two more hours. I walk into the consultation room just after 14h00 and spend 25 minutes with my doctor who, I hope, will be satisfied with my progress and prescribes my routine medicine and care. Stepping out, I pass patients still queuing and make a beeline to the reception where I make an appointment for my next visit. By now this queue has diminished somewhat, so finishing relatively quickly, I make my way to the pharmacy.

Chaos! It is peak hour and those sent from a host of clinics join walk-in patients in the waiting area. People push through the queues to get prescriptions filled. I sit down again. I check my watch. It's now 14h45 and I am thirsty, hungry and still feeling unwell, but dare not lose my place. A queue marshal takes my file, hands it to the pharmacy staff and I wait to be called up. At 15h50 I am called to the counter but feel too tired and frustrated to take in much of what the pharmacist is explaining. The glass barrier muffles the words stitched together messily by a distant mouth about how to store and take my medication. I am relieved to escape the mania. I wonder if the prescription has been correctly filled, but decide to worry about that later. I struggle past the crowd and find my way back to my transport. I join queues that lead me to a public taxi and by 17h20 I am heading home in a minivan, with 10 other people. There are elderly people and sick children travelling home from the hospital with me. We are utterly spent. Every visit is the same as the last. The next will be no different.

## Little is straightforward in public healthcare…

In the private health sector, activities are driven by profit and investment triggers growth to meet the changing needs of the market. Public healthcare is fundamentally a very different animal with its own unique challenges and victories. It requires a respectful, empathetic approach when it comes to change.

When meeting someone who works in public healthcare for the first time, you hear of the lack of resources, inadequate infrastructure and patient numbers that far outweigh the available capacity. When provoking a conversation about improvement, what returns is a palpable sense of complacency and a justification that unless the 'big things' are fixed, smaller changes are unlikely to make any difference. This seeming fixation with obstacles perceived to be outside of employee control has led to a staggering loss of morale and in some cases the wilful avoidance of activities linked to improvement. It is perhaps ironic that such escapism from change—for the better—exists in parallel to such overwhelming need for change.

## Is there hope?

o What if the patient experience could be different?
o What if there could be a different way of operating?
o What if improvement was a possibility even in the absence of 'big changes'?
o What if we could get past the defeatist attitude and consider that which is within our power to change?
o What if we could make the best possible use of the resources we have and utilise them more effectively?
o What could we do right now to improve the way we service our patients and make everything easier for ourselves in the process?

Do you need evidence that change is indeed possible? Try a simple experiment. Set aside 30 minutes to stand in one place and simply observe the work being performed in a public healthcare facility.

This is a technique Taiichi Ohno—also known as the father of the Toyota Production System—insisted be practiced, to help actualise the work being done and to better understand the issues at hand. Watch and document the flow of work being performed in the service of a patient. Each time you see inactivity or see someone searching for something that is not easily accessible, detect a delay or see a problem, take note of it and ask questions about **why** there is an obstacle to the flow. You will be astounded at how much avoidable waste creeps into our daily work, soaking up capacity and burning through time and energy. You will be surprised by how much we deviate from the standards ostensibly enforced, while we cope with everyday crises. Every small inefficiency adds up. Soon the system is overwhelmed.

Yet, the beauty in this chaos is that a single question changes it all: 'Why?'.

Every time a doctor has to stop a consultation to do something that could be done by the nurse, every time a clerk has to get up and move somewhere else to fetch stationery, every time a pharmacist has to stop their work to fix an error in a prescription the picker prepared, ask 'Why?'.

Once you learn to see the waste and interrogate the reality of inefficiencies around you, you will learn to banish these from operations and liberate resources.

You get the idea.

## You have to be brave!

I have seen young physicians begin their work in state healthcare facilities with absolute passion for the job and a vengeance for rooting out inefficiency. They raise every problem they encounter and offer practical solutions. They truly wish to make a difference. But, over time, even the most enthusiastic take strain when their every request is met with a counterargument reiterating that change is impossible due to a lack of budget or other obstacles. They throw their arms in the air in frustration and, exasperated, navigate the systems as they are. These staff are worn down and eventually become institutionalized, joining the ranks of all who have given up and accepted conditions they believe cannot be changed. I do not blame them for feeling this way.

Some medical professionals and support staff burn out. Others leave public healthcare for private employ. Yet, bravery is the key ingredient in the journey of change. When leaders have enough courage, determination and willingness to challenge the Current Condition, staff can be mobilized to undertake the incremental changes needed to collectively initiate a bigger breakthrough.

No one promises that change will be simple. Dynamic and lasting gains must take root and so are not acquired overnight. But, take heart. Choose to be brave. You too can *make a difference.*

# Are there any benefits to being brave?

I am always encouraged by brilliant results—and the case studies illustrated in this book prove there are many tangible benefits within your grasp. Measureable improvements are a credible indicator of progress towards the Vision for Change, but I am elated when I hear real comments coming from the real people who gave us their trust and time:

*'It is not always necessary to spend more in order to improve service delivery. I learned how to identify 'waste' that needs to be eliminated to improve flow. This training improved my confidence in how to plan for further reductions in waiting times.'*

*'The most useful part of this training was being physically involved and pooling ideas with other team mates.'*

*'We seldom have time to step back to look and see, analyse what we see, think critically, and identify waste.'*

*'The training helped me see and understand that waiting times can be reduced if the waste is being eliminated.'*

*'The most useful part of this training was to learn to see abnormal from normal, and to understand the value of time to the patients.'*

*'Each employee should understand that working smart is key. Knowing that every minute counts and that any time wasted has an impact on other departments.'*

*'The power of observation, limiting waste and trying again and again until you reach your desired outcome without quitting. We can apply the principles in any project.'*

*'This programme will improve service delivery if sustained.'*

Push through. Learn from every obstacle. Reap these benefits:
- o Patients see the difference, paying more compliments and reporting less complaints
- o Staff are engaged, involved, inspired and committed
- o Waiting times are slashed by up to 86%
- o Improvement gains fuel better cost-control.

# OVERVIEW OF OPERATIONAL EXCELLENCE

## A Strategy to Raise Performance

In public healthcare the LIA facilitators have experimented with Lean Thinking techniques, which have proven extremely effective in developing the thinking patterns that drive sustainable change. There are several philosophies available to advance improvements in organisations such as Six Sigma, Lean Thinking, Theory of Constraints, Agile and Best Practice, and each has its merits depending on the level and type of problem you are trying to solve. Public healthcare is plagued by problems, but many of them are solvable at the front line, and can be considered 'low hanging fruit'. This is the perfect climate for the tools and techniques Lean Thinking has to offer and in the context of Operational Excellence, which makes use of the right tool for the right job, the focus is on Lean Thinking for the work that is documented in this book.

Generically speaking, the concepts of Operational Excellence mean different things to different people. They could appear to be a runaway train of models, philosophies, principles, methods, tools, terms and acronyms. Industry experts place emphasis on different elements of the concept and there is really no one approach to what matters most in the way a problem is tackled. Interpretation and implementation vary and, of course, so too do results. It is therefore important to define Operational Excellence in a way that is unique to each environment to which it is applied, whilst preserving the fundamentals.

There is, however, an added challenge. You can only take your operations to new levels of performance by taking your people and your processes to territories that may be entirely unchartered and unfamiliar. People become the critical factor as real change will involve adjustments in the habits of those people who drive new processes needed. Without their support, their involvement and their true emotional connection and belief in the change at hand, they are likely to remain content and secure in the comfort zone of current or old ways—a frustrating reality for those people who are on-board and ready to set off into seas of change!

You are encouraged to view Operational Excellence as a management system that nurtures people's growth throughout the change effort. It is a system that respects five elements:

o PURPOSE
o PROCESS
o PEOPLE
o PROBLEM SOLVING
o PLANET

Together, these five elements drive the right balance of changes. Operational Excellence is also a system that creates what I like to call 'Thinking People'. Thinking People are capable of sustained on-the-job learning. They are people who continue innately to discover innovative ways to offer more value to the patient, long after a 'Lean' intervention is formally over.

In times of old, sailors were known to navigate by the Polaris Star or North Star. This bright star seen in the northern part of the sky almost exactly above the North Pole was of great reassurance to travellers that they were indeed heading in that direction. Creating a system of Operational Excellence begins with discovering your North Star by:

o Defining a clear understanding of why the organisation exists
o Pinpointing the areas where the organisation is currently prospering and excelling and where further development is needed
o Clarifying what true value means to a patient, a stakeholder and an employee.

Your North Star will provide much-needed direction to the improvement strategy and define the critical problems to which your organisation will allocate resources and time.

Progressing from that grand Vision for Change to something more practical, it is valuable to take a look at the previous year's goals and objectives to see exactly how well the organisation performed, and where it failed to meet expectations. Comprehensive diagnosis contrasts current performance to the potential for future performance or the ideals of the North Star, and clarifies the road map needed to achieve the improvement strategy.

The first element of Operational Excellence—PURPOSE, is then clear. Planning the practicalities of the strategy deployment effort will identify the goals that an organisation is striving to reach.

Once armed with clarity on the direction of change and a system with which to deploy this change, it is then possible to delve into the nuts and bolts. The PROCESS can then be better designed and managed to expose problems effectively and for the goals identified for Operational Excellence to become a reality.

Key to the strategy of Operational Excellence is absolute focus on activities that will achieve the desired outcomes. Only these are therefore assigned scarce resources. This in turn breeds a culture of continuous improvement in the areas that truly matter. Now you are ready to customise the changes needed in various key processes, in detail.

Having a plan and knowing which problems need attention is only the beginning. A critical cog in the machine is getting your PEOPLE, the third fundamental element in Operational Excellence, to understand their role in the process and helping them to achieve the improvement strategy. Change involves everyone—not only leaders and not only front-line staff. It requires creating an environment of teamwork, collaboration, problem-solving and learning, coupled with the strength of leadership skills to guide the right behaviour and to drive results. Changing the daily, weekly and monthly habits of all the people whose hard work keeps the ship of your organisation sailing high seas, will kindle a culture of continuous and sustainable improvement.

Experience shows that improvements soon decline if they are not actively sustained. This applies not only to the systems we put in place after a change event but also to how we worked through the improvement phases from the start. Each phase in the change is critical to ultimately determining whether or not the improvement will last. That is where

PROBLEM SOLVING Best Practices give us effective countermeasures to regression and structure outcomes needed to preserve effective changes.

A substantial part of the change effort involves banishing wasteful activities that do not bring value to the patient or organisation. An organisation that achieves this benefits from more efficient processes that meet patient needs, particularly through the buy-in and involvement of your people. This improvement directly influences how the organisation contributes to environmental sustainability and to the PLANET. So, the model is completed with a robust approach to delivering a cleaner, more responsible and environmentally friendly service.

Ultimately the five elements key to the 5P Model of Operational Excellence— PURPOSE, PROCESS, PEOPLE, PROBLEM SOLVING and PLANET—synchronise for sustainable change.

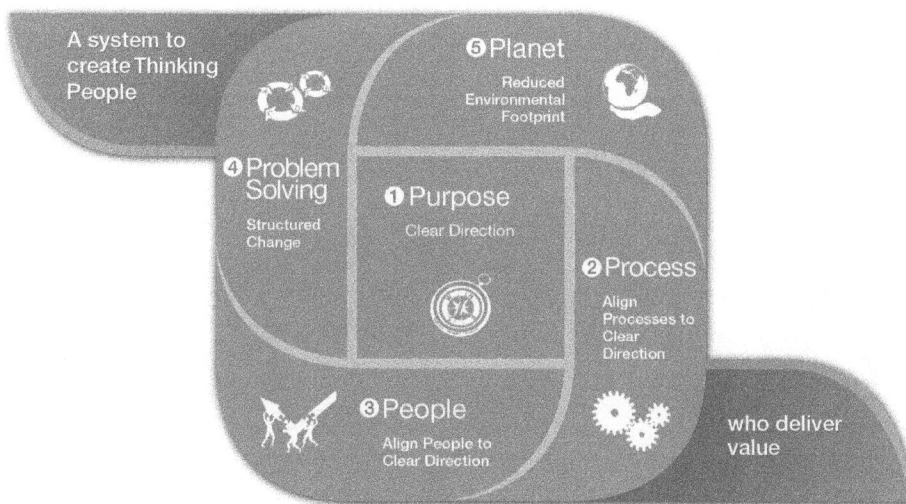

▲ The 5P Model represents the system that creates *Thinking People* who deliver value

In conclusion, developing each element of the 5P Model to support the level of organisational improvement required, will create a fit-for-purpose management system to create THINKING PEOPLE who deliver value.

*Making a Difference* captures the customised approach taken to solving the problems presented by the public healthcare facilities that took part in Cohort 1. This book explores those aspects of the 5P Model which proved most relevant to Cohort 1's learning, growth and improvement.

For more detail around the 5P Model refer to *Clear Direction* (Heathcote, 2014)

# HOW THIS BOOK GUIDES YOU

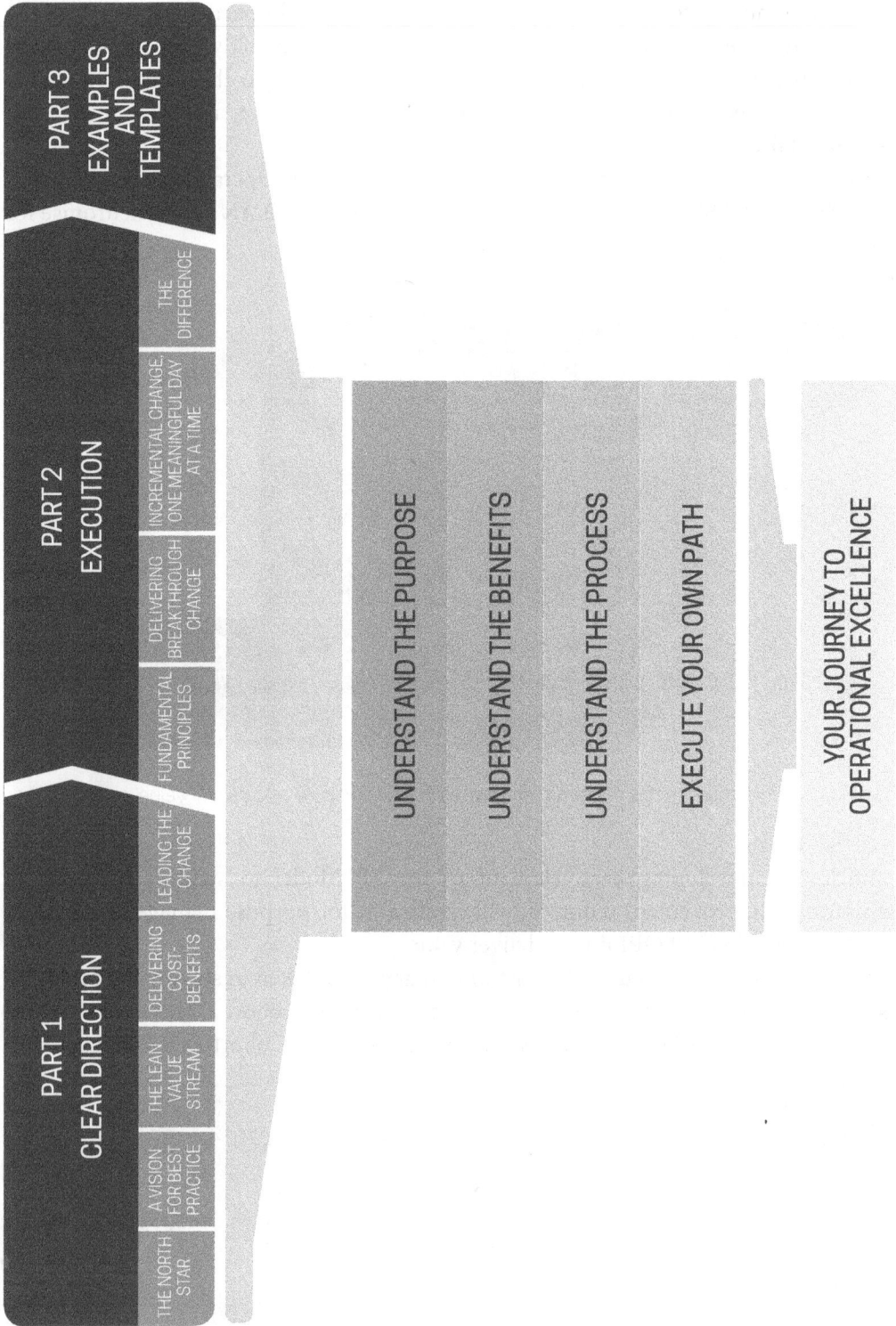

PART 3
EXAMPLES AND TEMPLATES

PART 2
EXECUTION

THE DIFFERENCE

INCREMENTAL CHANGE, ONE MEANINGFUL DAY AT A TIME

DELIVERING BREAKTHROUGH CHANGE

FUNDAMENTAL PRINCIPLES

LEADING THE CHANGE

PART 1
CLEAR DIRECTION

DELIVERING COST-BENEFITS

THE LEAN VALUE STREAM

A VISION FOR BEST PRACTICE

THE NORTH STAR

UNDERSTAND THE PURPOSE

UNDERSTAND THE BENEFITS

UNDERSTAND THE PROCESS

EXECUTE YOUR OWN PATH

YOUR JOURNEY TO OPERATIONAL EXCELLENCE

▲ **A Roman Cohort:** A cohort is a group of people banded together for a common cause. Chris Hani Baragwanath Academic, Leratong, Sebokeng and Kopanong Hospitals formed Cohort 1 in the GDOH Service Delivery Improvement Initiative.

*Act your way to a new way of thinking rather than think your way*
*to a new way of acting.*

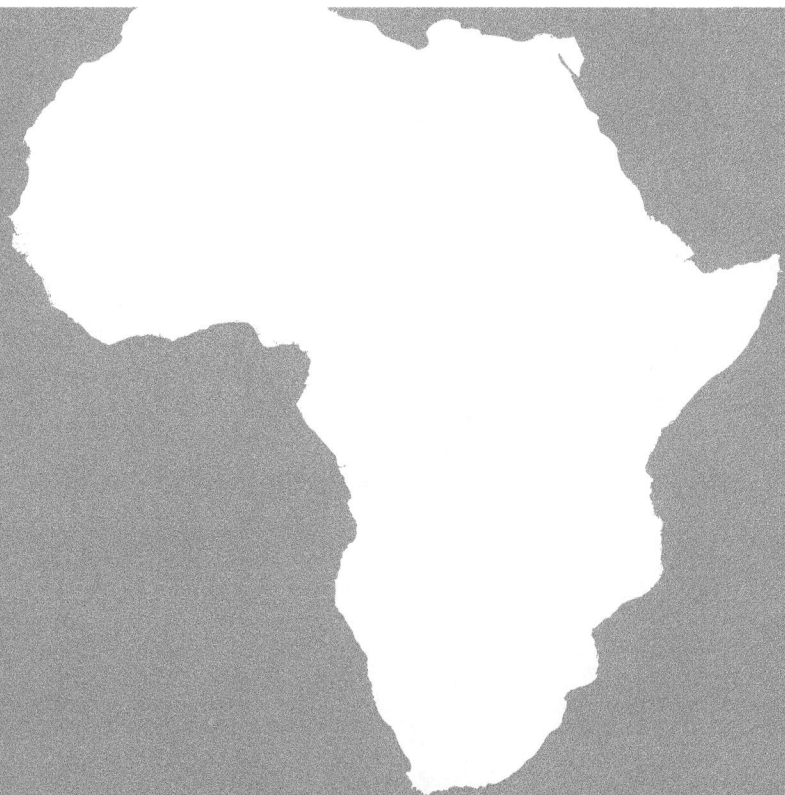

# PART I
## CLEAR DIRECTION

## Think about Purpose

It is indisputable that many public healthcare facilities, in emerging or developing economies, are plagued by a litany of everyday operational obstacles that result in sub-standard performance. But,

> Are all problems important?

are all problems important? Where do priorities start? Do you first address staff and get the right people doing the right things? Or, do you fix the layout of the route through which the patient journeys? Do you throw your energy into revising standards? Should you start with the booking-system and control the number of patients the facility sees? Should you focus on 'down-referrals' to lower level facilities first?

Launching improvement in the face of such a variety of obstacles, it is not always possible to see the wood for the trees. You want clarity of Purpose and Clear Direction with which to frame the problem-solving as, without this, you risk throwing time and effort into projects that are ostensibly commendable but which make no difference to patient care.

The challenge is to create a link between the strategic intent of the organisation, the indicators that disclose performance and problem-solving activities to ensure everyone is aligned and improving in the right direction—even in times of chaos.

---

**PRACTICAL ACTIVITY: Defining your Position**

Gather a team including senior management. Consider the following questions and discuss (Faull, 2014):

▸ What is the Purpose of your healthcare facility? What problem are you trying to solve?
▸ What are its economics? What drives cost, revenue and efficiency?
▸ What objectives does your healthcare facility aspire to?
▸ What is the vision for your facility three years from now?
▸ What is your Current Condition?
▸ How do you know how well you are performing?

The improvement strategy aims to drive action that compliments the Purpose. Through better definition of Purpose and the key activities that drive it, it becomes clearer which activities are value-adding and which do not contribute to Purpose.

---

# The Voice of the Hospital

The Voice of the Hospital (or 'Clinic'), represents the strategic intent of the organisation for future prosperity. It is the voice that defines the plan of action that will raise current performance towards specific goals. There is usually a three to five-year focus but this period can be longer.

The Voice of the Hospital seeks to understand the goals, objectives and any key initiatives already identified that will take the organisation forward. It also compares current performance to these objectives. This clear voice informs our focus and tells of the impact we are striving for through the improvement strategy. This voice is particularly helpful for the following reasons:

o We cannot define our problems until we know what constitutes them. By comparing our current performance to the goals and objectives we want to reach, the shortfalls become clearer and the improvement strategy takes on a strategic focus.
o The improvement strategy is closely connected to the organisational strategy and so leaders are able to voice Clear Direction and focus their people on the right activities.

o Employees develop faith that the leadership team is aligned to, and maintains, a constancy of Purpose.
o Performance improvement efforts can be measured for their impact.
o More focus leads to better use of scarce resources.
o The improvement strategy is not deemed a 'stand-alone' exercise by a 'stand-alone' department but a critical component in the achievement of the bigger-picture organisational strategy, to the benefit of all.

## PRACTICAL ACTIVITY: Hearing the Voice of the Hospital

Depending on the availability of a strategic plan and defined goals and objectives, capture the key components of the improvement focus using Figure 1.1 as a guideline:

▸ List the goals and objectives for the next one to three years.
▸ Establish which key initiatives are already in place for reaching each of these objectives.
▸ Confirm the current performance relating to each of the initiatives, using measurable, data-driven evidence.

There may already be good initiatives underway that simply require completion. It is wise to be aware of these before saddling teams with additional work. This process is also a means of evaluating initiative-loading so as not to overburden individuals. Your intention is to focus teams onto a few initiatives at a time to achieve quality execution, aligned to Purpose. If employees have too many focus areas, they may start many projects and finish very few, leading to unrealised outcomes.

# Goals, Objectives and Current Performance

| VOICE OF THE HOSPITAL | | | |
|---|---|---|---|
| Goal (Mar 2017) | Objective | Existing Initiative | Current Performance (Feb 2016) |
| Reduce infection rate by 25% | Improve cleanliness assessment to 85% | Staff awareness programme | Not measured |
| Reduce Patient Journey Time by 15% | Reduce Patient Affairs waiting time by 50% | None | 95 minutes |
| | Reduce Clinic waiting time by 20% | Introduction of smart phone app for blood results retrieval | 220 minutes |
| | Reduce Pharmacy waiting time by 30% | None | 69 minutes |
| Improve availability of medicines to 80% | Reduce avoidable stock-out by 50% | Implement re-order levels for A-Categories | No max and re-order levels |
| | | Streamline requisition procedures | 23-day lead time for requisitions |
| | | Remove obsolete stock | 20% of stock obsolete |

## Strategy

**Addressing the patient concerns:**
**THE SIX QUALITY PRIORITIES**

Based on the concerns raised by patients and the public, the National Department of Health has identified six priority quality areas for fast-track implementation and focus over the next 3 years:

1. **Improving values and attitudes – of staff, managers and patients**
2. **Cleanliness of our hospitals and clinics**
3. **Reducing waiting times and queues**
4. **Keeping patients safe and providing reliable care**
5. **Preventing infections being passed in hospitals and clinics**
6. **Making sure medicines, supplies and equipment are available**

In rapidly improving the situation in these six areas, the National Department of Health has chosen a few basic things that we are going to make sure work well NOW and in so doing improve the way patients feel about the care they are receiving.

*BACK TO BASICS TO MAKE HEALTH AND SOCIAL SERVICES WORK BETTER*

health and social development

Gauteng Department of Health

▲ **Figure 1.1:** An example of the way in which the 'Voice of the Hospital' or 'Voice of the Clinic' might be defined and taking into account the Gauteng Department of Health's Six Quality Priorities. These assist us in the identification of key 'Voice of the Hospital' initiatives.

# The Voice of the Patient

The patient is your customer. Lean Thinking teaches us to think *Customer First*, such that all improvement activities are directed towards bettering their experience. Before starting any improvement initiative, it is critical to understand the needs of your patients to ensure the changes pursued bring them real benefit.

> Think *Customer First*, such that all improvement activities are directed towards bettering their experience. What do your patients need?

> *'Patient requirements, as expressed in the patient's own terms, are called the Voice of the Patient. However, the patient's meaning is the crucial part of the message.'*

(Adapted from Evans and Lindsay, 1996)

You are encouraged not to proceed before first giving careful consideration to your patient's definition of 'requirement'. If at the end of this section of the book, you can answer the following questions, you are one step closer to understanding the Voice of the Patient:

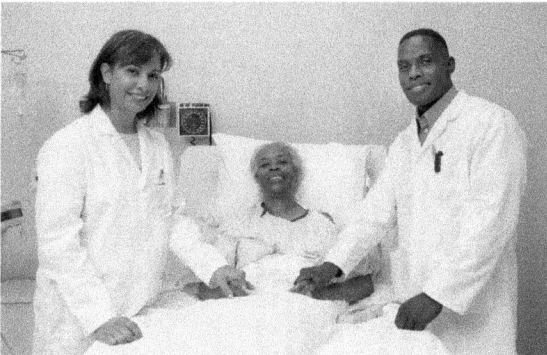

WHO are our patients?

WHAT do they want?

WHY do they want it?

WHERE do they want it?

WHEN do they want it?

HOW do they want it?

Bypassing the accurate outlining of patient requirements often leads to assumption and a skewed view of how to deliver services to them. Putting in the effort up-front will significantly help you to:

o   Figure out what your patients care about
o   Ensure your priorities and goals are consistent with patient needs
o   Determine patient needs that you can realistically meet.

If you service many different types of patients, consider grouping them into categories before exploring their individual needs. Quality guru, Joseph Juran suggests classifying customers into two main groups, namely 'the vital few' and 'useful many' (Juran, 1992).

Before analysing their needs, consider segmenting your patients as follows:
- o Condition type (Figure 1.2)
- o Clinic attended (Figure 1.3)
- o Chronic vs. acute
- o Physician or unit attending
- o Number or type of scripts.

EXAMPLE

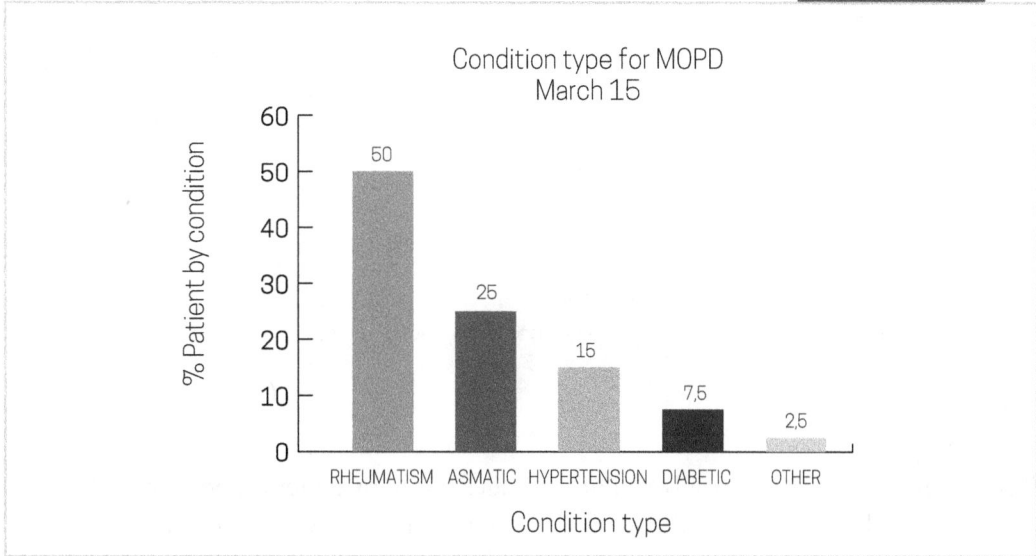

Figure 1.2: Classifying patients by condition type

EXAMPLE

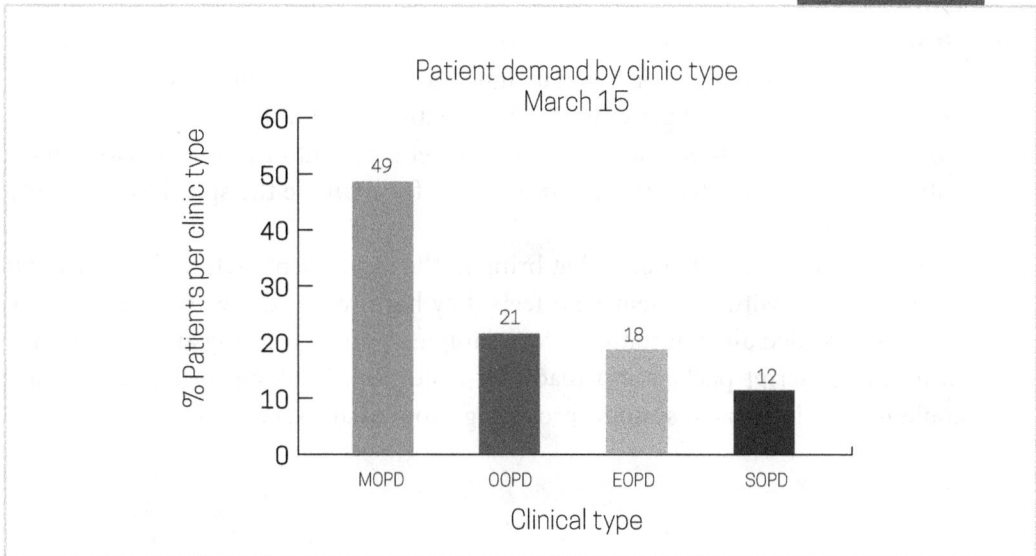

Figure 1.3: Classifying patients by clinic type

It is not always possible to resolve all of the issues raised by patients and staff. But, by filtering the results of your investigations, you can understand how much value the patient places on certain attributes of the service your facility offers.

Dr Noriaki Kano's so-called Kano Model talks to product development and customer satisfaction. It outlines three categories to consider which have been adapted to suit service improvement:

o *Dissatisfiers* are elements of service that reflect basic needs—for example the provision of a patient file or being assigned a doctor for a consultation. As these 'must-haves' are implied patients will not mention them unless they are absent.

o *Satisfiers* refer to elements of service that meet a patient's need for performance. Patient satisfaction will centre around these—for example the speed, cost, quality of care and more.

o *Delighters* are service elements that bring in the excitement factor. They earn you brownie points with a patient who feels they have received a world-class service that has exceeded all expectation—for example a patient arriving at the pharmacy to find their script packed and ready for collection. Looking to the future, care could involve integrated systems providing 'wow' factor service elements.

## PRACTICAL ACTIVITY: Identifying *Dissatisfiers*, *Satisfiers* and *Delighters*

Consider how much value patients place on particular areas of service. List each of their top requirements on individual Post-It notes and stick them onto the model in figure 1.4 to map out these priorities:

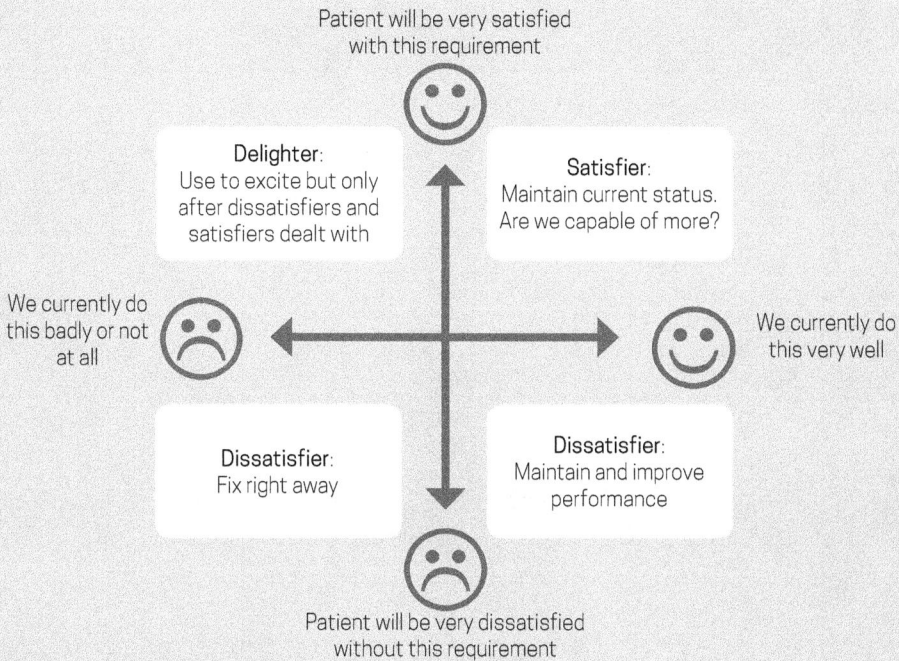

Patient will be very satisfied
with this requirement

**Delighter:**
Use to excite but only after dissatisfiers and satisfiers dealt with

**Satisfier:**
Maintain current status. Are we capable of more?

We currently do this badly or not at all

We currently do this very well

**Dissatisfier:**
Fix right away

**Dissatisfier:**
Maintain and improve performance

Patient will be very dissatisfied
without this requirement

▲ **Figure 1.4:** Kano Model adapted to suit service improvement

The activities you have completed have shed valuable light on your patient identities and needs. You are ready to capture the Voice of the Patient. See Table 1.1 for an example of how you might go about this.

| PATIENT GROUP | WHO is the patient? | THE VOICE OF THE PATIENT | | | | | | | |
|---|---|---|---|---|---|---|---|---|---|
| | | WHAT do they want? | WHY do they want it? | WHEN do they want it? | WHERE do they want it? | HOW do they want it? | VALUE how important it is | PRIORITY level for improvement focus |
| MEDICAL OUT-PATIENT | 49% of outpatient demand<br><br>50% rheumatism | Correct diagnosis and treatment | They need quality care that leads to improved health | At each visit | At the MOPD Clinic | Sufficient time with qualified physician | Dissatisfier | Very high |
| | | Quick service | They value their time | At each visit | Registration and Pharmacy | Wait for less than 30min | Satisfier | High |
| | | Prescription readily available | Stock-out forces patients to make multiple visits to receive their prescription | At each visit | At a dedicated counter | Repeat prescriptions ready in advance | Delighter | Medium |

◄ Table 1.1: Example of how to capture the Voice of the Patient

# The Voice of the Employee

Never underestimate the power of employee intelligence. They are at the coalface of everyday operations, experiencing both patient frustrations as well as their own. They bear witness to the problems, delays and inefficiencies inherent in the system and are in a strong position to summarise key challenges. And, when given a voice, they are usually very open to sharing their experiences. Not only is it important to listen to the Voice of the Employee, but also to ensure you provide them with feedback on what you have learned and how you will help them to better problem areas. It can be both demotivating and unnerving for employees to share their opinions only to have nothing come of their openness and trust.

For a well-structured, customisable climate-survey approach to gathering the Voice of the Employee, refer to *Clear Direction* (Heathcote, 2014).

## PRACTICAL ACTIVITY: Hearing the Voice of the Employee

Find a suitable time and place, and gather key personnel who work with the bulk of your patients. Ask them to complete the following exercise:

▸ On your own, list the top five obstacles that affect patient service.
▸ In groups of two or three, discuss your individual lists of obstacles and agree on three key issues to be addressed.
▸ Ask each group to give feedback to the team. Capture the results as closely as possible and in the words of your employees.

# Your North Star

The North Star (Polaris) has historically been used to navigate Northwards and to determine latitude. Should you find yourself lost on a clear night with no GPS technology or compass in hand, it remains a reliable gauge of the positioning of North. An interesting fact to note is that the North Star, although dependable in its constant position in the night sky, does shift slightly over time.

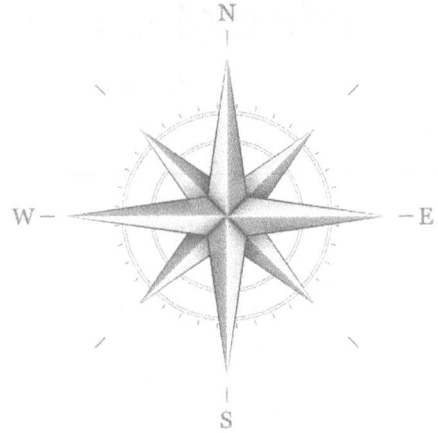

In the context of Operational Excellence, your North Star is your navigation guide, the beacon towards which sustained levels of improvement are directed. It remains a reliable reference to look to and guides the healthcare facility towards its goals. As with Polaris, it does not shift dramatically but rather, shifts gradually over time—not unlike your strategy should do. It represents the blue-print to raising performance and:

- o Providing the service levels that patients require
- o Driving change that supports stable employment
- o Deploying policy decisions throughout the organisation
- o Preserving the environment for future generations.

The North Star is not limited to the Voice of the Hospital, but also includes the Voices of the Patient and Employee. It captures all the voices that tell the story of the organisation's current positioning and the heights to which it must aspire. Capturing each Voice in a North Star summary provides a straightforward and tangible view of key areas of interest. It also provides members of leadership in an organisation with the Clear Direction needed to navigate each level of change.

*'Clear Direction is all about maintaining one's bearing even when everything blows up all over the place. It's about following a guiding star regardless of currents and reefs and shipwrecks.'*

(Ballé, 2009)

## PRACTICAL ACTIVITY: Articulating your North Star

Review the results from capturing the Voice of the Hospital, Voice of the Patient and Voice of the Employee. Impose the overall improvement focus onto your North Star (Figure 1.5). Update the North Star's focus as you discover additional areas for improvement over time, but always keep it simple, to-the-point and measurable.

**EXAMPLE**

Reduce patient waiting times — N

Reduce hospital spend

Reduce infection rate

Improve patient and staff safety — W

Improve medicine availability — E

Reduce IT downtime

Improve quality of care

Stabilise resource availability — S

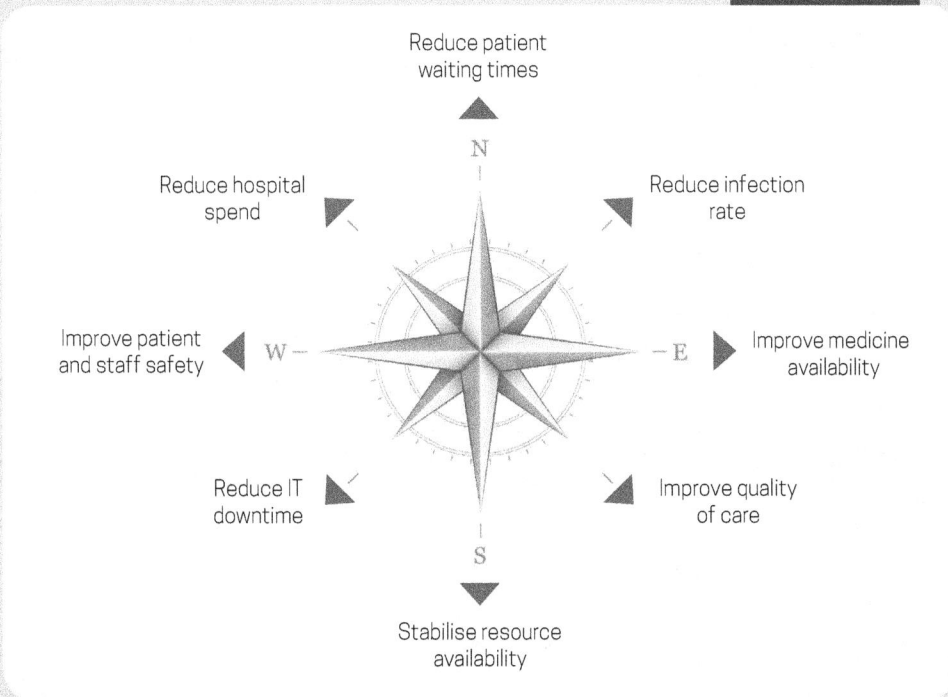

▲ Figure 1.5: Example of a North Star for Operational Excellence

# From Current Reality to Future Care

It is exhilarating to imagine the future of patient care. Having reviewed articles and publications and having listened to the views of journalists, doctors, information technology gurus and scientists, I remain mesmerised by the catalytic power of continuous improvement to create a better future state. Continuous improvement is capable of bridging the divides typically faced by public healthcare facilities going from their current reality to a future state of excellence (as depicted in Table 1.2).

| CURRENT REALITY | FUTURE CARE |
|---|---|
| Overburdened resources | Efficiently used capacity to meet demand |
| Reactive care | Preventative care |
| Short courses of treatment | Long-term patient relationships |
| Focus on illness | Focus on wellness |
| Silo-based thinking | Departmental collaboration |
| Manual, repetitive processes | Automation of streamlined processes |
| Crisis-management | Scientific principles guide problem-solving |
| Physicians work independently | Collaborative team problem-solving |
| Physician shortages and available capacity taken up by lengthy consultations | Decreased demands on physicians allow them to focus on their core areas of expertise |
| Patients rely on physician for all aspects of their care | Patients are more accountable for their own care and supported by smart technology |
| Disconnected and silo-based IT systems | Vertically and horizontally integrated IT systems |
| Lack of visible data pertinent to patient care | Sophisticated data capture transparently reflects performance, triggering problem-solving and healthy intra and inter-departmental competition |

▲ Table 1.2: A snap-shot of a current public healthcare facility's reality in contrast with the stretch goals of enhanced, future patient care

Those organisations willing to engage in programs such as Lean Management ahead of times of crisis, will be better equipped to implement the principles of continuous improvement. In a beautiful domino effect, they will be adept at rooting out waste and improving flow, leading to enhanced use of resources such as time, budget and facilities. As a consequence, processes and systems will be more efficient. The organisation will attract better skills and motivate its people to offer their best.

Remember that bravery is fundamental to a culture of continuous improvement. Weave the threads of Operational Excellence into the billowing sails of your organisation's ship as early as possible and as much as possible. This will provide a competitive edge in the face of imminent future challenges that test your ability to employ better process management when under pressure.

# How Big Can You Dream?

It is time to dream. BIG, BOLD DREAMS.

*Set doubt aside and fill the space once occupied by fear and uncertainty with a vision of what the organisation could become, given the chance. Can you see the significance of the change effort you have chosen to charter? Can you see the reality of your healthcare facility's future, world-class self?*

*Think big and imagine your organisation at its absolute best, steadily navigating the stormy seas—this identity now its daily norm. The sleek hull of your ship naturally rises and falls with the tide of daily challenges. Vast canvas sails catch every breeze and wind, every opportunity for innovation towards Operational Excellence in their path. Leaders guide teams to unexplored, prosperous shores. Witness the crew working in unison. Everyone understands the common vision, the PURPOSE of the journey at hand and works together to counteract every wave, every current and every storm with ease and calm. Imagine you have captured the heart of every employee to evolve PROCESSES that adapt to the winds of change. Burn with pride knowing that striving for Operational Excellence has uplifted all your PEOPLE and consequently, your patients. Can you feel the energy of successful PROBLEM SOLVING turning challenges into opportunities? How quickly are you generating more Thinking People? Everyone now wakes up to a new day with a feeling of fulfilment, as they are part of an organisation governed by integrity and PURPOSE. Your North Star beckons towards a better place and your facility sets the benchmark for others. Together, you serve humanity—starting with your patients— for the good of all. You are thinking beyond the now, moving forward in a responsible way, respecting the PLANET and paving the way for future generations.*

*With this dream in hand we are about to leap into the future and look at your organisation as it CAN and WILL BE—transformed by courage and fed by BOLD possibility.*

How do we make this future dream a reality? Let us step back into the present and investigate the tangible collection of activities that will take your organisation there. The next section deconstructs the meaning of Best Practice for you. Sink your teeth into the devilish detail that many prefer to avoid but that has the power to achieve the future you have begun to dream.

# What Defines Best Practice?

The word 'culture' is used in conversation and often in the context of comments such as 'The culture in this organisation is preventing us from improving', or 'We do not have the right culture for Operational Excellence' and 'If we could just change the culture, we could change the way we service patients'.

Various models and meanings describe the key aspects of organisational culture. For the purposes of this book, consider the definition of culture to be as follows: *The sum of people's habits related to the work they do* (Mann, 2005). So, by definition, if we want to 'fix' the culture, we need to improve the individual *habits* that combine to give life to the overriding culture within the organisation. These habits are rooted in the way people go about their daily work and also in how they perceive obstacles prevalent in a public healthcare environment.

> The definition of culture is the sum of people's habits.

Habits that build a culture typical of a world-class organisation are called Best Practices. A sensible fusion of these Best Practices, deliberately arranged around the 5P Model areas depicted in Figure 2.1, can elevate any facility to world-class standards.

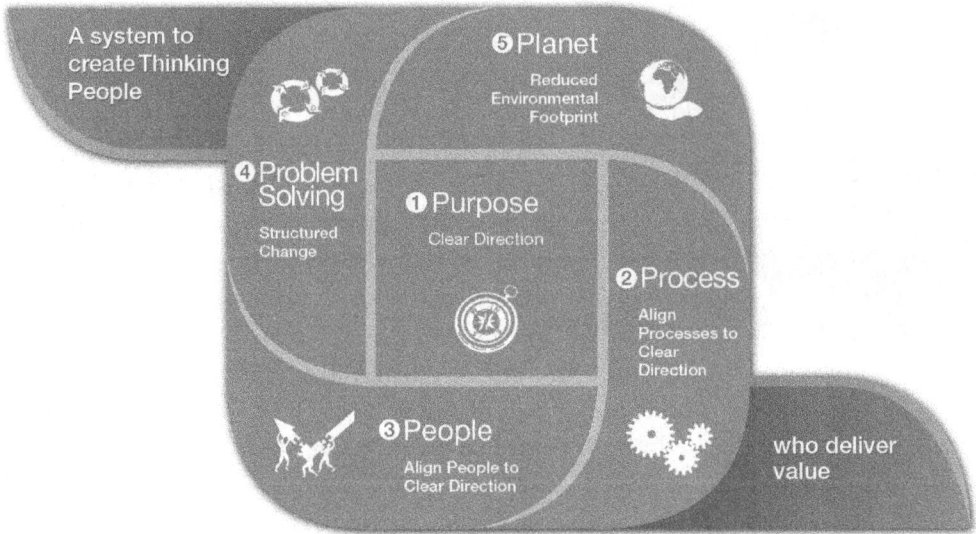

A system to create Thinking People

❺ Planet
Reduced Environmental Footprint

❹ Problem Solving
Structured Change

❶ Purpose
Clear Direction

❷ Process
Align Processes to Clear Direction

❸ People
Align People to Clear Direction

who deliver value

▲ Figure 2.1: The 5P Model encompasses the network of Best Practices needed to build a management system for world-class performance

Not only do Best Practices define processes and how we manage them, but they also extend into the network of activities that collectively drive a facility's heart and soul—the management system. These elements are illustrated in Figure 2.2, and include:

- o The improvement strategy and how it is deployed through operational levels (PURPOSE)
- o The Value Stream and how we design, develop and manage it to align with the strategy (PROCESS)

- o Our leaders, managers, supervisors, team leaders and frontline staff, and the routine work they do to bring the healthcare facility closer to its goals (PEOPLE)
- o How we identify and respond to obstacles and the structured approach we use to deal with them in a sustainable way (PROBLEM SOLVING)
- o The focus we place on reducing our environmental footprint and preserving what we have at our disposal for future generations (PLANET).

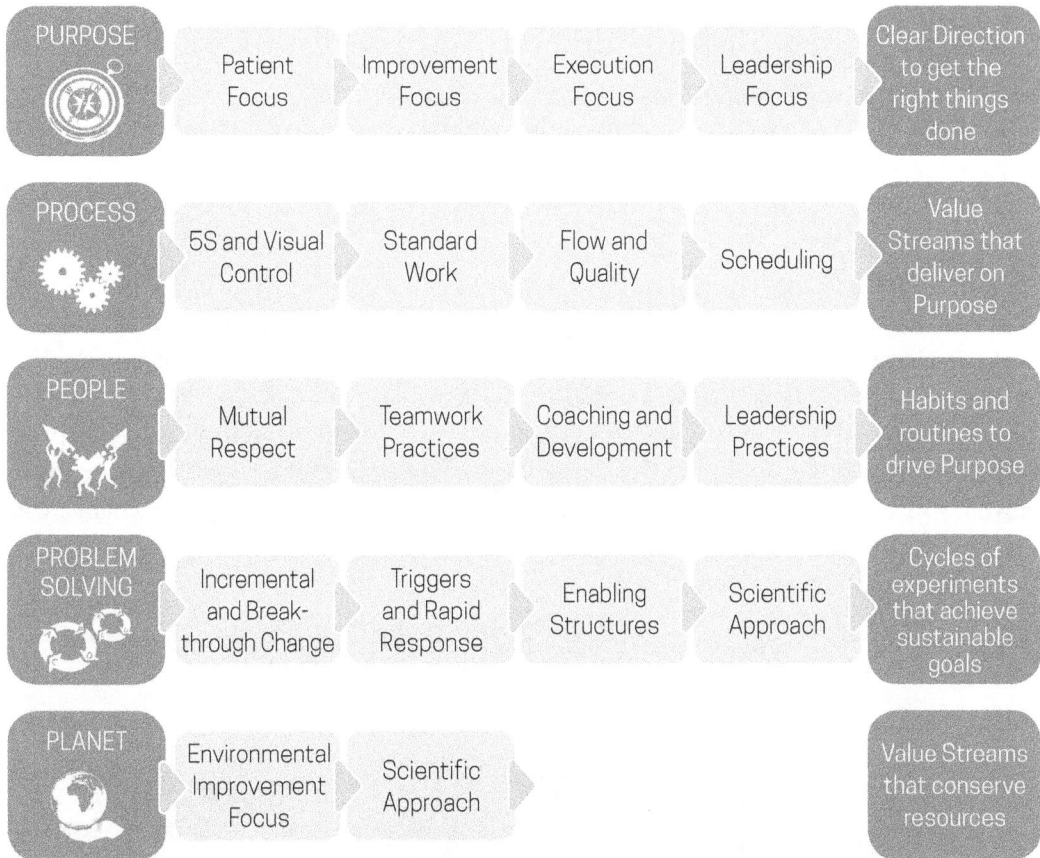

| PURPOSE | Patient Focus | Improvement Focus | Execution Focus | Leadership Focus | Clear Direction to get the right things done |
| PROCESS | 5S and Visual Control | Standard Work | Flow and Quality | Scheduling | Value Streams that deliver on Purpose |
| PEOPLE | Mutual Respect | Teamwork Practices | Coaching and Development | Leadership Practices | Habits and routines to drive Purpose |
| PROBLEM SOLVING | Incremental and Break-through Change | Triggers and Rapid Response | Enabling Structures | Scientific Approach | Cycles of experiments that achieve sustainable goals |
| PLANET | Environmental Improvement Focus | Scientific Approach | | | Value Streams that conserve resources |

▲ Figure 2.2: Key relationships between elements of the 5P Model

Developing organisational muscle to strengthen each of the 5P Model areas will kindle the fires of a culture that systematically encourages employees to think about their work from a different perspective. This allows your Thinking People to engage in activities that directly impact the true Purpose of the healthcare facility.

The 5P Model areas are akin to the steel skeleton that supports a skyscraper or, the scaffolding of bone, cartilage and connective tissue supporting different biological systems that make life possible. Mastering the 5P elements will make new management systems and improvements able to withstand the test of time.

# The Long-Term Journey to World-Class

If your healthcare facility were to devote time and effort to Operational Excellence, what would change? What novel activities would empower employees to solve problems, realise goals and ultimately achieve the future dream?

This chapter presents:

o First, the theory of optimal Operational Excellence: the full possibility of a future vision to aspire towards—what each of the 5Ps of Operational Excellence has the potential to deliver (illustrated in Figures 2.3 through 2.7).

o Then, the proof of performance: Each ideal scenario is illustrated by real-life input from Gauteng Department of Health, or GDOH, hospitals that took part in the GDOH Service Delivery Improvement Initiative.

This pioneering Gauteng provincial department, led by MEC Qedani Mahlangu, had the courage to believe that four key hospitals known as Cohort 1—Chris Hani Baragwanath Academic, Leratong, Sebokeng and Kopanong Hospital—could make the theories of Best Practice a new, daily operational reality. This chapter reveals both the elements they struggled with most and what was proudly accomplished.

You might feel overwhelmed when comparing your organisation to a Lean enterprise shaped by years of dedication to this cause. Never lose sight of the bigger, bolder picture of what you are setting out to achieve. Keep in mind that in the early stages of change you may only choose to tackle particular challenges. Simply define each stage as a stepping stone on the path to a far greater goal.

An experienced facilitator will be able to assist you in defining the Best Practice Current Condition and to chart tangible Target Conditions to meet the long-term vision. Remember that you can access a detailed 5P Assessment in *Clear Direction* (Heathcote, 2014).

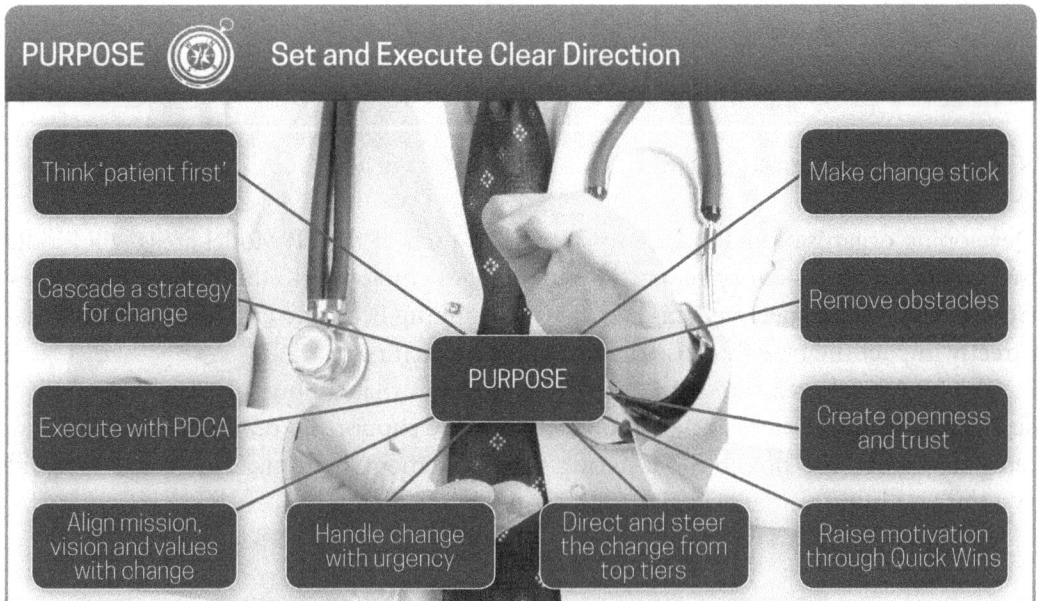

**PURPOSE** — Set and Execute Clear Direction

- Think 'patient first'
- Cascade a strategy for change
- Execute with PDCA
- Align mission, vision and values with change
- Handle change with urgency
- PURPOSE
- Direct and steer the change from top tiers
- Make change stick
- Remove obstacles
- Create openness and trust
- Raise motivation through Quick Wins

▲ Figure 2.3: A Vision for PURPOSE

### Patient satisfaction is the primary goal of employees and guides improvement behaviour.

The Voice of the Patient (VOP) is gathered, verified and defined from the perspective of the patient. The VOP guides improvement activities and is continuously reviewed.

### A clear strategy and plan aligns the focus of activities throughout the healthcare facility.

The strategy is available to all and leaders buy into the rationale. The strategic plan cascades through departmental- and team-level goals and alignment is clear, traceable and accountable. Employees can explain how their daily activities contribute to the goals of the team and the organisation.

### The Current Condition, Target Condition and key focus areas are clear.

Using assessments and Value Stream Maps the Current Condition, future state and key areas for change have been documented. Metrics track the improvements (visual dashboards and A3 reports). The Current Condition is periodically updated.

### A formal strategy-deployment system aligns strategy and execution.

A3 reports have been introduced and standardised to illustrate the thought process guiding improvements and structuring activities to align them to the strategic plan and evaluate implementation. There is no ambiguity as to what employees must spend time on to achieve set goals. Accountable employees regularly give their A3 feedback. A cycle of Plan-Do-Check-Adjust (PDCA) takes place in every improvement process executed.

### Purpose is clear, measurable, communicated and guides behaviour.

Goals and Key Performance Indicators (KPIs) have been defined for all levels and align with the North Star. The right number of KPIs maintain focus. The KPIs drive the right behaviours and influence incentives, bonuses, recognition and promotion opportunities.

### The mission, vision and values drive a patient-focus, respect for people and the environment, and continuous improvement.

The mission, vision and values are communicated to all and employees are able to explain them in their own words. Employees have an emotional connection to these values and this drives ethical behaviour on their part.

### There is a consistent, burning platform for change.

There is a defined need for change and the execution of actions is handled with urgency. Everyone is clear on why the change is needed and what each person can personally contribute.

### Senior management provides constancy of Purpose.

A Steering Committee (Steerco) has been set up to direct and steer the improvement strategy. Steerco meetings are structured, regular, focused and well-attended.

### A clear communication strategy is executed.

A formal communication plan is documented. Employees are well-informed of the improvement strategy and their role in its achievement. Communication flows freely between staff levels. Obstacles and anxieties regarding the improvement strategy are effectively dealt with. Trust grows between the employees and leadership and new communications are met with openness and interest.

### Obstacles are systematically removed.

A formal escalation and feedback process encourages employees to raise obstacles and allows leaders to provide timeous responses. Confidence in every employee's capacity to improve grows, more improvement activities are implemented than are abandoned and employees are empowered to act on the overall vision.

### Quick Wins raise motivation.

Improvements that produce the most benefits yield positive, short-term results. Recognition has been awarded to the teams and individuals responsible for the progress at hand. This stimulates further interest to engage in change. Employees can see the link between their effort and the results and impact on the patient, the healthcare facility and themselves.

### Change is made to stick.

Initial improvements hold firm. There is no desire or will to regress towards previous performance. All improvement efforts make use of the PDCA cycle and the management system does all in its power to nurture new levels of performance.

---

## PURPOSE AND THE GDOH SERVICE DELIVERY IMPROVEMENT INITIATIVE

*Directive: Improve staff efficiency, eliminate waste and reduce patient waiting times*

Before embarking on an improvement initiative we first consider **what** problem we want to solve, **why** it is needed and **how** it will be executed and supported. The GDOH Service Delivery Improvement Initiative was no different. In the early stages, the Lean Institute Africa (LIA) was issued a clear directive from MEC for Health, Ms. Qedani Mahlangu, as to what needed to change and how this would influence the Voice of the Patient. The MEC's focus: **Improve staff efficiency, eliminate waste and reduce patient waiting times**. First, a Steering Committee (Steerco) consisting of the key people from Gauteng Health provincial office was elected. Together they defined the way Cohort 1 would be formed and engaged. This message was successfully and consistently cascaded to each of the hospitals involved (Chris Hani Baragwanath Academic, Leratong, Sebokeng and Kopanong Hospitals) and in detail to the teams within each. Creating constancy of PURPOSE across all four facilities was a significant factor in the successes achieved, and helped maintain focus on the end goals.

The Current Condition, Target Condition and key focus areas for the overall goal of reduced waiting time were defined for each of the participating model areas using Value Stream Maps and other methods (further described in Chapter 3). In time, these would evolve into dashboards, and although this did not include all the Key Performance Indicators, this approach would form the basis for the Daily Management System and drive the right behaviours within teams.

The Heads of Department for each of the model areas began constructing A3 reports for reporting to the LIA facilitators and the executive team at each hospital. Initially these reports were only a means of outlining the work done, but over time they developed into invaluable documentation to assist teams in explaining their thinking patterns and decision-making.

Through Rapid Process Improvement and other workshops, the teams experienced their inherent potential to make a real difference to cutting patient waiting times. This built their confidence to seek out further improvement. Upfront wins yielded quick results which stimulated and galvanised the teams to take further, bold steps.

Standard Work remains a critical part of improvement behaviour. Tangible examples of policies, processes and procedures that held new standards of performance firmly in place and reduced the risk of their slipping back to old, inefficient ways, began to accumulate. (Chapter 3 outlines further examples from Cohort 1's successes).

Although not all elements of PURPOSE were achieved by Cohort 1, the initiative undertaken built a solid foundation for continued improvement. Further action on the part of the Provincial Office Steerco would take advances to the next level.

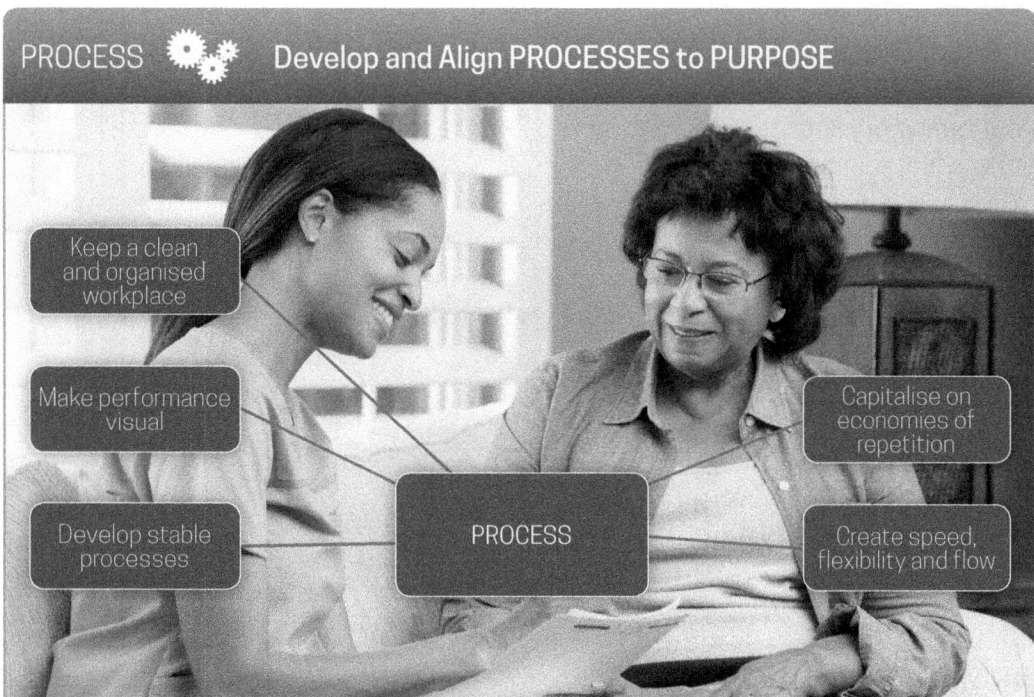

PROCESS    Develop and Align PROCESSES to PURPOSE

Keep a clean and organised workplace

Make performance visual

Develop stable processes

PROCESS

Capitalise on economies of repetition

Create speed, flexibility and flow

▲ Figure 2.4: A Vision for PROCESS

**The work area is well organised and conducive to safety, productivity, discipline and comfort. Problem areas are easy to identify.**

The work area is clean and maintained by a documented standard. Only necessary items are found here and they are cleverly located for easy access and retrieval. The team regularly audits their work area for improvement opportunities and these actions are displayed on the performance dashboard.

**Performance is visual and the improvement focus is clear and drives behaviour. Visitors and newcomers quickly understand operations.**

A meeting area is established and features carefully designed visuals that depict the improvement focus. Relevant metrics showing current and target performance are updated. Team members daily review the condition they are targeting, resulting in well-focused problem-solving and improved performance over time.

**Variation is stabilised. The best methods to carry out work are documented in a way that very specifically captures content, timing, sequence and outcome.**

Standards are developed for critical processes and employees are trained and assessed to comply with the requirements. Variation is reduced and the standards put in place are used as a baseline for further improvement.

**Speed, flexibility and flow are achieved throughout the Value Stream.**

Critical Value Streams are identified. Causes of Muda (waste), Mura (variation) and Muri (over-burdening) are highlighted and eliminated. Where possible, batching of patients is reduced to a minimum and patients are served one at a time, with minimal queuing time. The flow of the patients is managed by the operational system and not by individuals.

**Economies of repetition and improved flow are accomplished through scheduling principles.**

Where applicable, similar service types are grouped together so that simple, fast-moving Value Streams are not hindered by slow-moving, complex service offerings. Operations become highly responsive to the demand at hand, resulting in an improved flow of patients and successful attainment of the goal of reduced patient waiting times.

# PROCESS AND THE GDOH SERVICE DELIVERY IMPROVEMENT INITIATIVE

*Directive: Improve staff efficiency, eliminate waste and reduce patient waiting times*

With PURPOSE clarified, the teams from each of the participating hospitals were provided with guidance on how to develop and improve their PROCESSES. This entailed interrogating the critical steps in the process of servicing patients and deciding on key elements that could cut waiting times. Value Stream Maps were completed by each of the teams, unlocking hidden processes and obstacles for the teams to tackle. These visual activities allowed teams to discuss, debate and define new patterns of working.

Good 5S is a foundational practice that can effectively derail the success of change if ignored. Teams were therefore encouraged to de-clutter their environments. This included removing outdated documents from walls, cleaning up worktables and removing anything that was not necessary to get the job done. Registration counters were tidied and pharmacy worktables cleared. This made it possible for the teams to 'clear the window to their processes' and expose the waste that blocked the flow.

Allocating a dedicated area for team meetings is ideal but not always possible. Teams were able to set up dashboards close to patient service points around which to start their daily meetings. This was a challenge since boards were not freely available. The absence of budget and facilities did not deter the teams. They innovated and erected brown-paper boards as a starting point. These boards indicated patient waiting times, problem-solving activities and actions. With time the teams enhanced the boards to include additional components affecting patient waiting times.

Standards always seem to exist somewhere—especially in the public health sector. But what use are standards that are not readily available or easy to evaluate? A procedural document hidden away in a drawer is a pointless guide. When it came to conveying the ideal standards of service, Cohort 1 team leaders struggled to place the right information at employee fingertips. Visually depicting key elements of the standards and procedures at service points, was a challenge that some met better than others. But all teams must ideally have access to updated summaries of the Target Condition against which current performance can easily be compared (discussed in more detail in Chapters 3 and 6).

Achieving economies of repetition presents an interesting challenge and one to approach with careful consideration. At one of the Cohort 1 hospitals, the pharmacy team captured a Current Condition describing the workings of an Express Queue, historically set-up to service patients requiring a small number of items. When implemented a few years prior, demand patterns had been different and the Express Queue was the best way. When interrogated, this quick-checkout queue was no longer conducive to current demand patterns and the team adjusted the design so that any counter could assist any patient. It is therefore best to observe and measure the Current Condition in light of current obstacles and assign countermeasures to deal with these specific obstacles. What has worked in the past may not suit the present demand. Having said this, in other hospitals and clinics, an Express Queue may very well be the ideal solution to implement. Relevant solutions, customised to the needs of each facility, are therefore fundamental.

PEOPLE 🦋 Develop and Align PEOPLE to PURPOSE

Collaborate and coach

Devise a plan for excess capacity

Promote stable teams

Develop leaders into teachers

PEOPLE

'Go-see'

Develop successors and build staff flexibility

Recognise achievement

Help leaders standardise their work

Develop the 'Kaizen spirit'

▲ Figure 2.5: A Vision for PEOPLE

## Collaborative problem-solving between leaders and employees breeds mutual respect for knowledge and contribution.

Leaders and employees solve problems together. The leader respects the employee's knowledge and provides context and structure to assist in problem-solving.

## Operational Excellence and caring go hand in hand.

Improvements have a positive impact on human resources and more time becomes available to staff. Employees are confident that improvements will not result in job losses as leaders have formally communicated their strategy to deal with any excesses identified. These strategies for redeploying capacity include staffing new service lines, reducing overtime hours, reducing the hiring of temporary labour or re-allocating employee time to problem-solving activities. Capacity improvements are met with enthusiasm, rather than fear and negativity. Trust develops between employees and leaders.

## Performing teams align their activities to the strategic goals and achieve basic stability in the operations.

Stable, functional teams are formed with defined team leadership and clear roles and responsibilities. Teams align to a common goal for improvement and no longer operate in isolation. They develop a shared understanding of obstacles and solve problems together. Cross-departmental and cross-functional team-based problem-solving has become the norm.

## Coaching and development is focused, structured and delivers results.

Training and coaching needs are aligned to the improvement goals and are viewed as an investment in staff, and not as an added expense. A3 Thinking structures the coaching conversation that happens between leader and employee for Breakthrough Change. Coaching Kata structures the coaching conversation between a leader and an employee for consistent, Incremental Change (see Part II).

### Leaders become teachers and grow participation in employees.

Leaders observe, spend time, coach and assist employees to internalise the right routines. They spend 30 to 50 percent of their time on teaching and guiding employees to make improvements in their work processes.

### Urgency for patient satisfaction starts with leaders and cascades through the levels to every individual.

Leaders visit patient service points to gain insight into obstacles to service excellence. Every complaint is treated with urgency and is personally addressed by the line management, and not only by Quality Assurance personnel.

### All employees are now problem-solvers who daily remove obstacles and facilitate improvement goals.

Problems are seen as opportunities by every employee. They are everyone's responsibility. Every individual, from the lowest to the highest levels of a healthcare facility, has now been developed to solve problems. Managers and specialists are consequently free to concentrate on higher-level problems that require their expertise.

### Leaders 'go-see' to develop first-hand experience, grow participation and create a genuine understanding of the obstacles to positive change.

All improvement activities include 'go-see' as a fundamental part of PDCA and a standard part of a leader's work. Prior to accountability meetings, leaders perform walkabouts to see and hear of obstacles that staff encounter and to ensure improvement discussions include real facts from real observations. The workplace is becoming the teacher and the leader is closely connected to the process. Employees are confident in the leader's understanding of the issues they face on the frontline.

### Leaders ensure processes are managed for basic stability and improvement, and actively develop a 'Kaizen spirit' in the healthcare facility.

Normal and abnormal conditions are defined and the team is coached to respond to abnormality and achieve basic stability in the processes. Incremental improvement is evident in the focus areas and there is a foundation for bigger breakthrough improvement in place. Leaders and teams seek ways to improve on standards through Kaizen activities (Rapid Process Improvement events) and more time is spent on improvement than on managing crises.

### Leaders understand the balance between improvement tools and leadership principles to create a management system for Operational Excellence.

Leaders understand that Operational Excellence is not simply about Lean tools but primarily about the rationale, leadership attitudes and activities that support and guide Lean tools.

### Leaders maintain focus on the North Star and provide Clear Direction to the improvement activities.

There is a clear connection between strategy, the Current Condition, indicators and problem-solving activities. It is understood that some problems are more important than others. The Target Condition is clarified and leaders have identified the most important improvement activities so that teams solve only those problems identified as strategic and relevant to the change effort.

### Leader Standard Work (LSW) guides behaviour and stabilises the management system for Operational Excellence.

When leaders change or move, the management system governing continuous improvement is preserved. The system survives beyond the person. Key aspects of the LSW are captured, core tasks and routines are explicit and compliance is ensured.

### There is clarity about a leader's responsibility and the outcomes needed to support Operational Excellence.

Job descriptions for leaders include responsibility for continuous improvement and the promotion of leaders is influenced by competency in their expanded roles.

### Rewards and recognition both stimulate continuous improvement aligned to the improvement goals and foster teamwork.

At a minimum, non-monetary incentives are awarded for performance improvement. A monetary reward system is also aligned to team KPIs and individual performance. The system is considered fair and employees understand that targets are revisited to meet changing strategic needs.

### Succession planning is in place for critical positions in the healthcare facility.

Succession planning forms part of the leader's job description and a list of critical positions is created. Two employees have been identified for development into these positions (in case one of the employees is lost to a promotion, natural attrition or resigns). There is a smooth transition when a key person leaves a critical role.

### Employee flexibility and cross-skilling supports the improvement goals of the healthcare facility.

Where there is a need for employee flexibility and cross-skilling, a skills matrix has been developed indicating who will be skilled, in what, by whom and over which period. Development follows a defined training plan and competency acquisition process.

# PEOPLE AND THE GDOH SERVICE DELIVERY IMPROVEMENT INITIATIVE

*Directive: Improve staff efficiency, eliminate waste and reduce patient waiting times*

The development of PEOPLE to align with PURPOSE requires long-term investment. The behaviours and habits required to develop and sustain Operational Excellence take time to cement. Yet, there are some upfront practices that will advance these in the right direction.

Problem-solving collaboration between leaders and teams was not initially evident in each of the Cohort 1 hospitals. Rest assured, this is common to other sectors too. One reason for this lack of collaboration is that it is often seen as a manager's job to solve problems. Employees are expected to do the work, but not improve the work, and even if they want to make changes, they are often not equipped with the skills to do so. Jack Welch (retired Chairman of General Electric) was once approached by one of his employees who enlightened him by saying: *'For 25 years, you paid for my hands when you could have had my brain as well—for nothing.'* This profound statement illustrates the value of employee input.

Employees in each of the model areas were overjoyed at the opportunity to take part in problem-solving. They were not expected to just clock-in and leave their thoughts at the door, but were asked for their views, opinions and solutions to the obstacles faced. Through guided assistance from the LIA facilitators, teams and their managers at each of the Cohort 1 hospitals were able to visualise problems and solve them together during Rapid Process Improvement Workshops. It does of course require a concerted effort from managers to continue this practice going forward. It also requires diligence to distinguish between seeking employee input and abandoning employees to solve problems on their own.

In one of the Cohort 1 hospitals, registration counters were struggling with variation in employee numbers. Three employees were required at a minimum, to service patients. Each day this number varied either due to leave taken, absenteeism or because an employee had been 'borrowed' by another department. The impact of this irregularity on patient waiting times was significant and hindered the team from working together to remove obstacles. The improvement effort identified that stable teams were needed to manage patient queues and service them at the counters and to trigger innate problem-solving. Stabilising the patient service teams took several months, but once in place, also stabilised the Standard Work, routines and—crucially—the patient waiting times.

Coaching staff is not natural to every leader but it is one of the most important qualities to develop. To build this skill first requires a structure that will, over time, make coaching second nature. Coaching Kata was introduced (see Part II) and provided each manager with a set of questions to run through with the team. The outcome of this structure meant that teams were well-prepared to give their improvement feedback, and also meant that managers could prompt the right conversations leading to more effective coaching and problem-solving.

Finding enough time to solve problems will always be a challenge. It takes time to stop working, take stock, and reflect on performance to drive improvements. Initially, Cohort 1's teams struggled to dedicate time, every day, to their problem-solving. They had to be coached by the LIA facilitators to do this and then it was up to the teams to routinely practice problem-solving. Initially teams felt the need to negotiate, asking that 'problem-solving time' happen weekly rather than daily.

The question the LIA facilitators often asked, was 'How 'daily' is your Daily Management System?' Teams would smile and sheepishly admit that active problem-solving management didn't happen every day. Yet, incremental improvement relies on the daily management of processes. In Chapter 3 we investigate the impact of leaving a problem unresolved in more depth. In short, the longer it is left unresolved the more challenging it becomes to understand the root causes, and the more likely it becomes that its impact will be amplified. So, while teams managed to get their Daily Management Systems working, more effort was required to make this routine an ingrained habit.

Standard Work has typically been applied in processes where the employees doing the work need procedures to guide the quality and execution. However, to build new Lean practices into a management system requires that the leaders also perform activities they have not been expected to do before. The backbone of a team's Lean practices is formed of the structure of a leaders' Lean practices. As such, Leader Standard Work is as important as Standard Work at the frontline. Leaders and managers were identified in each of the participating hospitals and were encouraged to incorporate certain routines into their own daily work. CEOs were asked to perform periodic Gemba Walks to see first-hand the progress made and to offer support. Managers and CEOs were trained to use Kata cards to guide the conversations at the model areas. Heads of Department were asked to present A3 reports at hospital follow-ups arranged by the LIA facilitators. Managers were coached to use standard reports on the dashboards to create a common approach across departments. PDCA was repeatedly incorporated into conversations and standard reporting. As the leaders' routines became more consistent, the language for continuous improvement also evolved. Now when model areas are visited, there are strong similarities in what is being observed and discussed.

In one of the Cohort 1 hospitals, the performance structure was developed to incorporate the achievement of Lean practices. This had the desired effect of staff actively committing to the challenges that Lean Management presented. This could be taken a step further by re-defining the job descriptions and contracts of employees to ensure all aspire to Lean principles. While not simple or quickly achieved feats, these brave changes are necessary to feed progress.

These few examples of efforts initiated in Cohort 1 hospitals merely scratch the surface of what is possible. PEOPLE practices will mature as long as there is an on-going focus on the right behaviours for change to ensure they are indelibly ingrained into the fabric of the facility.

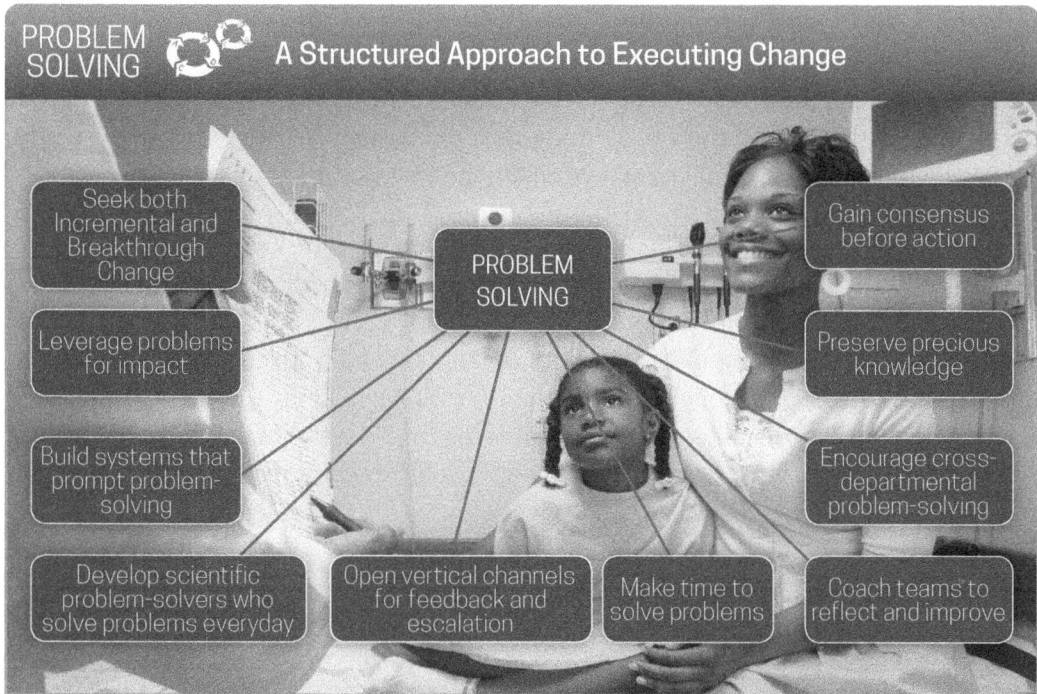

PROBLEM SOLVING — A Structured Approach to Executing Change

Seek both Incremental and Breakthrough Change

Gain consensus before action

PROBLEM SOLVING

Leverage problems for impact

Preserve precious knowledge

Build systems that prompt problem-solving

Encourage cross-departmental problem-solving

Develop scientific problem-solvers who solve problems everyday

Open vertical channels for feedback and escalation

Make time to solve problems

Coach teams to reflect and improve

▲ Figure 2.6: A Vision for PROBLEM SOLVING

### A strategy to address both Incremental and Breakthrough Change is deployed.

Daily measurement and problem-solving are entrenched in the routine and yield incremental improvement in areas that really matter. Periodic breakthrough Kaizen events are scheduled and executed by a dedicated team, to achieve leaps in performance. Pro-active problem-solving processes become the norm.

### Improvements are leveraged to focus all change activities toward improvement goals.

Leaders guide the teams to allocate the bulk of their energy to the top obstacles that hinder improvement goals. Employees are trained in a scientific approach that ensures the right problems are tackled through sustainable methods.

### Problem-solving triggers are well defined and support a culture of rapid response to problems.

A trigger system flagging out-of-standard processes prompts problem-solving activities. Employees at all levels are trained according to a structured approach to respond rapidly to difficulties. Processes are stabilising and improvement is absolutely evident in the indicators measured—to the delight of all.

### A tiered problem-solving model drives multi-level improvement, escalation and feedback.

The way in which problems are escalated, the conditions under which escalation happens, the handling of feedback and the attribution of accountability are all clearly communicated. Escalation and feedback are visually managed and empower employees to act on obstacles.

### Every problem is seen as an opportunity to stimulate continuous improvement, participation and personal growth.

Leaders create an environment that enables exposure to and learning from dealing with obstacles. Employees are thanked for bringing a problem to a leader's attention. The leader responds by providing support to solve the problem, following the principles of A3 Thinking and Coaching Kata. Although new problems continually surface, the recurrence of problems is declining.

### Time is made available to solve problems.

Dedicated problem-solving time is made possible and designed into the work schedule. Triggers prompt employees to respond to out-of-standard conditions and if the problem cannot be resolved immediately, the leader is alerted through an escalation procedure. If a longer time is required to solve a problem, a dedicated session is scheduled. If a 'quick-fix' has been implemented to stabilise a problem, sufficient time is allocated to address the root cause thereafter, to prevent recurrence and to remove the temporary 'Band-Aid'.

### An ability to continuously improve on all levels, in all areas, every day, has become possible.

Employees are trained in problem-solving methods relevant to their level. These might include tools such as the 5 Whys approach, Fishbone or Six Sigma methods. Those closest to the processes solve problems rapidly using the right techniques.

### Coaching and reflection is frequent and structured.

Leaders and employees share a dual responsibility for solving problems, and leaders use A3 Thinking and Coaching Kata to steer individuals through the learning process.

### Scientific data-driven thinking is embraced and drives every cycle of improvement.

Employees use PDCA to structure improvement activities. Before decisions are taken, data-driven and factual information feeds decision-making to avoid improvements based possibly only on the gut feel of a few individuals. Employees are becoming far more capable of solving problems effectively and this has a significant impact on improvement goals.

## Management-level Kaizen sets the example and encourages system-wide impact.

Department heads take part in problem-solving activities that cross borders into other functions, and are actively engaged in removing obstacles that are outside of the control of the teams. Leaders engage Kaizen techniques to improve systemic and strategic-level indicators. Their impact cascades through to situation-level improvements.

## Knowledge management preserves prior learning and creates cross-learning.

A policy to capture and share knowledge to preserve learning is initiated. A3 reports used in the coaching process capture the problem-solving story and detail how the knowledge is to be shared. Employees learn from others and deploy similar changes in their own areas. The rate of improvement in the healthcare facility is accelerated and learning survives beyond employee turnover.

## There is strong focus on accurate problem-definition, consensus-building and speed of implementation of solutions.

As part of the scientific, data-driven approach, employees understand the importance of defining problems accurately in the planning stages. While time is taken to understand problems with consensus from all parties, solutions are implemented quickly.

---

### PROBLEM SOLVING AND THE GDOH SERVICE DELIVERY IMPROVEMENT INITIATIVE

*Directive: Improve staff efficiency, eliminate waste and reduce patient waiting times*

Each of the four hospitals in Cohort 1 was awarded the opportunity to host a Rapid Process Improvement Workshop (RPIW). The RPIW follows the principles of Kaizen—a breakthrough event held over a short period of five days. During this time, teams were trained and coached to achieve an impressive reduction in patient waiting-times whilst maintaining quality of service. After each of these workshops had been completed focus fell onto each of the model areas to ensure that fragile new processes took root. It is not uncommon for performance to soon return to previous practices after a Kaizen workshop, so the LIA facilitators visited each model area consistently, to coach teams through the barriers to change and risks of regressing into old ways of doing things. To sustain the breakthrough performance, it was necessary for each model area to install a Daily Management System, which would effectively monitor short-term performance and ensure that they were continuously improving and not declining post the workshop. It is this dual-approach of breakthrough and incremental improvement that creates sustained leaps in performance. Without bigger Breakthrough Changes, the team cannot see the real potential of what they are doing and soon loses interest. But it is incremental, day-to-day changes and monitoring, that maintain progress and stimulate further improvement. The Cohort 1 teams achieved both.

---

As part of the problem-solving training, the teams were shown how to prioritise their changes, follow a scientific method (using PDCA) and iterate this approach towards improved levels of performance. They learned to understand the obstacles slowly, and supported by evidence, make decisions they could quickly implement. The five-day workshop was intense but well-structured. Day four saw teams able to test their countermeasures and draw conclusions ahead of the last day. This gave them the assurance that by following the process, they would get a positive result as a team.

The team learned to differentiate normal from abnormal performance, and each model area was able to understand the measures that would trigger improvement. They learned that batching patients made waiting times longer; that cycling the slowest process quicker would speed up the whole Value Stream; that waste steals time and prolongs waiting. They also learned about elements patients value and how the Value Stream delivers on these. They used this new knowledge to pro-actively debate new patterns of work.

Occasionally the teams would encounter an obstacle that they could not resolve. Many teams experienced difficulty with doctor starting times, the IT system's performance and the booking systems. These were obstacles that the team alone could not remove. They engaged with multi-disciplinary teams such as IT specialists and directors to collectively resolve the issues at hand. This collaboration paid off, and many changes were made that could not have been achieved in isolation.

**PLANET** 🌍 **Reducing Environmental Impact**

- Reuse, reduce and eliminate
- Visualise green opportunities
- Execute change with PDCA

▲ Figure 2.7: A Vision for PLANET

**A holistic approach drives improvement activities to reduce environmental impact.**

Improvement goals for reusing, reducing and eliminating materials are included in the improvement strategy and a quantifiable reduction in the footprint is achieved.

**The environmental impact is visible and tactical changes to achieve the Target Condition are executed.**

A Green Value Stream Map has been created to visualise the Current Condition. Opportunities have been identified, quantified and prioritised. The Future State Map has been developed with a phased implementation plan, and is in the process of being implemented.

**Environmental improvement projects use scientific problem-solving techniques to deliver sustainable changes.**

Environmental Health and Safety (EHS) representatives are trained in the principles and application of scientific problem-solving and actively use PDCA cycles to execute changes sustainably. Improvement in the environmental indicators is evident.

At the time of writing *Making a Difference*, no environmental projects had been identified. Yet, it is worth considering that certain cost-reduction projects and operational improvements could lead to reduced environmental impact. This is further discussed in Chapter 4.

# Best Practice and Performance in Tandem

## Invest in training that matters

Albert Einstein is broadly credited with the insightful genius that: 'The definition of insanity is doing the same thing over and over again, but expecting different results.' Despite a lack of proof that he truly coined the expression, the wisdom remains.

To achieve Operational Excellence and reach goals we have never before achieved, we will need to do new things we have never before done—do new Best Practices. To achieve new levels of performance in the 5P Model areas, we need also to learn new ways of working. But, how do you know that the training you invest in to promote PURPOSE, PROCESS, PEOPLE, PROBLEM SOLVING and PLANET, will translate into tangible benefits?

Many employees have uttered the words, 'Training, training, training! I spend so much time in training that there is no time to get my work done. How can that be good for service delivery? The free lunches are the only good thing about it all!'

Investing in training is certainly worthwhile. But what is the antidote to training that does not deliver results? Strive for well-focused development that is carefully designed to encourage the right behaviours, and therefore the right culture for change. If training is properly directed, the right practices will drive the right performance.

## Ready to take a leap of faith?

Consider which of the following states best describes your healthcare facility:

- o The wrong practices drive the wrong behaviours and our goals are not being achieved.
- o There are some good results but these are largely driven by one person, and when this leader leaves the performance will drop too.
- o A great deal of effort has been made to develop employees but the results are not manifesting in the achievement of our goals.
- o The right practices drive the necessary routines. This feeds and replenishes an ongoing performance culture that achieves our goals.

All of the Cohort 1 hospitals aimed to tick the last box. All world-class healthcare facilities strive for the same. If a balance can be struck between the routines created to run a facility and the performance achieved by a facility, not only are its breakthrough goals ultimately realised but they will be sustainable too. This is why it is so important to develop a management system that drives both performance and Best Practice in tandem. Together, these will take your organisation to new heights and steer the billowing sails of your Operational Excellence to bright, new shores.

Remember: See your organisation as it CAN and WILL BE. Be transformed by BOLD possibility. Believe in your potential for excellence. Be brave. Dream BIG. And, above all, cherish the journey.

# 3 THE LEAN VALUE STREAM

## What is Lean?

The survival of today's manufacturing entities, service enterprises and public sector facilities requires continuous improvement for the better. Organisations therefore look to trusted and established philosophies, tools and techniques for wisdom with which to meet the challenges at hand. Lean Thinking is one approach available and has, time and again, proven a highly effective means of bringing about positive and sustainable change.

Simply speaking, Lean Thinking means maximising customer and patient value while minimising waste—providing more value while using fewer resources. Lean is however, not meant to be *mean*. Employing fewer resources does not translate to doing more whilst cutting heads or unfairly squeezing stretched budgets. But realistically, if there is less demand for a service, then the organisation may need to make difficult decisions around its free capacity. Lean Thinking engages staff—both head and heart—in the process of change, so it is assumed that Lean is being attempted in a relatively stable environment, where demand for the product or service truly exists. Lean should not operate alongside *meaner* strategies such as headcount-reduction but it will lead to improved use of capacity and organisations may require strategies to deal with excesses created—for example:

o Allocating additional capacity to Value Streams that require support
o Reducing staff overtime hours and hiring of temporary labour
o Promotion from within the employee body before hiring outside people.

# A Formula for Lean

Is it possible to measure how Lean your facility is? As part of his introduction to Lean at the opening workshops with the GDOH participants, Prof. Faull presented the Efficiency Matrix depicted in Figure 3.1.

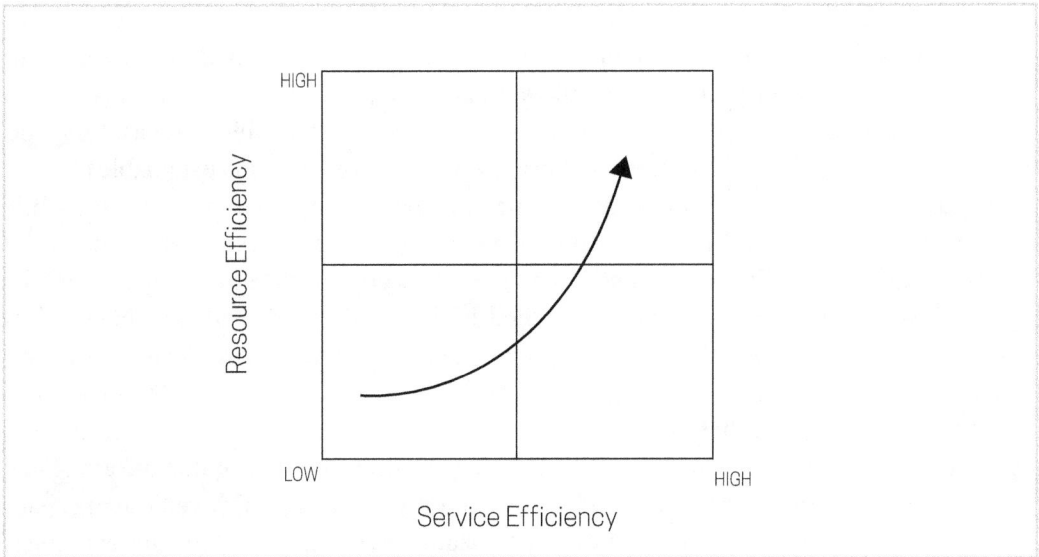

▲ Figure 3.1: Efficiency Matrix (Modig and Ahlstrom, 2012)

The Efficiency Matrix is truly at the heart of operations. It illustrates that becoming Lean involves improvements in both Resource Efficiency:

$$Resource\ Efficiency\ \% = \left( \frac{Actual\ Output}{Rated\ Output} \right) x\ 100$$

and Service Efficiency:

$$Service\ Efficiency\ \% = \left( \frac{Total\ Service\ Time}{Total\ Journey\ Time} \right) x\ 100$$

When Resource Efficiency is at its best, then what employees are doing is aligned with what they should be doing. Say a pharmacist is capable of dispensing 65 scripts within a certain time frame, but only manages 45 scripts. Their Resource Efficiency % is therefore

$$\frac{45}{65} x\ 100 = 69\%$$

Service Efficiency compares the amount of time spent attending to a patient to the amount of time a patient spends on the full patient journey. The longer they spend in queues or waiting, the longer the journey, and the worse the Service Efficiency.

Say a patient spends 25 minutes with the nurse and doctor, but spends 4 hours (240 minutes) in the clinic overall. Service Efficiency % is calculated as

$$\frac{25}{240} \; x \; 100 = 10\%$$

The patient is serviced for a mind-boggling 10% of the time they spend in the clinic. This presents a significant opportunity for improvement on patient waiting times.

If you can support your employees to perform closer to their actual capacity, and if you can take out the waste that increases the patient's journey time, you are targeting both elements of the Efficiency Matrix, bringing you closer to a Lean Value Stream.

Now consider Figure 3.2. where variation can attack the Value Stream and effectively damage both Resource and Service Efficiency.

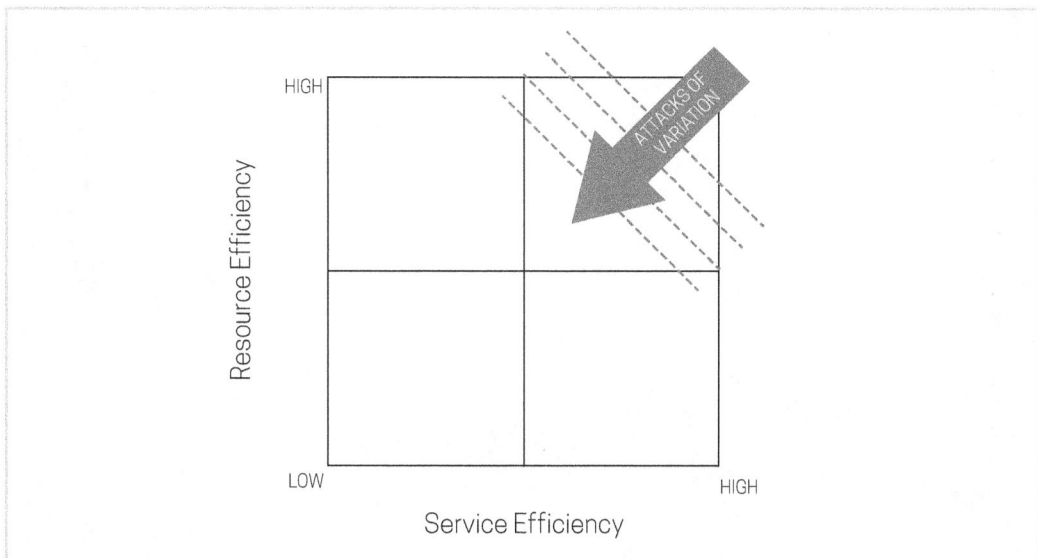

▲ Figure 3.2: Attacks of Variation on the Efficiency Matrix

Variation is a common condition and appreciating its impact can open up new improvement dimensions. Does your facility experience extreme changes in patient numbers? Are nurses not certain what time doctors will arrive to open the clinic every morning? Do you find the patient administration system to be slower on certain days and, in extreme cases, not available at all? Perhaps new staff members perform work differently to more experienced staff leading to longer service times and quality issues. Stop to think about it for a moment. Does patient service flow in exactly the same way each day—in a predictable, productive manner? Or can you see examples of variation that affect an employee's ability to perform to the rated output and that result in a patient waiting longer than is necessary? The latter is most prevalent in many organisations that have seen the slow creep of abnormal conditions becoming the norm.

To develop a Lean Value Stream in your healthcare facility, you want to target both Resource and Service Efficiencies by stabilising operations, reducing attacks of variation and improving the flow of patients. The chapters to follow will guide you through a battle-ready strategy to counter attacks on the frontlines.

# When Abnormal becomes Normal

One of the key points Lean Thinking teaches us is to be able to distinguish the abnormal from the normal. At first glance the differences may not be obvious, but when you stand and watch a process, eventually you start to see the unwelcome and harmful critters that have wormed their way in.

▲ Figure 3.3: The 'abnormal' amidst the 'normal'

The cat in Figure 3.3 is the 'abnormal' amidst the 'normal'. Imagine the chaos the cat could cause if left to integrate into the meerkat mob? It is best for the survival of the mob that he be removed before causing long-term, irreparable damage. If he were to remain and perhaps attract more of his kind to the group, not only might the problem of his abnormal presence escalate, but with time it will also be more difficult to determine how he got there in the first place.

Figure 3.4 was adapted by Prof. Faull from a presentation given in 2013 by John Shook, Lean Management guru and the first American manager at Toyota's operations in Japan. It illustrates the point that if a problem remains undetected, over time the effect of the problem amplifies. The longer a problem festers, the more difficult it will be to establish what caused it in the first place as evidence tracing its origins will no longer be fresh or available.

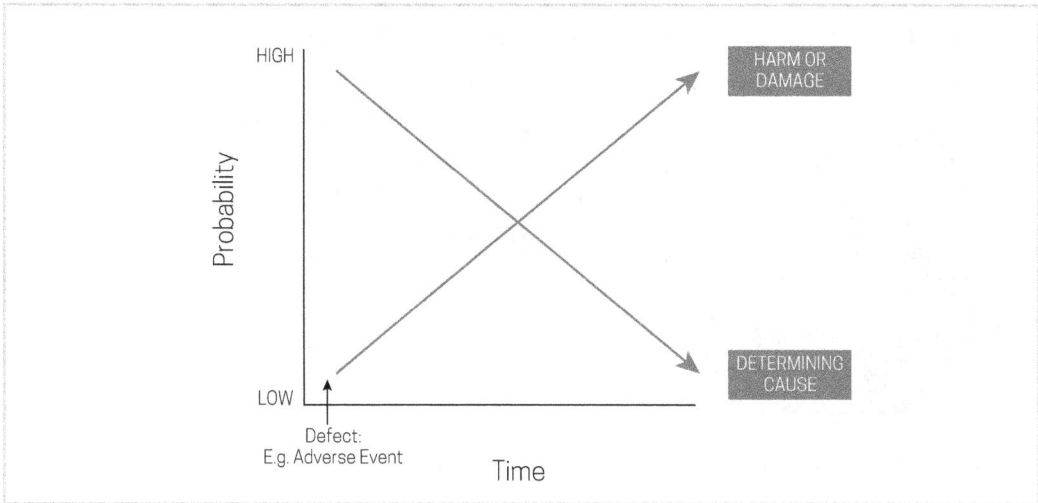

High

Probability

Low

Defect:
E.g. Adverse Event

Time

HARM OR DAMAGE

DETERMINING CAUSE

▲ Figure 3.4: Impact of an abnormal process

Lean Thinking is therefore a powerful weapon in the arsenal of change, not only allowing an organisation to deliver value with less effort, but also encouraging the building of systems that expose abnormal performance, leading to better reliability and quality. If we build systems that do this for us, we will master the art of very quickly distinguishing normal from abnormal, and be able to respond immediately (Faull, 2014).

> Lean Thinking allows an organisation to deliver value with less effort. Build systems to expose abnormal performance, leading to better reliability and quality.

# The Current Condition

## Patient Demand Patterns

A very real example of how attacks of variation challenge public healthcare facilities is that of patient arrival patterns. The queues swell at different times of the day and week making it difficult to plan for staff numbers, coordinate staff breaks and ensure there is a smooth flow of patients from one area to the next rather than a stop-start motion. As a point of departure, it is good to understand what this pattern looks like and how big the problem of variation really is, to prompt staff to work in alternative ways that suit Patient Demand Patterns. In the short-term, healthcare facilities can plan their staff numbers, staff break times and processes to deal with the surges, but in the long-term they should investigate what can be done to stabilise and reduce the variation. Forward-thinking hospitals and clinics are finding innovative ways to deal with this challenge. Figures 3.5 and 3.6 illustrate documentation of weekly and monthly patient registration and the categories of patients typically dealt with on a particular day, shedding light on the variation at hand at one of the Cohort 1 hospitals. This is the first step in stabilising the system.

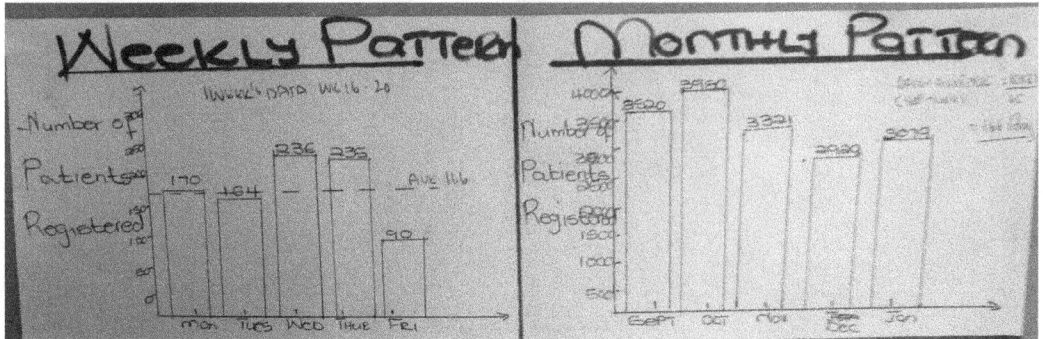

▲ Figure 3.5: Weekly and monthly patient registration patterns

| ME | ORTHO | PENSION | GERERAL | CASHIE |
|---|---|---|---|---|
| 7h00 | 18 | 42 | 44 | 9 |
| 9h30 | ... | ... | ... | ... |
| 0h00 | 6 | 24 | 27 | 6 |
| 10h30 | 6 | 13 | 19 | 4 |
| 11h00 | 2 | 6 | 10 | 2 |
| 11h30 | 2 | 0 | 3 | 1 |
| %. | 19 %. | 30 %. | 51 %. | |

▲ Figure 3.6: Categories of patients dealt with

At face value it may seem there is little to be done about patient arrival times, and in the short-term this may be true. There are however countermeasures to be explored before abandoning a clear opportunity for improved processes.

## Clinic Schedules

Reviewing patient arrival patterns could justify changes to clinic times or changes to the days on which clinics run, so spreading the workload more evenly across the week and across shifts. Often clinics will experience that from Monday to Thursday, they see a heavier patient load leading to excessive waiting times and dissatisfied patients. Yet Fridays might be remarkably quiet. For the sake of both patients and employees it may be worth evaluating such opportunities for resource re-allocation according to demand. If clinic schedules cannot be changed, clinics and hospitals may find other innovative ways to use the quieter time more effectively, perhaps for problem-solving or better organising all areas of the workplace so that busy days run more smoothly.

## Patient Arrival Times

Many patients arrive early in the morning prior to administration office or clinic opening times. This is both due to transport constraints and the belief that the earlier they arrive, the sooner they will be serviced. Some healthcare facilities are investigating implementing specific patient arrival time slots to more evenly stagger the hospital's workload. Others have implemented rosters so that certain patients are seen earlier in the day by a skeleton staff of doctors and nurses. Once ward rounds have been completed more doctors arrive as the day progresses. This system means some patients are dealt with earlier in the shift and that more doctors are available later in the day, at the busiest times to see more patients, so reducing the overall congestion.

## Cross-functional problem-solving

It is not uncommon to observe patient administration, the clinics and pharmacy operating in complete isolation. Key to achieving a Lean Value Stream is working across departments—one large team striving towards a common goal. Practically, this means understanding issues and solving problems across the Value Stream, and ensuring that an improvement in one area is not detrimental to patient waiting times or quality of service in another.

Consider the example of an EOPD or Eye Out-Patient Department, at one of the Cohort 1 hospitals, which was experiencing excessive patient waiting times in the first four hours of the day. This not only resulted in distressed patients, but also in overloaded nurses and doctors. Patients needing attention far exceeded the available medical staff capacity and patients would often be sent home without having had a consultation at all. After a few rounds of problem-solving, it was decided that the patient booking system would be redesigned to spread the workload across the day and stabilise the patient numbers by matching them to staff and doctor capacity. These sorts of decisions and innovative new systems cannot be implemented in isolation. Support from the governing hospital department is key to incorporating the new system and work routines into daily Best Practice. If there is a common inter-departmental understanding of the problem faced by all divisions, it is possible to agree on mutually-beneficial countermeasures. This approach should also extend to include inter-healthcare facility problem-solving across multiple state hospitals facing similar challenges in different geographical areas.

## Planning for Predictable Peaks and Troughs

Patient demand tends to pick up and slow down at different times of the year. This could be influenced by public holidays, the festive season or seasonal changes. As such, healthcare facilities experience relatively predictable annual spikes in patient numbers.

Once this seasonal demand pattern has been defined, it is possible to pro-actively plan for these spikes. Consider a pharmacy at one of the Cohort 1 hospitals that annually takes in a group of new learners during a holiday period. It takes time to train them and ensure their performance is up to the standards required. Predictable, annual surges in patient demand following the holiday period expose novice learners to pressure they may not be ready to handle and result in much longer patient waiting times. The requisite counter-measure introduced at the pharmacy in question, focused on fine-tuning the induction of new staff to make them competent sooner and prepare them to meet the coming demand surge. New staff were therefore ready to perform to standard and at the required speed and the impact on the patient was diminished or went largely unnoticed.

To establish the patient demand your facility is dealing with, it is necessary to access data detailing the number of patients serviced every hour, each day of the week and each month, by each department. This will help to visualise how patient numbers change across various periods, allowing you to extract patterns and implement systems to best meet the demand patterns now laid bare.

‣ If system data is reliable, gather three months' data and sort it into a spread-sheet as follows:
  » Number of patients seen each day
  » Number of patients seen each hour on the busiest clinic day
‣ Develop graphs (see Figure 3.7) to illustrate:
  » Hourly patient demand for each busy clinic day
  » Daily patient demand for each month
  » Weekly patient demand (show the load for each day of the week)
  » Monthly patient demand (show the load for each month of the year)
  » Indicate the minimum, average and maximum range for each graph
  » For pharmacies, include the number of scripts and patients dealt with
‣ Review the trends experienced and document peaks and troughs. Discuss the reasons for the patterns observed. More studies may be needed to understand the causes, but use this exercise to start highlighting the opportunities and potential to reduce attacks of variation.
‣ In your discussions, continue to think 'Value Stream'. Will an improvement in one area result in an improvement impact on the entire patient journey? There is little value in saving time in one area only to amplify queues in the next.

**EXAMPLE**

**Monthly Patient Demand - Pharmacy**
**November 15**

Min: 842
Average: 1377
Max: 1945

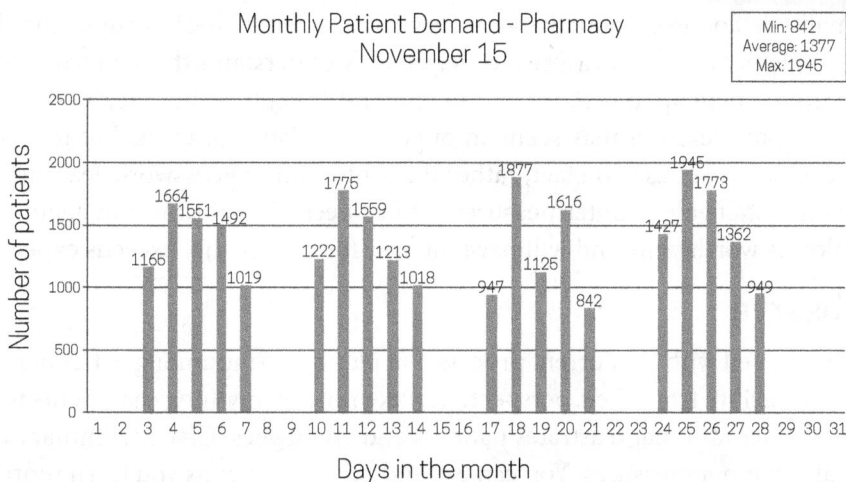

Figure 3.7: Example of a monthly demand pattern in a pharmacy

# Daily Measurement Systems

Patient waiting times tell part of the story of a patient's experience. Yet, they give little insight into what is driving the waiting time duration and causing any delays experienced. As such it is useful to differentiate between input and output measures (Figure 3.8). Output measures refer to the service the patient has received and the outcome of their experience and encompass all the things that matter to a patient. Patients are not concerned with how many people arrived for work on time, how well processes are designed or the reasons for system downtime. The only thing that interests them is how quickly and effectively they can be seen and helped. Input measures refer to the contributing factors that affect the output measures. They teach you about the elements to control in order to achieve more stable outcomes.

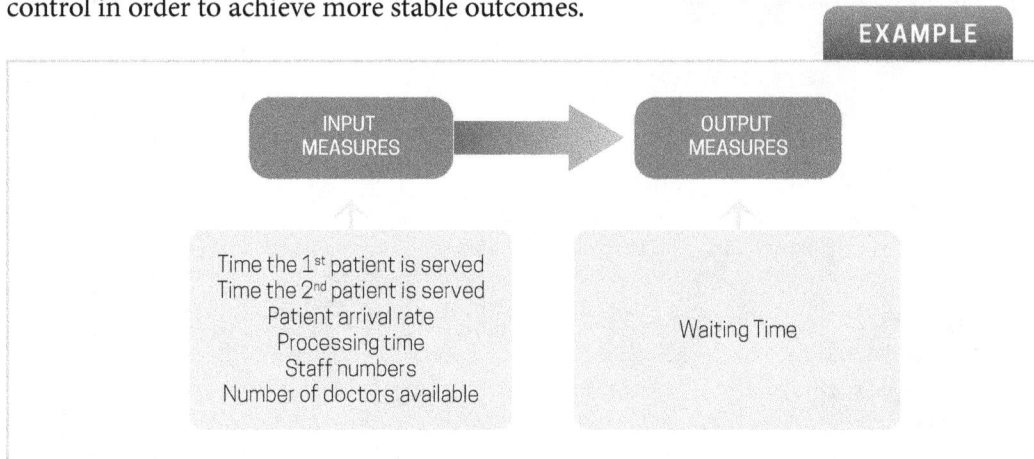

**Figure 3.8:** Example of the input measures that drive the output measure of waiting time

Waiting time is only one example of an output measure. Quality of service should also be measured. Doctors often voice concerns that improving flow without maintaining service quality is counterproductive—and rightly so. Every healthcare facility has the power to implement input measures to help teams understand the 'abnormal' in more depth, and to set them up to succeed in resolving the difficulties they face. Gathering data that defines input measures may seem an ongoing and laborious task, but it also means decisions can be made based on fact, rather than intuition or guesswork, leading to more effective and sustainable countermeasures. It has been shown time and again that this upfront effort is worthwhile and will pave the way for change that exceeds expectation.

## First Observe

Familiarise yourself with the current processes at play by sitting among patients and experiencing your facility from their perspective. Take note of anything that seems to hinder the flow of service and that frustrates patients and employees. Give preliminary thought to potential key input measures. You can expand on them later as you learn more.

## Install a Data-Gathering Sheet

As mentioned previously, if data is not available or reliable, it is necessary to make use of a data-gathering sheet, a method to gather raw data and better understand the input measures. It is essential to identify individuals who can dedicate time to this somewhat drawn-out endeavour. Table 3.1 is designed to capture four areas of data that are central to a public healthcare facility's processes:

o How quickly each area makes ready to serve patients in the morning
o Queue sizes and how these change over the course of the day
o Total patients seen each day and each week
o Challenges observed that will need solutions.

## MEDICAL OUT-PATIENT CLINIC DAILY MEASUREMENT

DATE RANGE:

| START-UP MEASURE | | M | T | W | T | F | AVERAGE FOR THE WEEK | OBSTACLES OBSERVED |
|---|---|---|---|---|---|---|---|---|
| TIME 1ST PATIENT SERVICED | | | | | | | | |
| TIME 2ND PATIENT SERVICED | | | | | | | | |
| QUEUE MEASURE | | M | T | W | T | F | AVERAGE FOR THE WEEK | |
| 07H00 TO 07H30 | NO. PATIENTS SERVICED | | | | | | | |
| | NO. OF PATIENTS IN QUEUE | | | | | | | |
| 07H30 TO 08H00 | NO. PATIENTS SERVICED | | | | | | | |
| | NO. OF PATIENTS IN QUEUE | | | | | | | |
| 08H00 TO 08H30 | NO. PATIENTS SERVICED | | | | | | | |
| | NO. OF PATIENTS IN QUEUE | | | | | | | |
| 08H30 TO 09H00 | NO. PATIENTS SERVICED | | | | | | | |
| | NO. OF PATIENTS IN QUEUE | | | | | | | |
| 09H00 TO 09H30 | NO. PATIENTS SERVICED | | | | | | | |
| | NO. OF PATIENTS IN QUEUE | | | | | | | |
| 09H30 TO 10H00 | NO. PATIENTS SERVICED | | | | | | | |
| | NO. OF PATIENTS IN QUEUE | | | | | | | |
| 10H00 TO 10H30 | NO. PATIENTS SERVICED | | | | | | | |
| | NO. OF PATIENTS IN QUEUE | | | | | | | |
| 10H30 TO 11H00 | NO. PATIENTS SERVICED | | | | | | | |
| | NO. OF PATIENTS IN QUEUE | | | | | | | |
| 11H00 TO 11H30 | NO. PATIENTS SERVICED | | | | | | | |
| | NO. OF PATIENTS IN QUEUE | | | | | | | |
| 11H30 TO 12H00 | NO. PATIENTS SERVICED | | | | | | | |
| | NO. OF PATIENTS IN QUEUE | | | | | | | |
| 12H00 TO 12H30 | NO. PATIENTS SERVICED | | | | | | | |
| | NO. OF PATIENTS IN QUEUE | | | | | | | |
| 12H30 TO 13H00 | NO. PATIENTS SERVICED | | | | | | | |
| | NO. OF PATIENTS IN QUEUE | | | | | | | |
| 13H00 TO 13H30 | NO. PATIENTS SERVICED | | | | | | | |
| | NO. OF PATIENTS IN QUEUE | | | | | | | |
| 13H30 TO 14H00 | NO. PATIENTS SERVICED | | | | | | | |
| | NO. OF PATIENTS IN QUEUE | | | | | | | |
| 14H00 TO 14H30 | NO. PATIENTS SERVICED | | | | | | | |
| | NO. OF PATIENTS IN QUEUE | | | | | | | |
| 14H30 TO 15H00 | NO. PATIENTS SERVICED | | | | | | | |
| | NO. OF PATIENTS IN QUEUE | | | | | | | |
| 15H00 TO 15H30 | NO. PATIENTS SERVICED | | | | | | | |
| | NO. OF PATIENTS IN QUEUE | | | | | | | |
| 15H30 TO 16H00 | NO. PATIENTS SERVICED | | | | | | | |
| | NO. OF PATIENTS IN QUEUE | | | | | | | |
| SUMMARY MEASURE | | M | T | W | T | F | AVERAGE FOR THE WEEK | |
| TOTAL PATIENTS TODAY | | | | | | | | |

▲ Table 3.1: Example of a data-gathering sheet

This sheet can be customised to bring in additional information required. For example, doctor or staff numbers can be tracked for each period indicating how resource-loading affects the patient waiting time. Clinics can include data on the number of patients booked but who do not show up or patients who arrive without an appointment, so affecting the queues. Data from the measurement sheet can be converted to very useful visuals such as graphs and trend maps.

Figure 3.9 illustrates how well the registration area at one of the Cohort 1 hospitals starts up in the morning as well as the interval between successive patient registrations. Controlling this input measure means patients will be consistently serviced as the doors open.

**EXAMPLE**

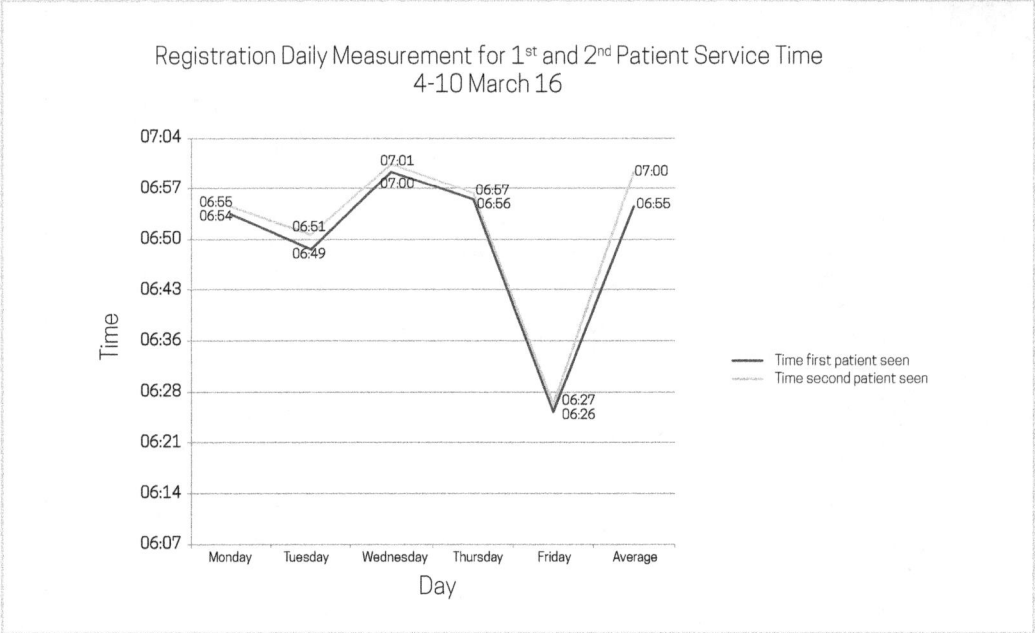

Registration Daily Measurement for 1st and 2nd Patient Service Time
4-10 March 16

▲ Figure 3.9: Example of a registration start-up daily measurement

Figure 3.10 illustrates the productivity per team in an Out-Patient pharmacy and includes both data on the patients served and number of scripts dispensed. This allows the team to monitor their daily performance and to ensure equitable workload distribution between service lines.

Take time to define measures for the process. By controlling the input measures you will achieve more stable output performance.

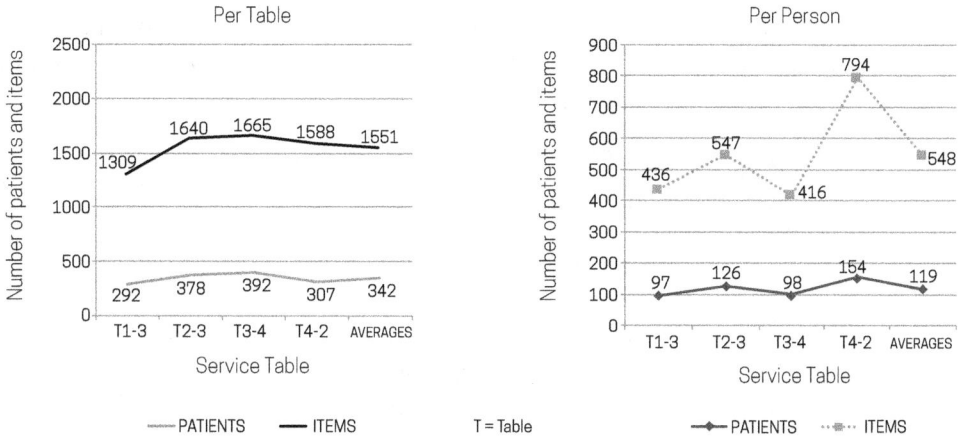

Patients Served at OPD Pharmacy on 6th May 2016

▲ Figure 3.10: Example of productivity and loading per pharmacy line

Figure 3.11 tracks daily times at which doctors begin their work at one of the Cohort 1 hospitals. A roster ensures the right number of doctors are available to consult at the heaviest patient demand times. This graph could also track clinic start times, differentiating nursing data from doctor-patient consultation data.

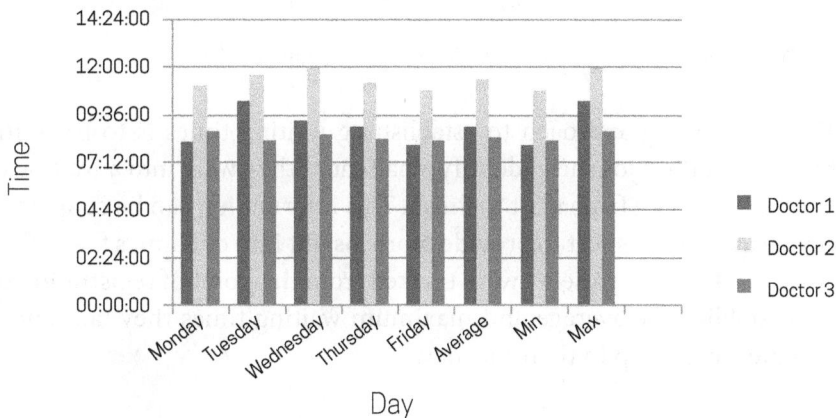

MOPD Doctor Start Times
June 16

▲ Figure 3.11: Example of doctor starting times for a Medical Out-Patient Clinic

Figure 3.12 manually illustrates average patient waiting times at a clinic. It is not critical that graphs be digitally compiled. There is tremendous benefit to completing graphs manually as the process does not require advanced word processor skills and can be updated in real-time. Staff completing a graph manually become connected to the process as they engage with the data and what it could signify. Figure 3.12 is a particularly good example as the nursing staff include reasons for spikes in the waiting time captured, which is beneficial to problem-solving.

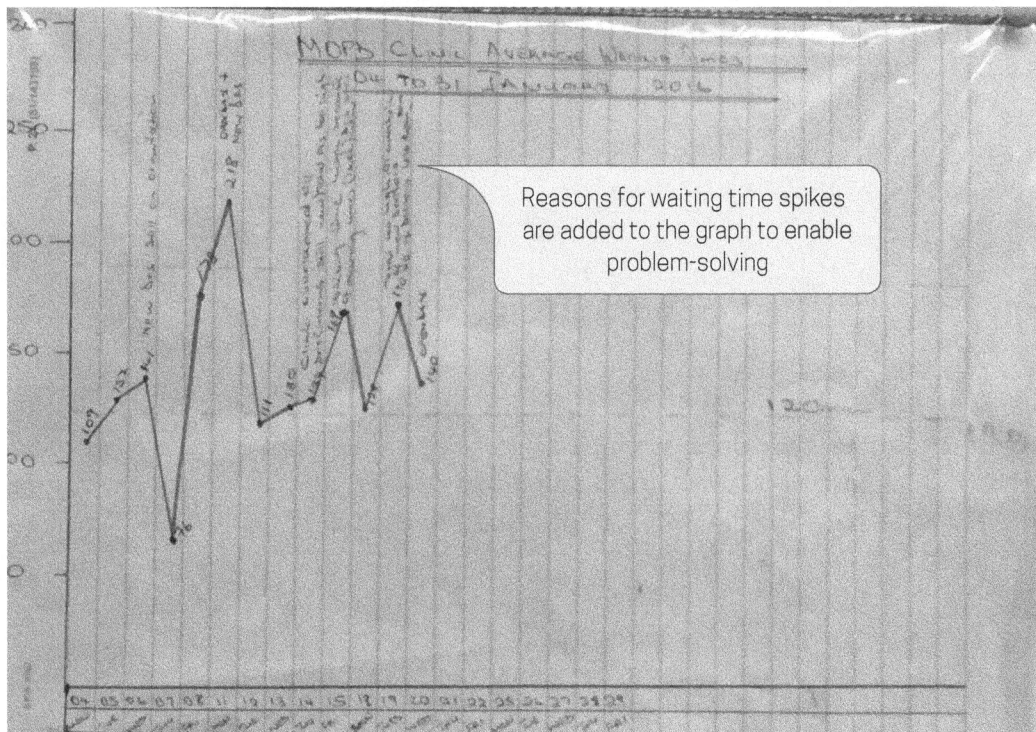

Reasons for waiting time spikes are added to the graph to enable problem-solving

▲ Figure 3.12: Manually capturing patient waiting times and reasons

A more time-consuming approach to establishing waiting times is to track individual patients throughout their journey. Identify a patient as they walk into a waiting or reception area, and follow them from start to finish. This information can be coupled with data from a daily measurement sheet to provide more insight into dynamics that affect waiting times. In Figure 3.13, eight patients were tracked from the point of registration on a busy clinic day to establish the average and maximum waiting times they face and the time taken to complete each step in their journey.

> Staff completing a graph manually become connected to the process as they engage with the data and what it could signify.

▲ Figure 3.13: Tracking eight patients through a Patient Journey

The team summarised the data gathered into the graph seen in Figure 3.14. The impact that file collection waiting time was having on the overall process became apparent as did areas of the registration process that needed work. With more individual patient samples this exercise could provide additional information on the variation in waiting times between clinics to prioritise clinic-specific interventions—a handy focusing-tool when the team is overwhelmed and unsure of where to begin making changes.

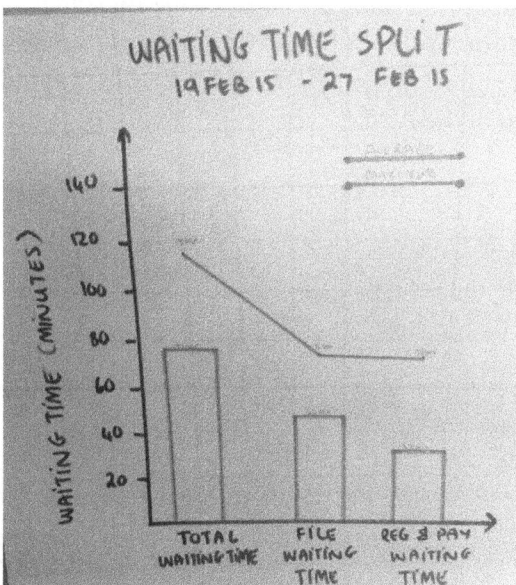

◀ Figure 3.14: Summarised data from eight aggregated patient journeys reveals factors affecting patient waiting times

# 'Go-See' Gemba Walks

As a leader, no matter how confident you are of your facts, always personally 'go-see' the actual condition of processes you manage and speak to the employees and patients in the areas visited (see Figure 3.15). Dated and biased opinions may lead to a vague interpretation of the issues at hand. But 'go-see' provides you with up-to-date and truthful information with which to make informed decisions. The hospital CEO, heads of department and staff involved in making improvements should all include 'go-see' as part of their regular work routine.

▲ **Figure 3.15**: The Gemba is the actual place where work takes place

Prof. Faull shared an explanation with a team from one of the Cohort 1 hospitals, of the Gemba Walk as described to him by his Japanese mentor, Furuhashi-San. The mentor explained that, in Japan, 'Gemba' means both the location where work is done and also the location of a crime scene. A good detective will never attempt to solve a crime from the safety of a police station office. A good detective goes to 'Gemba', to the scene of the crime and questions potential witnesses, gathers evidence and seeks the truth at the place where events took place. Armed with key facts and forensic evidence gathered for analysis, the detective unfolds the most likely scenario. This is no different to what the 'go-see' aims to achieve in the workplace.

Executing the improvements that lead toward a vision for Operational Excellence requires several iterations of a particular cycle of experimentation. We scientifically formulate hypotheses and then test them with information gathered from repeated 'go-see' episodes. The process of experimentation is depicted in the PDCA cycle (Figure 3.16). In the diagram, 'go-see' is central to all four steps of the PDCA cycle (see Chapter 6).

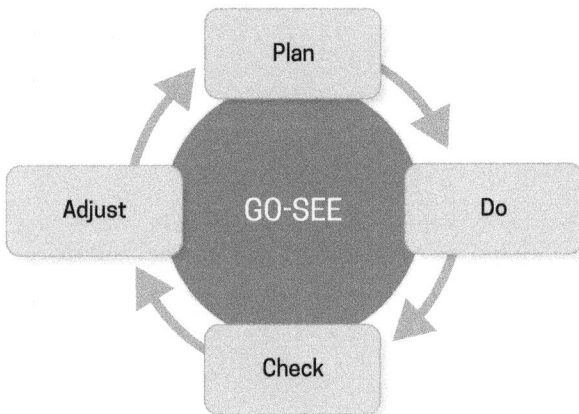

◄ **Figure 3.16**: Go-see and the PDCA cycle

# Spaghetti Diagrams

As discussed above, the best way to fully appreciate both a patient and staff member's experience of any site, is to 'go-see' the Gemba. The data obtained there is then best captured in a Spaghetti Diagram. As the name suggests it will look similar to a bowl of spaghetti when completed—a sumptuous mix of information, substance and flavourful depth through which to work. The Spaghetti Diagram maps the layout of the area through which a patient or patient file travel and the path they follow. It is also useful to track the path of the employee to establish any potential obstacles in the current flow of work. Once the diagram is complete, distances are mapped in detail to highlight any excessive motion, transportation and handling taking place. The team is then ready to discuss and improve upon the Current Condition.

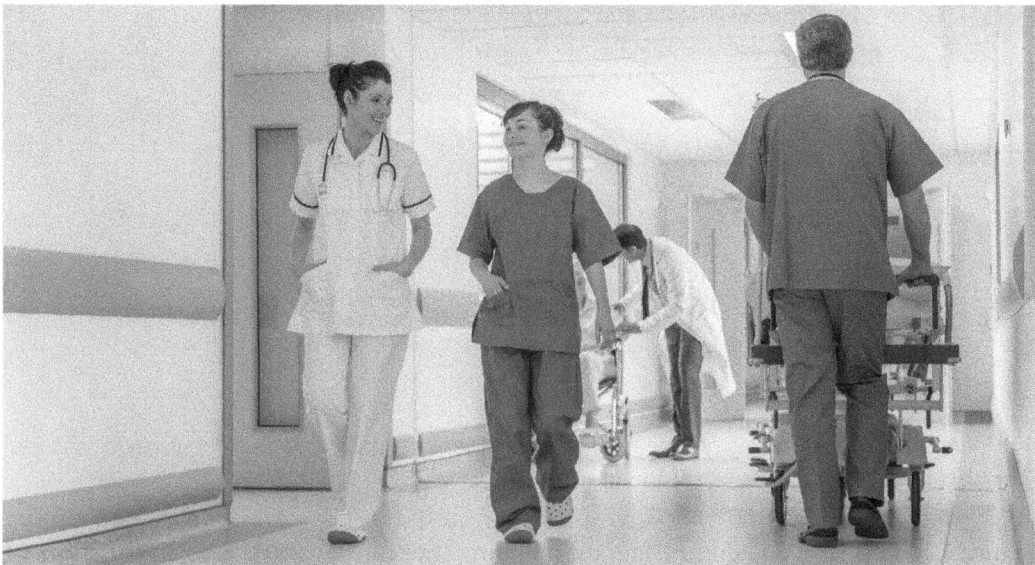

Excess motion (distances walked to carry out work or to go between departments) is one element of waste typical of many processes. It always presents a potentially significant opportunity for improvement and could be considered an easy win or 'low-hanging fruit'. In the public sector we are accustomed to layouts that have grown organically over time, to the extent that process efficiency is hindered by the way in which departments, and the processes that connect them, are laid out. It is not unusual to find staff and patients walking long distances between departments to fetch forms, to pick medication and to access vital equipment or computer systems.

The team responsible for the improvement of a registration process at one of the Cohort 1 hospitals found that the distance between registration counters and the cashier required excessive walking to traverse. For every patient serviced, the clerk would walk to the cashier with the patient's file. The cycle time to register each patient manually took, on average, 6.8 minutes per patient (with a maximum of 14 minutes per patient). The counter was idle for up to one minute each time the clerk walked to the cashier. The team developed the Spaghetti Diagram in Figure 3.17 to illustrate this clear waste, and to quantify the impact. The registration process was flagged as a priority for improvement, so the team discussed options to reduce the walking time and so reduce time wasted. Various changes were implemented and the resultant reduced walking time had a 40 percent impact on cutting the patient registration cycle time by 38 percent.

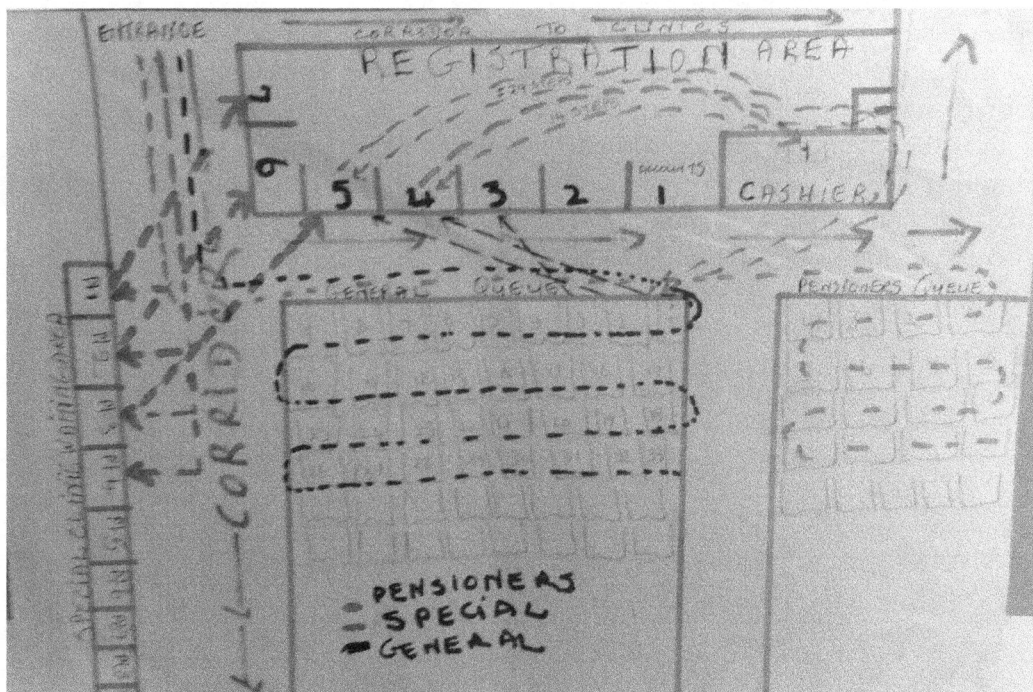

▲ **Figure 3.17**: Spaghetti Diagram constructed at the Gemba exposing motion at registration and the waiting areas

Figure 3.18 depicts a Spaghetti Diagram mapping the team's 'go-see' walk in the shoes of pickers who collect scripts in an Out-Patient Pharmacy. The team began by drawing the basic layout, and then followed a number of samples until they had a firm handle on the typical flow. Their immediate reaction was one of disbelief. They were astounded at the distance each picker walked each day to complete their work—100 000m or the equivalent of walking the distance from Soweto to Pretoria over the course of a year—just to fill a standard script! They evaluated the demand for particular drugs over the previous year, and captured this data into a spreadsheet they could manipulate. They identified the 20 percent of drugs that made up 80 percent of the demand, and then reviewed how these items were laid out on the Out-Patient Pharmacy shelves. Relocating commonly used items closer to the tables on which the drugs were packed, eliminated a substantial amount of walking. Within the workshop, walking was reduced by half and the team maintained improvement efforts to reduce this further over time. Although this was not the only change implemented, the reorientation of key drugs and other countermeasures cut patient waiting time by over 40 percent. It is clear that Spaghetti Diagrams hold great potential not only for the benefit of the patient but also the wellbeing of the staff.

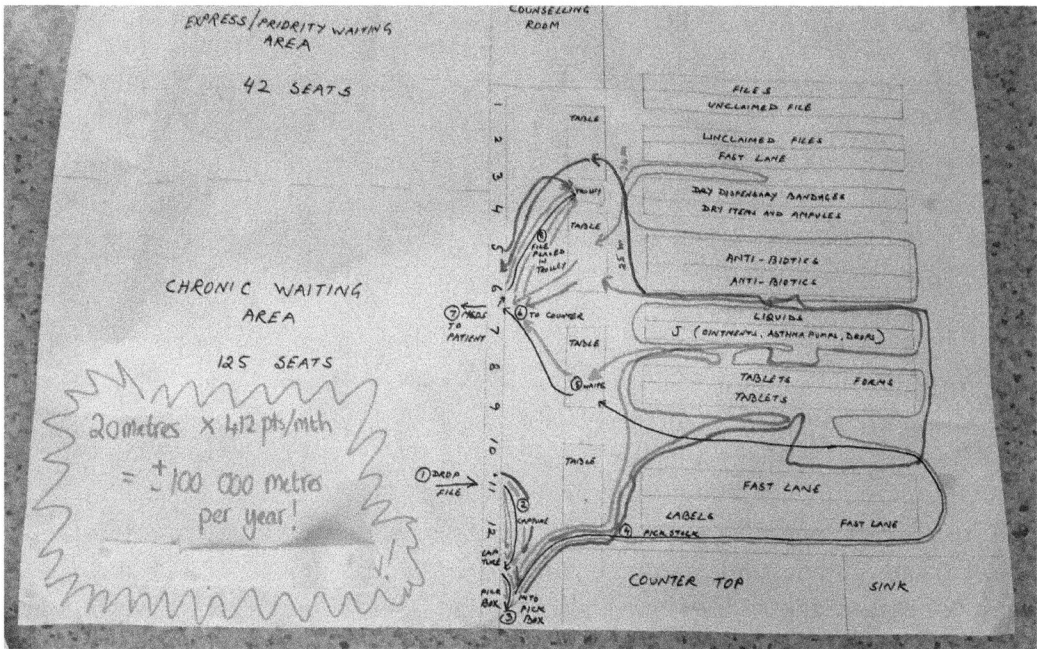

## PRACTICAL ACTIVITY: Creating a Spaghetti Diagram

▸ Go to Gemba and draw a sketch of the plan-view layout on a flipchart or A3 paper. Include labels on the layout to ensure the content of the sketch is explicit. A good day to do this is on a particularly busy day to capture a typical flow.

▸ Using coloured pens, mark the various routes of at least 10 samples. You will either be following a patient, a folder (or some other document) or an employee.

▸ Calculate the distance travelled for each element of the journey. If you do not have a distance-measuring wheel, use the number of footsteps taken as an indicator.

▸ Total up the entire journey, and if applicable, show the minimum, average and maximum distances travelled.

▸ Highlight areas that appear excessive and discuss obstacles, causes and options.

▸ On the diagram, indicate the potential saving that can be attained and how.

It is often not possible to make major layout changes due to infrastructure and budget constraints. It is important that the team not become disheartened by things they cannot change. Instead, they should be steered towards options they can impact. As in the example provided above, simple, low-cost changes could lead to leaps in performance improvement where many small changes add up to significant results.

# The Current Best Method

Quite often, we enthusiastically dive into making improvements without considering the current standard in place. The path to improvement requires an understanding of the Current Best Method and establishing how well the workplace adheres to it—how 'normal' is the performance? It is risky to implement change before first stabilising the Current Best Method. Once you have current standards in place and your staff performs their work to those standards with no abnormalities in the mix, you have a controlled platform from which to launch improvement efforts.

At one of the Cohort 1 hospitals, a team focused on the reduction of waiting time at a Patient Administration process. The team was unable to find a documented standard for this process and this made the evaluation of the true Current Condition that much more challenging. What the team was able to discern were key factors driving waiting times in the Patient Administration process, which included:

o   The starting times of the administration office
o   The number of staff allocated to service counters
o   Ensuring that patients were waiting in the correct queues
o   Ensuring that patients had the correct documentation with them
o   The time taken to process each patient.

It was clear that if these elements were properly controlled, waiting times would stabilise to less than half of those identified in the Current Condition. Although it took time to assign the right number of regular staff to the counters, once this was achieved the supervisor was able to coach them according to the best methods of patient service. He carefully monitored the cycle times for each counter and each time the process took longer than 90 seconds this abnormality triggered investigation of the cause and further coaching of staff. Over time, these efforts resulted in an impressive 80 percent reduction in waiting times. Most importantly, this was sustained going forward. The supervisor documented the Current Best Method into a standard, and this became the daily work routine followed by all the staff. Figure 3.19 illustrates the standard followed—essentially the baseline for further improvement, a training tool for new staff and a means through which to evaluate performance and obstacles. As a guideline, a well-written standard will include a description of the work to be done, the sequence in which it should be done, how long it should take and the quality of the expected outcome.

**GAUTENG PROVINCE**

HEALTH
REPUBLIC OF SOUTH AFRICA

## Operation Procedure for Registration clerk on Lean Project

1. Patients received greeted and file perused for compliance.
    a. Proof  of Address
    b. Proof of income
    c. Proof of identity
    d. Patient's details for correct classification identified and corrected.( GDF 4  and GDF 5 )
2. Visit booking checked for the day.
   **(un-booked patients  sent to  respective clinic for instruction to proceed or rebook )**
3. Patients file visit registered
4. Patients  requested to pay for service
5. Patient reminded of outstanding bills
6. File returned to patient to proceed to clinic  for service

Measured processing time

= 55 second minimum

= 1min 30 sec -  maximum.

▲ Figure 3.19: Example of a Current Best Method standard

# Time Studies

Time studies are an effective way to get to grips with the current process—how long does it take to service a patient? The time you spend observing work also presents clues as to improvement areas to be pursued. Prioritise Time Studies—the information gleaned will be invaluable to several studies going forward.

At this stage, it is not necessary to perform the sort of detailed capacity study undertaken by Industrial Engineers and Work Study Officers. For now, what we need is a reasonable indication of where work flow inhibitors are to be found. Should one particular element of work stand out as problematic, a more detailed study can then be performed focussing on that area. As such, initial Time Studies are simple and not excessively time consuming.

The time you spend observing work presents clues as to improvement areas to be pursued.

# Work Balance Charts

With Time Studies completed, you have a good idea of how long each process takes. Now, it will be particularly useful to visualise this information and use it as a discussion point. A Work Balance Chart is a means through which to show the work distribution amongst employees. Some processes take longer than others and some employees have more work to complete than others. By understanding this picture, you can make decisions about how to better distribute their work for improved flow.

A Work Balance Chart is also a powerful tool to put times into perspective. Sometimes we think speeding up a process will reduce waiting times, but unless we have picked out the slowest process and are directing efforts towards it, we could be cycling a faster process that will have no overall impact on the patient.

Think about a rowing team (Figure 3.21). If the third team member from the front is rowing faster than everyone else, will they get where they are going any faster? Not likely. His 'over-performance' may very well slow them. But, if the team is rowing in the same synchronised way, with an even pace, they will be in a better position to win—as a team.

◀ Figure 3.21: A rowing team synchronised for optimum results

When servicing patients, we want everyone to be 'rowing' at a similar pace, in tune with the patient arrival rate, so that when a patient arrives we can cycle them through their journey with both speed and Purpose. This means we first need to understand the Current Condition. How evenly-distributed is the workload? Of course we cannot just move work from one employee to another if they are not qualified or skilled to perform this function. We need to keep healthcare compliance in mind when deciding on new and innovative ways of creating flow.

Figure 3.22 is an example of a Work Balance Chart and indicates the workload distribution, times, number of staff and the Patient Demand Rate (PDR). The PDR is an indicator of how often a patient needs to be serviced in order to keep up with demand. It is a useful indicator against which to compare current patient processing times. If a process takes longer than the PDR, the employee will not be able to keep up and the queue will grow. If the process takes less time than the PDR, there will be excess employee capacity to service patients and cope with some fluctuation in demand

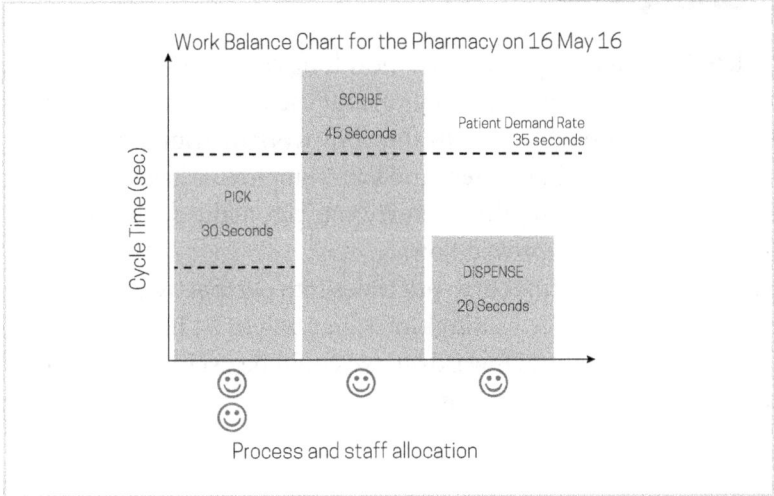

**EXAMPLE**

◀ Figure 3.22: Work Balance Chart for a Pharmacy

Work Balance Chart for the Pharmacy on 16 May 16

Cycle Time (sec)

SCRIBE
45 Seconds

Patient Demand Rate
35 seconds

PICK
30 Seconds

DISPENSE
20 Seconds

Process and staff allocation

At the pharmacy depicted in Figure 3.22, the scribing process takes the longest. Although the picking time averages 30 seconds, that workload is halved between two employees. The dispensing process is therefore second in line in terms of loading. For the team to improve the flow of this process, they need to find ways to accelerate the scribing process. For example, at a particular pharmacy it was found that the pharmacists were performing tasks that could have been done by an assistant under supervision. When the work was passed on to the assistant, it increased their workload marginally, but improved the speed of the scribing process substantially and therefore the overall Value Stream improved. The reduced scribing time increased the speed of flow, and removed pressure on the pharmacist giving them more time to check the quality of the scripts being dispensed. Everyone wins!

To calculate the Patient Demand Rate (PDR):

$$PDR = \frac{Available\ Time}{Patient\ Demand}$$

Where:
*Available Time is the shift time less any planned breaks and meetings*
*The Patient Demand is the number of patients seen during a shift*

Example:

$$PDR = \frac{480min - 45min}{745\ patients\ per\ day} = \frac{435min}{745\ patients\ per\ day} = 0.58\ min$$

*Multiply 0.58 min by 60 to convert to seconds:*

$$PDR = 35\ sec$$

In other words, the staff must service a patient every 35 seconds to keep up with the Patient Demand Rate. Practically, aim to service the patient in less than this time (for example 10% less) to allow for demand fluctuation and obstacles that may arise. In the example above aim for a cycle time of 31 seconds as the Target Condition.

Change agents do differ on their advice as to how to calculate and apply the PDR. Some prefer to calculate it for peak times only, since an average PDR will not truly reflect the high variation in queues throughout a shift or day. It is therefore useful to think about what the staff loading should be during peak times versus quiet times as depicted in Figure 3.23. It is also a good opportunity to discuss how improving the prevalent demand patterns can also even out the workload. Figure 3.23 shows how the staff allocation will change under different demand scenarios.

> To calculate the PDR at your facility, select the available time and patient demand for the same time-period. If you use the Available Time for an hour, be sure to use the Patient Demand for the same hour. The same for a shift, a day, a week or a month.

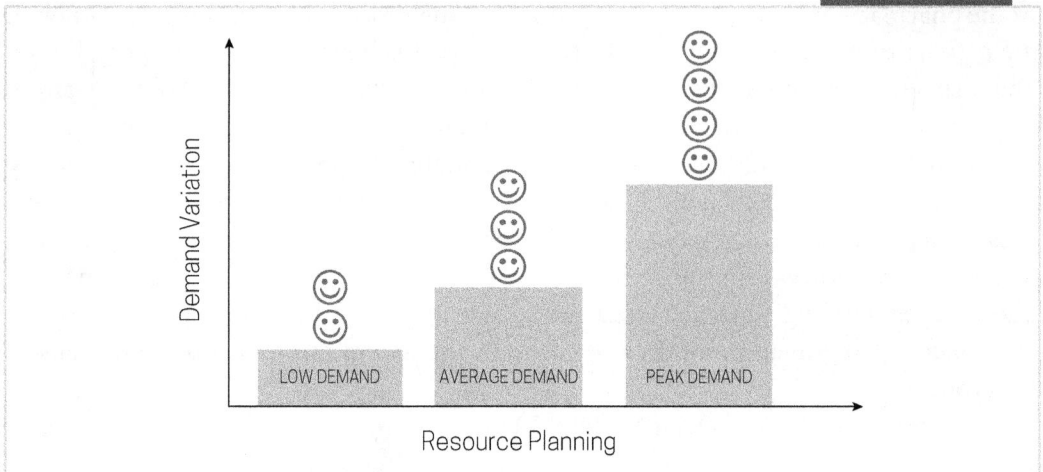

▲ Figure 3.23: Staff allocation meets Patient Demand Rate variation

## PRACTICAL ACTIVITY: Identifying the Bottleneck Process

▸ Use the summary times from the Time Study, and capture the current distribution of work onto the Work Balance Chart.
▸ Calculate the Patient Demand Rate and include it on the chart.
▸ Identify the bottleneck or the process that restricts the flow of patients.
▸ Discuss options to even the work flow and reduce the bottleneck time.

# Value Stream Mapping

It can be daunting to be tasked with improving a problem area and reducing patient waiting time. There may be hundreds of problematic issues that need to be addressed and it is ambitious to think they all might be tackled simultaneously. It is helpful to have a tool through which to visualise the current state of the area and to help focus the team on the most critical changes needed. That is where the Value Stream Map comes in. It is a valuable tool to help conceptualise work being carried out and chart a future vision for improvement to meet the needs of the patient.

*'Whenever there is a service for a patient, there is a Value Stream.*
*The challenge lies in seeing it.'*

(Adapted from Rother and Shook, 1999)

The Value Stream Mapping tool has several advantages that make it an attractive method for sketching obstacles and charting the Target Condition:

o   It shifts focus onto fixing the whole Value Stream and not just its constituent parts.
o   It shows the storyboard of workflows, and how they are linked.
o   It offers a visual evaluation of the Current Condition and relevant metrics, such as queue sizes and waiting times.
o   The visual nature of Value Stream Mapping makes it possible to share so as to seek the wisdom of the majority of the team and not just individuals.
o   It becomes possible to see waste and process-disconnects, their impact on the system and, in many cases, the sources of the problems revealed.
o   It prioritises what to fix, why, by how much and in what order.
o   Processes are better documented and understood so encouraging debate, consensus-building and learning using a common language.

> The visual nature of Value Stream Mapping makes it possible to share so as to seek the wisdom of the majority of the team and not just individuals.

## The High-Level View

To get started on a Value Stream Map it is first key to understand the total journey the patient undertakes. At this stage it is not necessary to have all the metrics in place, just the high-level flow that you are dealing with. Figure 3.24 depicts the out-patient journey at one of the Cohort 1 hospitals, from the time a patient arrives in the reception area to the time when they have received their script and are ready to leave the hospital.

Select a flow—for example the Medical Out-patient Department (MOPD)—to begin the Value Stream Mapping process. Then, 'go-see' at the Gemba and personally observe the flow of patients or folders while you sketch the map. The Value Stream Map will be more credible if you use a busy clinic day to illustrate the extent of the queues and blockages in the process. Sampling a quiet day will not give a true reflection of the challenges faced and the team will most likely miss out on critical evidence of waste in the system.

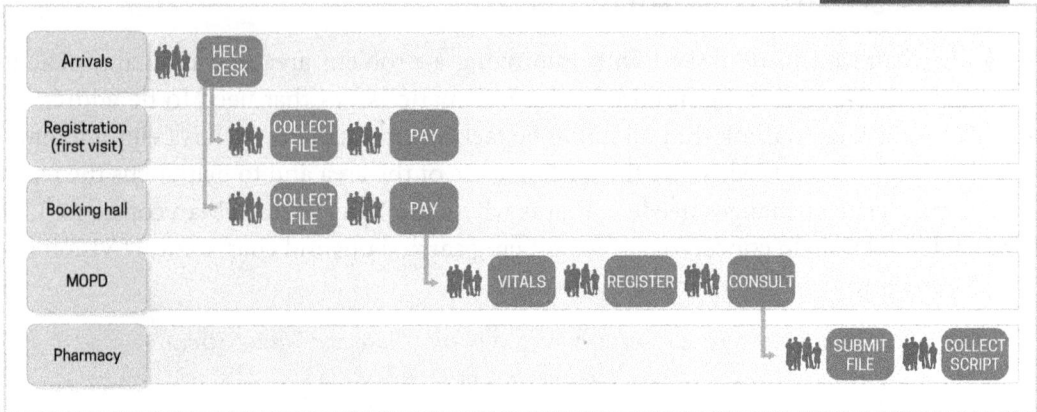

▲ Figure 3.24: Example of an out-patient journey

## Respect for People

It is human nature to feel uncomfortable when under observation. It is important to therefore ensure the mapping team approaches staff and patients with respect and empathy. If the staff feels as though they are being checked on and that the observations will lead to complaints, then they may be inclined to perform the process differently and not be open to sharing their obstacles, jeopardising a key source of ideas for improvement. Remember that, in the context of Lean Thinking, Respect for People also involves showing staff that their opinions are valued. This fosters collaborative problem-solving. Upfront communication, openness and a willingness to listen will build confidence in the improvement initiative.

## This is Reality

The Value Stream Map is a snapshot in time, and the Current Condition is captured as it is seen on the day of the activity. It is common for team members and staff

> The challenge lies in seeing each process for what it truly is—seeing both its valuable inputs and its wasteful, unnecessary activities.

to defend any negative performance documented by declaring that 'this is not how things usually look'. In truth, what is observed is almost always a true reflection of reality and, although some days are better than others, it is important to capture the current reality as it was observed.

At first-pass, the Value Stream Map may not tell you too much. The reason for this is that it is often difficult to see the issues in a process because our eyes are so accustomed to seeing the 'normal' presence of a persistent 'abnormal' condition. The challenge lies in seeing each process for what it truly is—seeing both its valuable inputs and its wasteful, unnecessary activities.

# The 3Ms

A vital step in fixing problems is to admit that the problems exist. Begin by defining what 'value' means to the patient. Then evaluate how all activities in the chosen Value Stream are influenced by three problems known as the 3Ms (Figure 3.25), namely Muda (waste), Mura (variation) and Muri (overburden). This will help you recognise and eliminate these problems and all that they embody, in a very structured way.

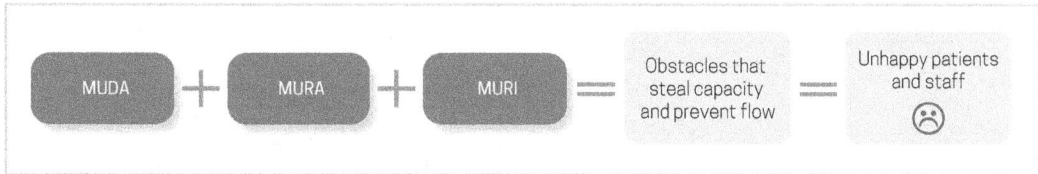

▲ Figure 3.25: The impact of the 3Ms

Consider the meaning of value from the perspective of the patient, always referring back to the Voice of the Patient. In the example provided in Chapter 1 the out-patient expects the following:

o Correct diagnosis and treatment
o Quick service
o An easily available and quickly filled script

Ultimately, patients want to be helped or cured, and any part of the service that takes them closer to this end and improves their quality of life will be viewed as 'valuable'. Anything that does the opposite or disregards their time will be seen as 'waste'. With this in mind, it is clear which of the processes an improvement team should look to interrogate in the Value Stream. The 3Ms provide you with additional clues as to elements that erode the performance of the Value Stream.

*Muda* = Waste

Lean Thinking is not limited to finding and eliminating waste. If we do not understand the context in which this waste is taking place, we may fix many problems but with little, tangible impact on the healthcare facility and zero change to the experience of the patient.

Father of the Toyota Production System, Taiichi Ohno provided us with a guideline, a lens, through which to contextualise common waste found in processes. New ways of thinking have added to the guideline over time but Ohno's basic principles remain. The point to remember is that seeing waste is not enough. You need to see the context it infects and weakens, understand the source of the waste and then permanently eliminate it, pruning out its root cause. Consider the *Muda* typical of public healthcare environments as listed in Table 3.2.

| MUDA (WASTE) | DESCRIPTION | EXAMPLES |
|---|---|---|
| Excess inventory | Ordering more stock than is required or 'just-in-case' stock | Excessive stock levels in the pharmacy and kitchen leading to expiry, congestion and added cost. |
| Waiting | Idle time where the patient, doctor or staff are waiting | Evident in long queues. Waiting for information, doctors to arrive, test results, admission and vitals. |
| Transportation | Excessive handling of patients, materials or information | Carrying files around the hospital, patients being transported long distances between departments, moving stock items long distances. |
| Over processing | Taking unneeded steps to complete the service | Filling out the same information several times when one copy complies with hospital requirements. |
| Unnecessary movement | Any motion that does not add value to the patient service | Walking to fetch items that could be located where they are needed most. Bending under the table to fetch a label for a script. Stocking frequently used items high on the shelf. |
| Errors | Not doing the work right the first time | The pharmacist gets up to re-pick the script because it was not done correctly. Incorrect file numbers leading to duplication. The patient is issued with the incorrect medication. |
| Unused employee creativity | Losing learning opportunities by not engaging with or listening to employees | Not allowing and enabling those directly involved in the work to help solve the problems. |

▲ Table 3.2: Typical *Muda* found in the public healthcare environment

*Mura = Unevenness, fluctuation and variation*

Mura results in inconsistency in the operations, which makes it difficult to plan, keep costs under control and provide a reliable service to the patient. Ultimately, Mura will cause Muda. Examples of Mura include:
- o Poor and unpredictable availability of equipment or systems
- o Errors that mean work has to be redone leading to cycle time variation
- o Last-minute changes to doctor schedules

*Look for waste*

o   Variation in Patient Demand Patterns
o   Daily variation in staff capacity impacting on patient service
o   Variation between employees and how they perform the work causing inconsistent service.

*Muri = Overburden*

Muri occurs when the available capacity – people, systems or equipment – is overloaded. Evidence of this can be found where:

o   Machines are planned to run at maximum capacity with no downtime, stealing from critical preventive maintenance periods and putting additional strain on the equipment.

o   People are continuously scheduled to work overtime affecting their ability to perform. Morale drops, absenteeism increases and additional strain on the system results.

o   An excessive amount of work – more than employees or equipment can handle – is released into the system. The result is confusion, an inability to prioritise and ultimately the creation of a crisis situation where employees lose focus on value. This occurs when the number of patients consistently exceeds the available capacity. While acceptable for this to happen periodically, it should not become the norm.

This may sound severe, but if you have been observing a process for an hour and have not seen any problems at all, you need to look more closely at the detail. Do not fall into the trap of becoming a 'process tourist'. Get into the habit of respectfully asking questions and continuously comparing performance to the documented standard.

As you observe the operations and develop the Value Stream Map, keep your eyes peeled for tell-tale waste, variation and overburden that, once removed, could make service flow that much quicker, with fewer errors and decreased costs, resulting in far happier patients and employees.

As you observe the 3Ms, consider the sources of each and make a note of these, to be used later in problem-solving activities.

# The Current Condition Value Stream Map

Armed with focus and knowledge of the 3Ms, you are now in a position to map the process in its Current Condition. Figure 3.26 illustrates the construction of a Value Stream Map. It indicates the queue size before each process, each step the patient follows during the journey and the cycle times at each service point. This information is then summarized to show the Total Journey Time and also the Total Service Time.

PROCESS 1
30 sec

PROCESS 2
45 sec

PROCESS 3
20 sec

50 patients in queue
25min to process queue

80 patients in queue
60min to process queue

15 patients in queue
5min to process queue

25min

60min

5min

0.5min

0.75min

0.33min

Total Journey Time = 25+0.5+60+0.75+5+0.33 = 91.6min
(or convert the decimal point to 91 min and 35 sec)

Total Service Time = 0.5min + 0.75min + 0.33min = 1.58min
(or convert the decimal point to 1 min and 35 sec)

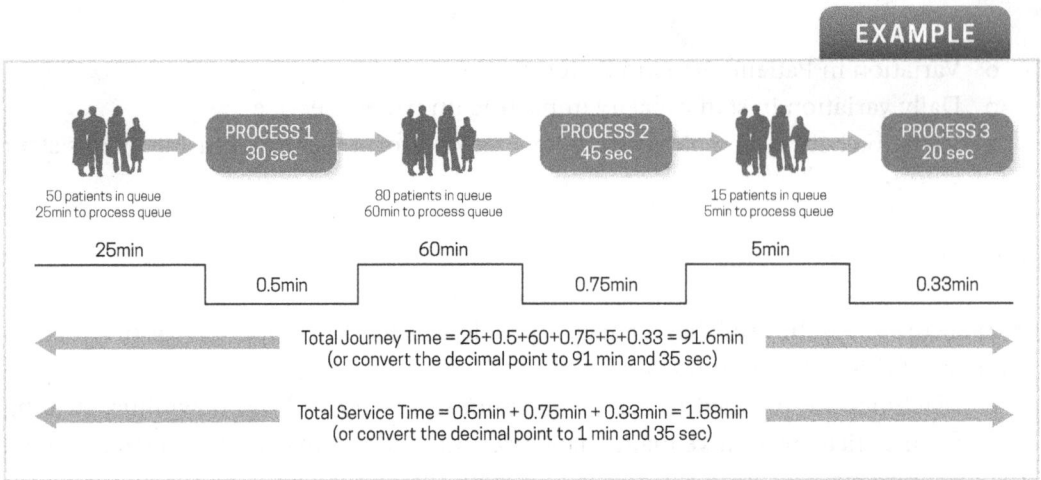

▲ Figure 3.26: Patient journey Value Stream Map

Although there a several methods to choose from, a simple and often preferred method of determining patient waiting time is to use both the number of patients waiting in a queue and cycle time to process each patient as follows:

*Waiting Time = No. of Patients in the Queue × Cycle Time per Patient*

The example provided in Figure 3.27 shows how to calculate the Waiting Time each patient goes through before reaching Process 1. Apply the formula as follows:

PROCESS 1
30 sec

50 patients in queue
25min* to process queue

Waiting Time = 50 patients × 0.5 minutes
= 25 minutes*

▲ Figure 3.27: Calculating patient Waiting Time

Once waiting times have been calculated for all queues a patient waits in, they can be added up to calculate the Total Journey Time (in the above example: 91min 35sec) through the Value Stream.

Service Time refers to the amount of time for which a patient is actually being assisted—for example, the time spent in consultation with the doctor or time spent in direct contact with a pharmacy employee to dispense a script. Adding up each of the service times in our example brings us to a paltry 1min 35sec. Although the patient spends 91min 35sec minutes in the Value Stream, only 1min 35 sec of this time period is value-adding to them. This is excellent evidence of waste! The next time you stand in a queue at Home Affairs, the bank or at an airport, try the formula out and work out how long you are about to wait.

Once the Total Journey Time and the Total Service Time have each been established, it is possible to calculate the Service Efficiency %, a measure of how Lean the Value Stream truly is (revisit the Efficiency Matrix: Figure 3.1):

$$Service\ Efficiency\ \% \ = \ \frac{Total\ Service\ Time}{Total\ Journey\ Time} \times 100$$

Using the information from Figure 3.26, Service Efficiency % is determined as follows:

$$Service\ Efficiency\ \% \ = \ \frac{1.58\ min}{91.6\ min} \times 100 \ = \ 1.72\%$$

An eye-opening 1.72%! Put yourself in a patient's shoes and imagine the frustration.

Remind the team that developing the Current Condition Value Stream Map is only the beginning. Guide them through the debates, discussions and problem-solving towards the vision for the future—or your North Star—and a defined Target Condition Value Stream Map. Without actions to achieve the Target Condition, this is just an interesting but isolated mapping exercise and of no real value to the patient.

> The Current Condition is only the beginning. Without actions to achieve the Target Condition, this is of no real value to the patient.

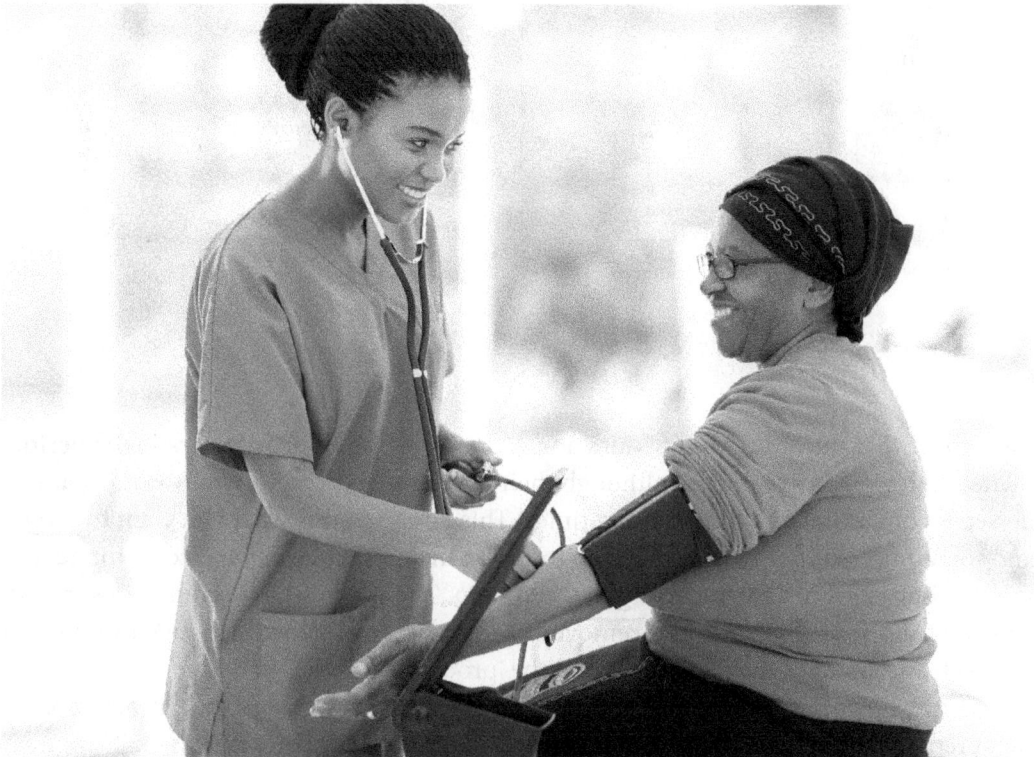

## PRACTICAL ACTIVITY: Creating a Current Condition Story Board

Developing the Current Condition may be a detailed, time-consuming process, but the information that it provides will give the team much substance to work through. Make up a story board by consolidating the findings and observations. Print and display them on a large sheet of brown paper so that the team can review what they have learned and begin discussing the way forward. Figure 3.28 is an example of a story board that includes:

▶ Patient Demand Patterns
▶ Daily measurements and graphs
▶ Personal observations and photographs with comments
▶ Current Best Method and work patterns
▶ Time Studies
▶ Work Balance Charts
▶ Spaghetti Diagrams
▶ Current Condition Value Stream Map

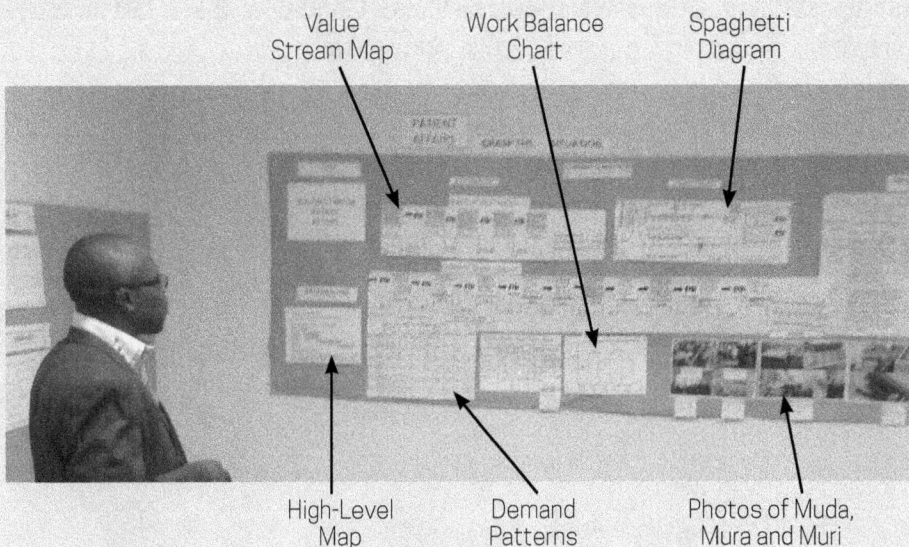

▲ Figure 3.28: Creating a Current Condition Story Board

Remember that the 3Ms (Muda, Mura and Muri) have the ability to degrade the performance of the Value Stream, and although their root cause is not always obvious, what you do see is congestion and long waiting times. This congestion is what you want to target, and sometimes the simplest way is to go to where the most congestion is to be found and look for options available to decongest the system. The process has become 'constipated' and the team must seek ways to remove the blockage and allow the work to flow—to complete the analogy, the team must find the 'process laxative'.

Cohort 1 teams took a closer look at the Service Efficiency % and the Current Condition prepared in their hospitals, and identified 'organisational constipators' that lengthen the journey and that hinder flow. Key learning from their investigations were noted as follows:

o Find a process that usually takes longer than others, a point at which patients experience congestion. Interrogate the detail of this process and find ways to simplify it, combine it with other processes or eliminate it altogether.

o Although a process may not be the longest in overall cycle time, errors of some sort have crept in to create a bottleneck. Investigate why the errors occur and what can be done to reduce them. Sometimes this is referred to as 'failure demand'—a failure has occurred creating more work or demand on the system. 'Failure demand' steals capacity and is avoidable.

o Finding ways to cycle a bottleneck process faster will result in better flow through the Value Stream. Bear in mind that once a bottleneck has been cleared, the congestion shifts and a different process will become the new priority bottleneck, and so on. Be extremely cautious of concluding that insufficient resources are to blame at a bottleneck process. Much of the time it is found that the process itself contains waste and, with this waste removed, staff or resource levels are found to be sufficient. It is a grave mistake to throw people at a problem (including ramping up queue marshal presence) without first addressing the true obstacles and waste.

o A loss experienced at a bottleneck is a loss to the Value Stream as a whole. To support a bottleneck area, always ensure it is not starved

> A loss experienced at a bottleneck is a loss to the Value Stream as a whole.

of work and is also protected from idle time. Support it with the best skills you can spare and ensure that the work released into a process that features a bottleneck does not exceed its capacity to carry out the work.

o If patients arrive in surges and congest the area, investigate how staff numbers can be adjusted to suit this pattern and captured into a more appropriate roster—without adding new staff. Investigate staff break times and leave schedules to see how these can be adapted to support the influx of patient numbers. Discuss whether the patient numbers can be spread out evenly over the shift or the week through a novel patient booking system.

o Evaluate how effectively the administration office, clinic or pharmacy kicks off each morning. Are their start-up systems prompt? Can patients immediately be serviced, efficiently and with a steady rhythm? If there is start-up delay, this will worsen the congestion.

o If the Information Technology system is slow, try to understand what makes it slow down and whether this can be amended. Perhaps a system back-up, which could be scheduled at a quieter time, is taking place during peak hours?

o Whenever a process is interrupted, ask why this happens and devise alternative ways of carrying out the activity. If the pharmacist has to move away from the workstation, find out the reasons for this. If a doctor leaves the consulting room to look for something they need, find a way to prevent this from happening. If the clerk has to get up to fetch something that should be within close range, ask what can be done to avoid this. We want staff to be adding value to the patient, not dealing with waste. This is particularly important at a bottleneck.

o Files are often retrieved for patients the day before they arrive for scheduled appointments. Should the no-show rate be high, evaluate whether the time taken to return files and the congestion this causes justifies changing the system. If more than 80 percent of patients honour their appointments, consider retrieving files for them before they arrive to reduce waiting times. This could apply to x-rays and blood results too.

o If un-booked patient numbers are high, measure the extent of this problem and devise methods to bring this figure down. How can they still be serviced and provided care, but without negatively affecting the waiting times of all patients in the same queue?

o Evaluate the categories of patients coming in. Is it possible to deal with less complex or high-volume patients in separate queues, and to separate lower-volume, more complex patients into their own queues? In this way, the long process times needed for complicated cases do not get in the way of fast-moving patients. Be sure to first understand the demand patterns before adjusting this.

o If a counter needs to be permanently manned by three staff members, but staff availability varies each day, it should be stabilised to suit the demand patterns. In some cases, staff are 'borrowed' by other units, are on leave or simply absent. If they work at a bottleneck process, the manager needs to have plans in place to stabilise staff numbers to match demand and to facilitate flow.

o Some work areas are cluttered and disorganised directly affecting the productivity of the employee and likely resulting in quality errors. By clearing unnecessary items, and positioning needed items correctly, staff can perform their work more efficiently and effectively. Cohort 1 hospitals reversed poor workplace organisation at typical areas including service counters, notice boards, filing systems, storage systems and pharmacist stations. This is discussed further in Part II.

o Using Visual Management, managers can help teams see when patient waiting times are exceeding desired waiting time standards, and prompt problem-solving. It is key to make the abnormal visible to stop waste creeping in and constipating flow. This is discussed further in Part II.

o Booking systems for appointments are often a point of contention. Either the bookings made are not clearly visible or easy to access, or the booking numbers are not well managed leading to over-booking and under-booking. In some cases the way in which patients are allocated to doctors is also not well balanced. By evaluating these flaws more closely, it is possible to devise better ways to manage and communicate patient booking numbers, and to closely match this with available staff numbers. In this way, operational areas are better equipped to plan for the following day's demand patterns.

o Often, the devil is in the detail. Observing consultations with doctors may expose challenges that cause bottlenecks such as overlooked systemic problems, slow access to blood results and x-rays, and long periods spent cleaning and preparing consulting rooms. These processes will all have significant impact on clinic waiting times and ultimately affect the morale of staff and patients. In some cases, doctors duplicate information on forms which, according to hospital guidelines, could be simplified. Observe the detail and dig out the devil of waste.

o  Nurses, doctors and pharmacists influence each other's work directly. They are in effect each other's customers and consumers of each other's services. As such, staff or 'customers' from different areas of the hospital need to come together to solve problems that touch all of their departments. Sometimes the actions of a doctor may influence the ability of a pharmacist to assist a patient, and vice versa. Have you identified obstacles apparent in the Value Stream that need cross-departmental attention?

o  Walking distances are often overlooked mostly because healthcare facilities are laid out in a specific manner that cannot be changed. However, there are examples of poor flow and processes requiring excessive walking that can be avoided just by relocating critical items. Wherever possible, the most used items (stock, equipment, paperwork) must be situated in more accessible and logical locations. The less walking required for staff to fetch frequently-used items, the less the waiting time of the patient.

o  Well-meaning staff members might take on tasks they are unqualified to perform, simply to meet escalating demands and particularly at a bottleneck process. This can result in poor quality and poor flow. Ensuring the correct allocation of duties is an important part of achieving standardised work.

o  One of the greatest flow inhibitors in a healthcare facility is the practice of batching work. A section has been dedicated to this topic below.

It is important to remember that the answer to continuous improvement is not to blindly copy a solution used elsewhere into your process. Examples of other facilities' successes certainly help to get your team thinking about possibilities, but at the end of the day the team must discover countermeasures to their particular obstacles. If your facility experiences an issue identical to one solved elsewhere, then by all means test a countermeasure proven elsewhere. But be strict with your team and be sure to follow the principles of PDCA through to completion to ensure the countermeasures you implement deliver on the unique obstacles identified and really bring value to the patients you serve.

> The answer to continuous improvement is not to blindly copy a solution used elsewhere into your process.

## The Batching Dilemma

Batching is a popular activity in public hospitals and clinics. It refers simply to moving patients and files through processes, in groups. Common examples of batching include:

o  Picking a batch of files for patient registration
o  Taking a batch of files to finance for billing
o  Preparing a batch of patients for vitals
o  Collecting x-ray and blood results in batches
o  Gathering a batch of files in the pharmacy for picking.

At first batching may not seem like such a big deal, but when the impact on the Total Journey Time is considered, the practice takes on another level of meaning. Often staff members believe batching to be the most efficient means of servicing patients. In reality batching only makes it easier for the person doing the work, and is not always in the patients' best interests. To be fair, there are indeed some examples of batching that contributes to flow. This includes controlled batching—the limiting of maximum batch sizes. It was mentioned earlier in this chapter that the bottleneck (slowest process) should never be starved of work. A controlled batch or buffer against starvation is therefore best implemented at a bottleneck process.

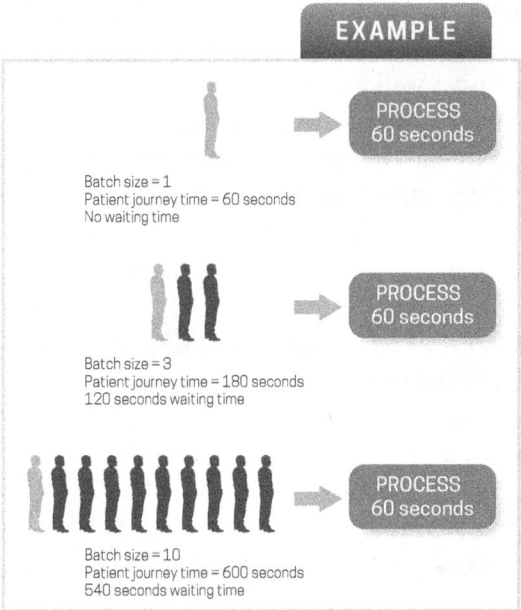

**EXAMPLE**

Batch size = 1
Patient journey time = 60 seconds
No waiting time

PROCESS
60 seconds

Batch size = 3
Patient journey time = 180 seconds
120 seconds waiting time

PROCESS
60 seconds

Batch size = 10
Patient journey time = 600 seconds
540 seconds waiting time

PROCESS
60 seconds

▲ Figure 3.29: Impact of batching on patient waiting time

Figure 3.29 illustrates the impact of bigger batches on waiting time. If the patient is not part of a batch and does not have to wait, their processing time is 60 seconds—the extent of their journey. If the patient is grouped within a batch and is number 10 in the queue, their waiting time becomes 540 seconds.

It seems logical that there will always be a queue, so why make such a fuss of batching? To answer this question, picture an administration process where the files first need to be picked and then delivered to the patient for their registration process. The picker walks to the box where the appointment cards are located, gathers 20 cards and proceeds to the filing room. Though there are 20 appointment cards, the picker is able to find only 15 of the corresponding patient files. Five of the files are problematic, misfiled or missing. The picker spends time trying to find the elusive five and meanwhile all 20 patients wait for their files to arrive. Instead of returning a smaller batch of 15 files so that patients whose files have been found can proceed through the process, they all have to wait for all 20 files to be found. Collecting and delivering one file at a time may also not be the answer, especially where there are long distances to be travelled to retrieve files, but there is always an optimum—often smaller—batch size to be considered.

Another view is the net effect that batch size has on a patient's Total Journey Time. Figure 3.30 shows the batch size before each processing point and a resultant Total Journey Time of 91.55 minutes. If the batch sizes are growing, the waiting time also increases and so the overall journey lengthens. By allowing excessive amounts of work into the system without adding support mechanisms to meet the swelling demand, we congest the Value Stream further, resulting in a longer patient Journey Time.

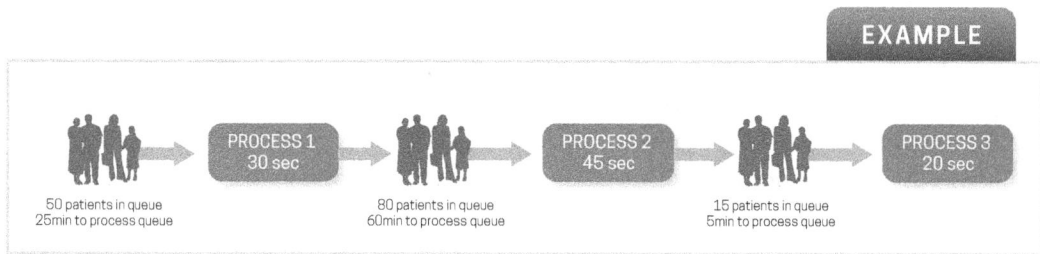

| 50 patients in queue<br>25min to process queue | PROCESS 1<br>30 sec | 80 patients in queue<br>60min to process queue | PROCESS 2<br>45 sec | 15 patients in queue<br>5min to process queue | PROCESS 3<br>20 sec |

▲ Figure 3.30: Net effect of batch sizes on waiting time

Figure 3.31 depicts the way in which a batch that is better controlled decreases Total Journey Time. In this case it becomes 47.05 minutes representing a commendable 49 percent reduction which adds value to the patient, straddling both the Kano Model's *satisfier* and *delighter* criteria.

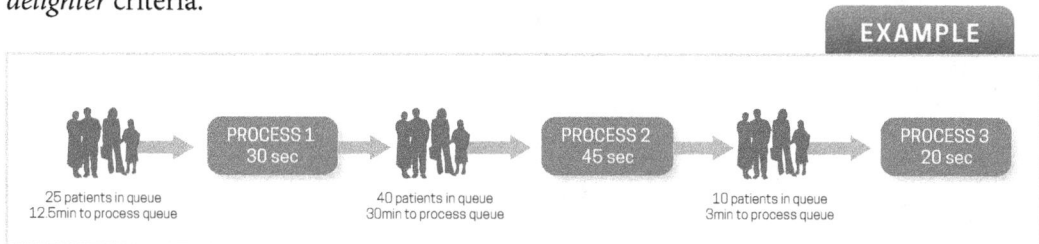

| 25 patients in queue<br>12.5min to process queue | PROCESS 1<br>30 sec | 40 patients in queue<br>30min to process queue | PROCESS 2<br>45 sec | 10 patients in queue<br>3min to process queue | PROCESS 3<br>20 sec |

▲ Figure 3.31: Controlled work-in-progress decreases waiting time

If batches are well-controlled throughout the journey of the patient, although the numbers of patients arriving does not change, the way in which they are spread across the Value Stream will become more manageable. Surges and starvation are replaced with an even flow of patients that is far easier to combat with available capacity.

# The Target Condition

Chapter 1 introduced us to the concept of the North Star with the words: 'In the context of Operational Excellence, your North Star is your navigation guide, the beacon towards which sustained levels of improvement are directed. It remains a reliable reference to look to and guides the healthcare facility towards its goals. As with Polaris, it does not shift dramatically but rather, shifts gradually over time—not unlike your strategy...'

Healthcare facilities undertaking a journey of Operational Excellence are encouraged to develop their North Star to guide the improvement strategy and maintain a steady course for the teams on board with the change effort. The North Star usually guides a change process with a three to five-year outlook. In some instances, the process spans periods even longer than this. Yet, very long-term strategies can be overwhelming and therefore difficult for teams to digest.

The journey towards the North Star should be broken down into manageable chunks for teams, to enable them to take many smaller steps towards their shoot-for-the-North-Star goal. In this way they will experience highly motivating interim successes whilst maintaining their focus on the ultimate destination.

Figure 3.32 (adapted from Rother, 2010) describes the thought process whereby the North Star provides Clear Direction, the Current Condition is known and interim Target Conditions have been set to guide a team through a longer-term change process. The team will then work their way through the obstacles, with guidance and support as they reach for the North Star.

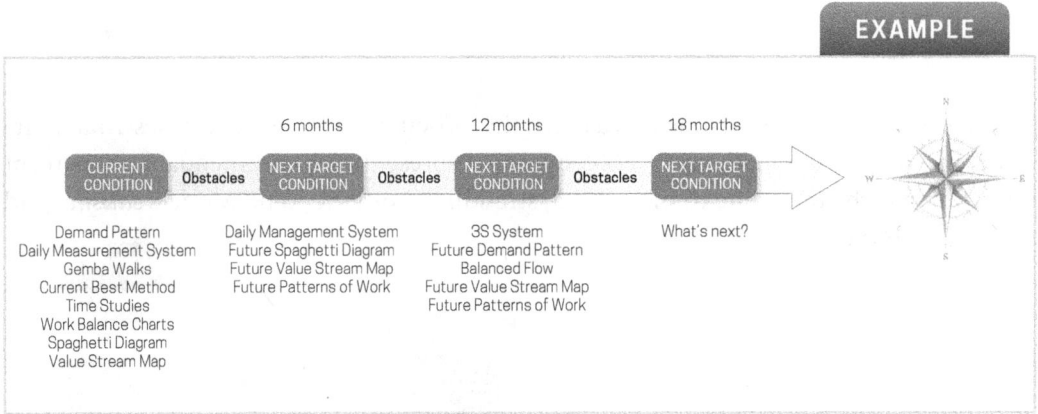

EXAMPLE

▲ Figure 3.32: Journeying towards the North Star

Figure 3.32 makes it clear that uncovering the Current Condition is only the beginning. It is an important first step and will lay the foundation for decisions made moving forward, but is of no value on its own. It is critical that the team develop their Target Condition, so that they are clear on what the future design will look like. A future Value Stream Map is one example of the analysis required. Once countermeasures to current challenges are put in place the team can test the results of the new measures against the expectations clarified in the Value Stream Map.

Figure 3.33 provides an example of a team's Target Condition for a Medical Out-Patient Clinic in one of the Cohort 1 hospitals. Although not depicted in the photo, the Target Condition should also specify a target date. The team in this example revisits this Target Condition every month and compares it to current performance. Their Target Condition covers more than the output measure of Waiting Time. It includes input measures to drive patterns of work and ultimately influence their patients' waiting times for the better.

A theoretical example of a Current Condition Value Stream Map and Target Condition is provided in Figure 3.34. Once the team has identified the 3Ms preventing them from achieving the Target Condition (Figure 3.35) they can then delve into the obstacles, establish root causes and construct a future Value Stream Map as detailed in Figure 3.36. With this in hand, they would be in a position to develop a detailed plan of action with the agreed countermeasures.

**TARGET CONDITION**
- Clinic starting time: 8h00
- 1st patient to be seen at 8:05
- 100% compliance on TTO sheets
- INR results: 50 minutes
- Average waiting time aimed at 55 minutes
- Journey time aimed at 90 minutes

▲ Figure 3.33: Example of a Target Condition

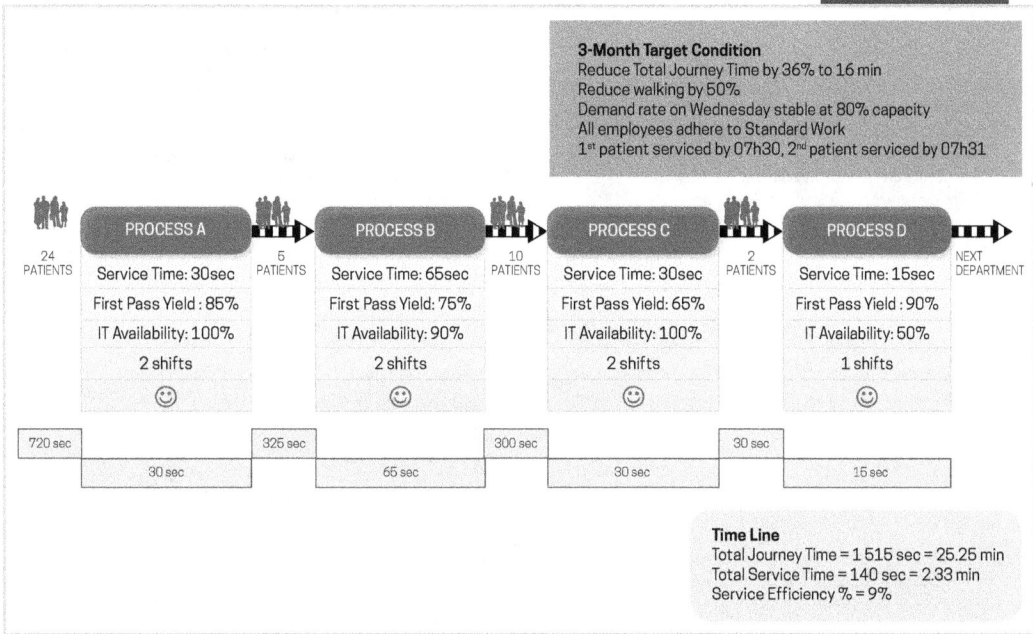

**3-Month Target Condition**
Reduce Total Journey Time by 36% to 16 min
Reduce walking by 50%
Demand rate on Wednesday stable at 80% capacity
All employees adhere to Standard Work
1st patient serviced by 07h30, 2nd patient serviced by 07h31

| | PROCESS A | | PROCESS B | | PROCESS C | | PROCESS D | |
|---|---|---|---|---|---|---|---|---|
| 24 PATIENTS | Service Time: 30sec | 5 PATIENTS | Service Time: 65sec | 10 PATIENTS | Service Time: 30sec | 2 PATIENTS | Service Time: 15sec | NEXT DEPARTMENT |
| | First Pass Yield : 85% | | First Pass Yield: 75% | | First Pass Yield: 65% | | First Pass Yield : 90% | |
| | IT Availability: 100% | | IT Availability: 90% | | IT Availability: 100% | | IT Availability: 50% | |
| | 2 shifts | | 2 shifts | | 2 shifts | | 1 shifts | |
| | ☺ | | ☺ | | ☺ | | ☺ | |

720 sec — 30 sec — 325 sec — 65 sec — 300 sec — 30 sec — 30 sec — 15 sec

**Time Line**
Total Journey Time = 1 515 sec = 25.25 min
Total Service Time = 140 sec = 2.33 min
Service Efficiency % = 9%

▲ Figure 3.34: Example of a Current Condition Value Stream Map and Target Condition

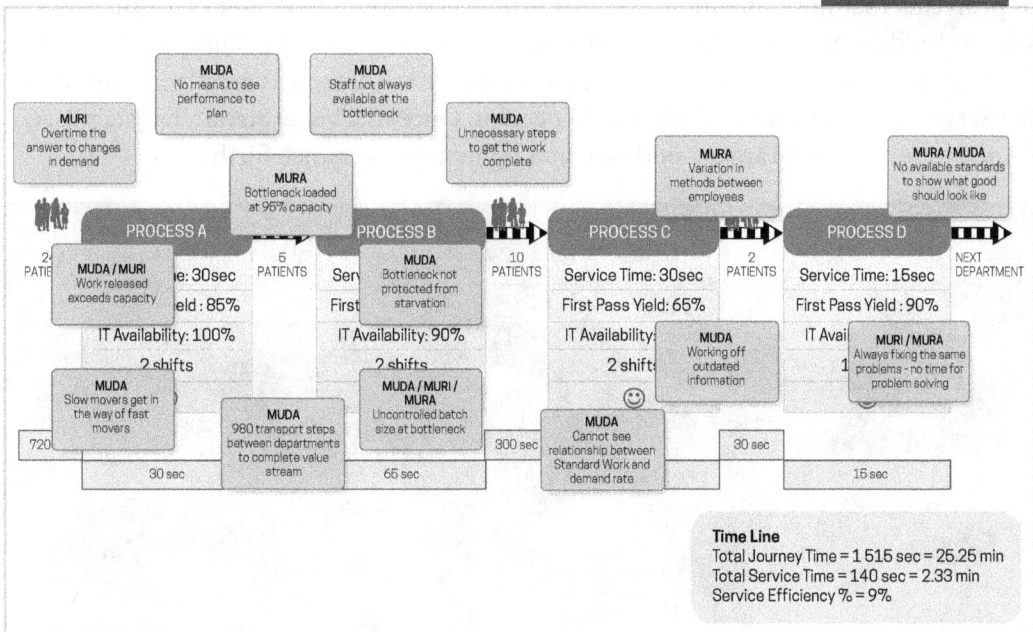

**MURI** Overtime the answer to changes in demand

**MUDA** No means to see performance to plan

**MUDA** Staff not always available at the bottleneck

**MUDA** Unnecessary steps to get the work complete

**MURA** Variation in methods between employees

**MURA / MUDA** No available standards to show what good should look like

**MURA** Bottleneck loaded at 95% capacity

| | PROCESS A | | PROCESS B | | PROCESS C | | PROCESS D | |
|---|---|---|---|---|---|---|---|---|
| 24 PATIE | e: 30sec | 5 PATIENTS | Ser | 10 PATIENTS | Service Time: 30sec | 2 PATIENTS | Service Time: 15sec | NEXT DEPARTMENT |
| | eld : 85% | | First | | First Pass Yield: 65% | | First Pass Yield : 90% | |
| | IT Availability: 100% | | IT Availability: 90% | | IT Availability | | IT Avail | |
| | 2 shifts | | 2 shifts | | 2 shifts | | 1 | |

**MUDA / MURI** Work released exceeds capacity

**MUDA** Bottleneck not protected from starvation

**MUDA** Working off outdated information

**MURI / MURA** Always fixing the same problems - no time for problem solving

**MUDA** Slow movers get in the way of fast movers

**MUDA** 980 transport steps between departments to complete value stream

**MUDA / MURI / MURA** Uncontrolled batch size at bottleneck

**MUDA** Cannot see relationship between Standard Work and demand rate

720 — 30 sec — 65 sec — 300 sec — 30 sec — 15 sec

**Time Line**
Total Journey Time = 1 515 sec = 25.25 min
Total Service Time = 140 sec = 2.33 min
Service Efficiency % = 9%

▲ Figure 3.35: Identifying the 3Ms preventing achievement of the Target Condition

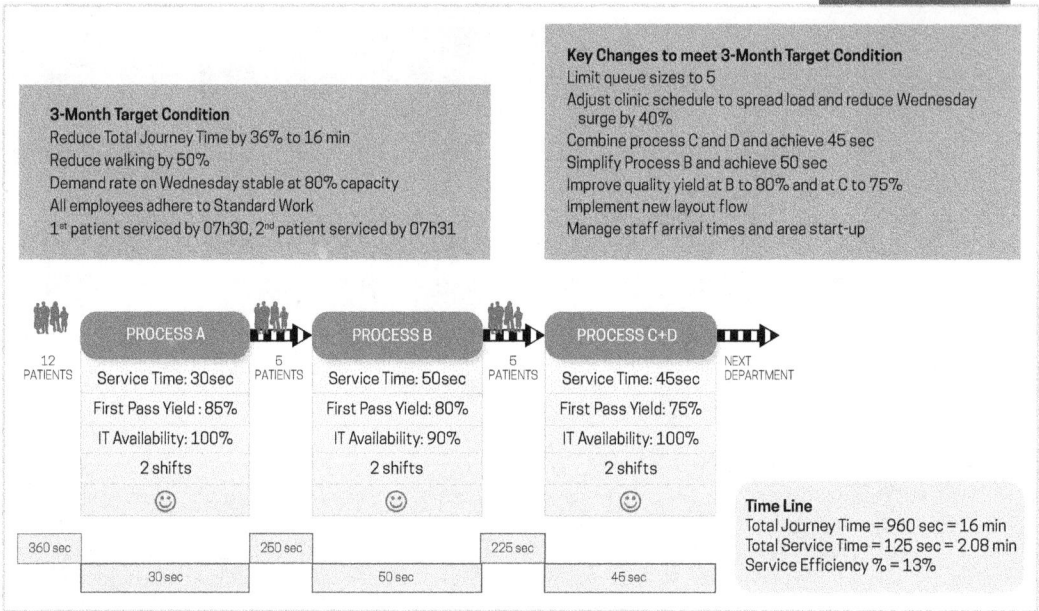

**3-Month Target Condition**
Reduce Total Journey Time by 36% to 16 min
Reduce walking by 50%
Demand rate on Wednesday stable at 80% capacity
All employees adhere to Standard Work
1st patient serviced by 07h30, 2nd patient serviced by 07h31

**Key Changes to meet 3-Month Target Condition**
Limit queue sizes to 5
Adjust clinic schedule to spread load and reduce Wednesday
  surge by 40%
Combine process C and D and achieve 45 sec
Simplify Process B and achieve 50 sec
Improve quality yield at B to 80% and at C to 75%
Implement new layout flow
Manage staff arrival times and area start-up

| 12 PATIENTS | PROCESS A | 5 PATIENTS | PROCESS B | 5 PATIENTS | PROCESS C+D | NEXT DEPARTMENT |
|---|---|---|---|---|---|---|
| | Service Time: 30sec | | Service Time: 50sec | | Service Time: 45sec | |
| | First Pass Yield : 85% | | First Pass Yield: 80% | | First Pass Yield: 75% | |
| | IT Availability: 100% | | IT Availability: 90% | | IT Availability: 100% | |
| | 2 shifts | | 2 shifts | | 2 shifts | |
| | ☺ | | ☺ | | ☺ | |

| 360 sec | | 250 sec | | 225 sec | |
|---|---|---|---|---|---|
| | 30 sec | | 50 sec | | 45 sec |

**Time Line**
Total Journey Time = 960 sec = 16 min
Total Service Time = 125 sec = 2.08 min
Service Efficiency % = 13%

▲ **Figure 3.36**: Creation of a future Value Stream Map

It may feel counterintuitive to set the Target Condition before understanding the causes of problems that need attention, but this is the very activity that will drive the team to seek and address the right obstacles, and continue looking for more *Mura, Muda* or *Muri*.

The future Value Stream Map (Figure 3.36) shows the process is greatly improved, but the Service Efficiency % is still only at 13 percent. Once this Value Stream has stabilised it is time to set the next Target Condition and tighten performance further.

# PRACTICAL ACTIVITY: Developing your Target Condition

The team is now prepared to develop the Target Condition. At this stage they should not concern themselves with the root causes and countermeasures relating to problems, but rather focus on identifying the flow inhibitors and interim Target Conditions that will complete each stage of the journey towards the North Star.

▸ Review the results from the Current Condition and the *Muda*, *Mura* and *Muri* identified in the Value Stream.

▸ Discuss in more detail those flow inhibitors that have the greatest impact on the key focus areas. If the team is tasked with reducing waiting times, discuss and highlight the 3Ms that will have a direct and significant impact on this focus area. Park the other obstacles for later problem-solving and only deal with them if these issues become more significant.

▸ Develop the Target Condition for the team to achieve. This should include time frames for each step of the Target Condition and measurable indicators. The Target Condition should also include patterns of work that will be needed to achieve the indicators—for example set a Target Condition for the Total Journey Time, but also that the first patient is to be served promptly at 7am (Figure 3.37).

| MEASURE | CURRENT | TARGET FOR FRIDAY | TARGET FOR 2 WEEKS | TARGET FOR 4 WEEKS |
|---|---|---|---|---|
| Journey Time | Ave = 77 min / 72min backed usm<br>Max = 118min / 1usmin | Ave = 55 min<br>Max = 85 min | Sustain average of 55 minutes<br>Max = 85 min | Ave = 45 min<br>Max = 75 min |
| Batch Size | Ave = 11<br>Max = 16 | Ave = 5<br>Max = 5 | Collect batches = 10<br>Deliver batches = 5 | Sustain |
| Registration Cycles | Ave = 6.5 min<br>Max = 8 min | Ave = 6 min<br>Max = 6 min | Ave = 4 min<br>Max = 6 min | Sustain |

| PATTERN OF WORK | CURRENT | TARGET FOR FRIDAY | TARGET FOR 2 WEEKS | TARGET FOR 4 WEEKS |
|---|---|---|---|---|
| Batches of cards<br>Delegation of duties<br>1st Patient | Officers collect any amount of cards<br>Need dictates delegation of duty<br>1st Patient Served at registration 07h11<br>1st Patient Served at cashier at 07h11 | Officer receiving records 8 batches of 5<br>My staff receiving<br>2 staff recording<br>1st Patient Served Other at registration<br>1st Patient Served Other | Sustain<br>1st Patient Served by 07h05<br>1st Patient Served at cashier by 07h05<br>Leader co-ordinates capacity to meet queue size | 1st Patient times sustained<br>Implement DMS<br>Commence Recces Area improvement<br>leader co-ordinate capacity to meet queue size |

▲ Figure 3.37: Example of the development of a Target Condition

# Why Does Cost Reduction Matter?

The public health sector is not famous for getting behind the wheel of cost-reduction vehicles in the race to efficiency and improvement. If anything it is infamous for cost chaos rather than containment. A cost-reduction focus is far more typical of commercial healthcare companies. Their survival depends on delivering ever higher profit margins and shareholder value in a competitive economy. Private healthcare companies, some listed entities on stock exchanges, must keep Lean and adapt continually to stay one step ahead of the game. This however does not mean that costs, and the impact they have on the bottom line, are unimportant in the public sector space. Cost management is crucial in public health. Speak to anyone in this sector and the word 'budget'—or the lack thereof—is bound to come up. Making ends meet in a budget-driven state-owned operation represents an ongoing struggle. Every budget cut or resource reassignment will invariably hurt something or someone, impacting the healthcare facility in one division or as a whole, and ultimately affecting employees and patients alike.

It is short-sighted to believe that status quos will remain and that cost-reduction will never become a primary directive in public health. Change is always in the air! Consider the implementation of South Africa's planned National Health Insurance (NHI) which aims to strengthen both service delivery platforms and overall quality of care in the public health sector. Numerous planned initiatives will be launched in tandem with the NHI to improve the management and governance of primary healthcare and hospital facilities. This will include scrutiny of costs, financial management practices and ensuring health-care resources are allocated and used in a manner that optimises value for money. And, to reiterate all that we have learned up to this point, it will be 'value' as defined through the eyes of the patient that will drive the improvement strategy.

Lean tools and techniques provide a powerful way to reduce costs. When implemented effectively, they offer an alternative to the knee-jerk cost-cutting measure of laying off staff and simultaneously improve quality of care for patients. Think of Lean as the ultimate lie detector. Once connected to the organisation's heart and soul, it scans the pulse and ambient pressure of every vein and artery of daily operational flow. As Lean's tests unfold our processes, it notes the issues, the waste and the abnormal—the *Muda*, *Mura* and *Muri*. Abnormal processes drain budgets. Can you see the aspiration towards truth that is cost reduction?

Lean encourages everyone to get involved in making improvements to processes and delivering better value to patients. It is these all-embracing practices that have a profound impact on cost saving.

Do not be fooled into thinking of Lean

> Think of Lean as the ultimate lie detector. Once connected to the organisation's heart and soul, it scans the pulse and ambient pressure of every vein and artery of daily operational flow.

only as a means to cost reduction. We are obligated to stakeholders and patients to provide more value through the better use of existing resources. If this is done in a data-driven, responsible and mutually beneficial manner, it will assist in moving the healthcare facility to new heights of performance and pave the way for further growth. If patient satisfaction and focus on the long-term reach-for-your-North Star goals remain on centre stage, cost reduction will take place effectively alongside real long-term benefit to the healthcare facility, environment, stakeholders, patients and employees.

# When Cost Reduction Fails

No doubt, cost reduction has a bad name. The worst form of cost reduction is the blanket approach taken during a crisis that sees management enforce across-the-board percent-age-based budget cuts. This reactive way of cutting costs invariably destroys value in the following ways:

- o Operations are cut to the bone to the extent that service levels to both inter-departmental clients and patients are affected.
- o Managers respond by padding budgets to compensate for future cuts, leading to unrealistic costs-projections and unnecessary fund allocations.
- o Good people move on to greener pastures opening a haemorrhaging skills gap.

o Long-term growth plans such as employee development and investment initiatives are put onto the backburner. Short-sighted, short-term benefits are achieved. But long-term, the sacrifices made eat away at Operational Excellence and patient service.

Cost reduction is often misdirected and aimed purely at lower-level employees. The organisation requires support from all staff to achieve true cost reduction strategies and this is best achieved when staff can see the same, if not more, effort being applied to cut costs at the higher levels of an organisation. Improvement pains are best shared.

Finally, certain investments may not necessarily align with strategic needs but may find strong internal support from a particular individual. Staying focused on the North Star objectives is critical to filtering out gratuitous cost driving activities (Bragg, 2010).

Improvement pains are best shared.

# Spend Reduction Opportunities

Lean Management tools and techniques drive Operational Excellence and naturally bring down cost drivers. It is however, helpful to define typical areas where financial losses are made in state healthcare facilities and their offending cost drivers. Typical areas of waste that lead to financial loss include:

o *Lost Revenue*: In public healthcare this may not seem a top priority, but revenue in the bank certainly counts when your facility is run using funds from the state coffers. Public healthcare budgets come from the hard-earned wages of citizens you serve and are accountable to and there is therefore a moral, ethical and statutory obligation to use every penny efficiently. If patient billing is problematic and incorrect monies are collected at the payment process, this translates to lost revenue. Longer than necessary in-patient stays drain the available capacity and ability to bill for another patient translating to lost revenue—and so on.

o *Lost Inventory*: Overstocking and poor management of inventory leads to unnecessary cost, unnecessary space usage and the risk of stock expiry or damage.

o *Lost Available Time*: Downtime on systems and equipment results in an inability to service patients and unnecessary expenditure on equipment brought in to cope with the demand.

o *Lost Labour Time*: Inefficient use of staff time leads to a need for more staff or overtime work and labour costs.

o *Lost Material*: Poorly managed consumables result in unnecessary waste and purchases. Forward-thinking hospitals and clinics are investigating options around sterilising and re-using certain devices, to reduce costs and medical waste.

o *Lost Money Flow*: To cope with increases in demand, hospitals and clinics look to expanding facilities and equipment. Using Lean Management to make better use of existing resources defers, and sometimes eliminates, the need for capital expenditure (CAPEX) for expansion.

Interrogating the management accounts will shine the spotlight firmly on the most influential spend- and cost-driver offenders. It is always helpful to understand the top 20 percent of costs that cause 80 percent of spend. Also bear in mind that many small savings add up, so targeting lesser costs you have immediate influence over will also add value.

Let us take a look at a selection of cost drivers and how to confront them:

# Unnecessary Investment

In some instances, plans to allocate CAPEX to a particular project should be deferred so that funds can be allocated to the correct focus areas, or spend avoided altogether. This is not about cutting CAPEX. Investment is indeed critical to growth. This is about ensuring the funds in question are allocated to the right projects, at the right time and linked to the organisation's strategic intents. Construct a list of all planned CAPEX and interrogate which of these projects is truly needed, which could be delayed, and which is revealed to be unnecessary when exposed to the clear light of the North Star's objectives.

# Poor Capacity Utilisation

Evaluate how well any bottleneck processes are performing by calculating the Overall Effectiveness % (OE%). OE% is a complex metric influenced by several variables. Its true value is in demonstrating the net effect of all the losses draining a process and influencing the ability to perform. It not only looks at the rate of quality output, but also the performance and the availability of systems and equipment. The lower the figure, the more impacted by loss the process has become. Figure 4.1 details the formulae used and the typical elements influencing each type of loss.

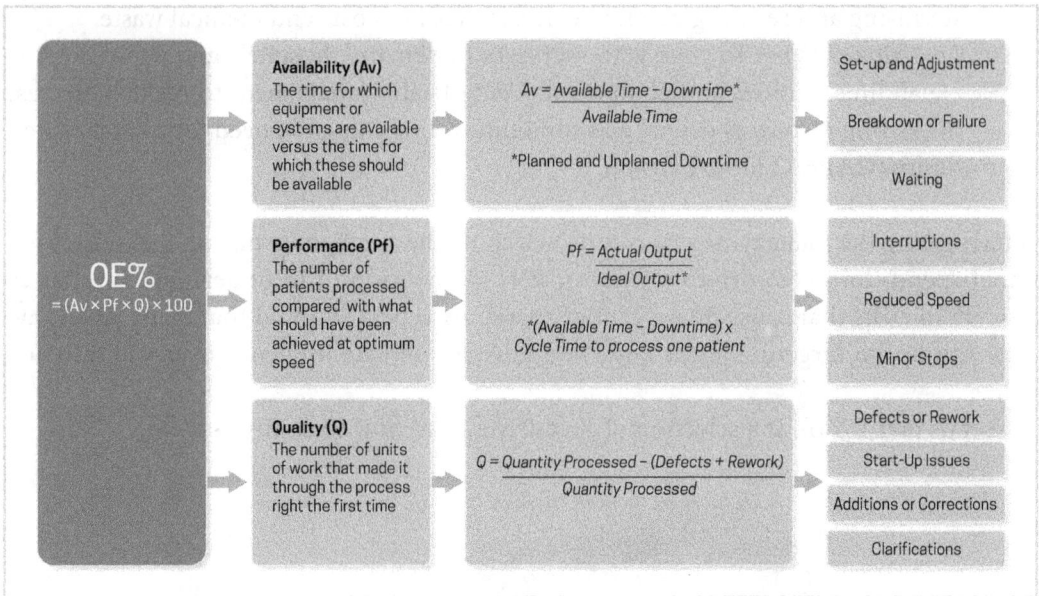

▲ Figure 4.1: Calculating the Overall Effectiveness % at the bottleneck process and establishing the key loss factors

By improving the elements negatively impacting on the OE%, capacity utilisation can be increased. Depending on the nature of the loss, this could reduce costs such as:

o Overtime worked
o Use of temporary labour
o The need for hiring new staff
o The need to purchase additional equipment
o Cost of material (such as consumables and inventory) as a result of not doing the work right the first time.

# Poor Inventory Management

Detailed analysis is the best way to understand the current systems and possible changes around inventory management. But, let us consider a simpler technique that can assist in whetting the appetite for exposing improvement opportunities.

Not all inventory held is truly needed to service patients and realise revenue. Its value is constantly declining. It is therefore critical to balance keeping inventory as low as possible but at levels that ensure patient service remains optimal. It is advantageous to have accurate information on the true consumption of inventory by patients and employees so that informed decisions can be made about the right stock levels to hold. Forecast accuracy improves the ability of procurement to make these stock levels available going forward. To get a view of the current situation and possible over-stocking culprits, consider the following approach:

o Create a spreadsheet listing all stock items under evaluation.
o Categorise each stock item according to its usage:
  - A-items are constantly in use and should always be in stock.

- B-items show a moderate frequency use and lower stock should be held.
- C-items are hardly in use and no, or extremely low, stock should be kept. These should be ordered as and when required.

o Compare the ABC categorisation with what is actually held in stock on average and highlight the 'over-stocked' items. Calculate the cost of the excess and include the carrying costs of this inventory (insurance, warehousing space, interest charges, staffing costs and so on). You may find reviewing the stock holding mid-month to be more representative or determine your own suitable method.

o During the comparison consider the types of stock you are dealing with and highlight additional opportunities uncovered. What decisions can be made to optimise the spend? Typically inventory includes:
- Current stock used in servicing patients
- Excess or obsolete, non-returnable stock
- Excess or obsolete, returnable stock
- Consumable stock
- Maintenance spares.

o Review the acquisition of overstocked items and estimate how much of this pattern is avoidable. Perhaps smaller, more frequent deliveries help to reduce inventory holding?

Invariably over time inventory wastes creeps back into processes. So, it is worth performing an audit of inventory activity at least once a year—if not more frequently.

# High Cost of Misaligned Services and Processes

Some services may have been designed without much evaluation of the true needs of the patient or the healthcare facility. Reviewing and eliminating those that are wasteful has a direct impact on service costs:

o Processes that add no value to the service—documenting the same information several times on different forms

o Specifications higher than those required by compliance standards

o Scarce resources wasted on work that could be done by a lower-level, less qualified person—a pharmacist performing the work of a picker during peak patient demand times.

The above scenarios clearly result in ineffective use of available capacity and increased service cost. It is important to mention that these suggestions of service streamlining must be met with careful consideration. Any changes must conform to hospital compliance standards.

# Poor Energy Usage

Energy waste comes in various forms. The result will be a negative impact on both the organisation's environmental footprint and associated costs. Typically energy usage is observed in the consumption of electricity and fuels to power electronics, machinery, lighting, heating, ventilation and air conditioning and so on, and can be quantified by examining monthly bills. Companies that specialise in energy-efficient conversions will advise on ideal solutions. Yet, energy-related cost drivers can be managed by countermeasures as simple as awareness campaigns among staff to reduce unnecessary energy consumption, insulation to reduce heat loss, automated lighting systems triggered by movement and other easily-implemented power-saving solutions.

# Unnecessary Temporary Labour

This type of labour is frequently used to buffer demand patterns and is understandably a necessary evil. Conversely, the bad habit of throwing temporary labour at every demand-driven problem in public healthcare represents a common addiction worth scrutinising:

  o Evaluate trends in temporary labour hiring over the past three years to establish whether this habit is on the rise or decline.
  o Evaluate the reasons behind use of temporary labour. Does it buffer absenteeism, increased patient numbers, lack of skills, an increase in the complexity of processes or other key challenges?
  o Be brutally honest in evaluating how efficiently current capacity is being employed. Is the use of temporary labour to compensate for a lack of capacity truly justified? How can this be improved?

# Transport Waste

Are you in the business of servicing patients or are you in the transport business? If transport is not your core service focus, ensure it is also not one of your greatest cost drivers. Transportation waste refers to any excessive transportation—an 'abnormal' norm—to move patients, employees, materials, documents or supplies in the name of service to patients. Constructing the Spaghetti Diagram explained in Chapter 3 may provide clues to areas of transportation waste. Also consider the following costs to assist you in evaluating the full effect of the transport inherent in your processes:

  o Cost to transport between processes, departments or healthcare facilities (forklifts, trucks, buses, ambulances, couriers, company cars)
  o Cost related to bringing in materials, tools and supplies
  o Freight bills, if applicable.

# Managing Absenteeism and Poor Leave Cover

Unplanned staff absenteeism is a fact of life but patients should not feel the effect of staff absences. Employees will get sick, and will need to take leave. Your employees are also entitled to annual, family responsibility, study leave and so on. Good planning around staff leave, whether planned or not, can reduce the unnecessary and avoidable losses that impact your organisation's ability to service patients consistently. The intention is not to prevent staff leave. Rather, proactively deal with staff absences by:

- o Evaluating leave applications over the year and where possible spreading the leave loading so that patient service levels are not impacted
- o Introducing contingency plans for periods when staff are on leave or off sick
- o Checking attendance at the start of each shift to accommodate the knock-on effects of any unplanned absenteeism in good time
- o Managing attendance through Visual Management.

Over time, excessive absenteeism and unplanned leave could lead to the employment of more temporary and permanent staff than is required. It could also increase the amount of overtime required of permanent staff.

# Managing Procurement Costs to your Advantage

There is significant cost associated with the procurement process itself. Streamlining at this juncture usually yields significant cost savings. If this has been a focus of your Value Stream Mapping, then consider quantifying the following losses as you refer back to the mapping exercise results:

- o The detrimental impact of long procurement lead times on patient service
- o Additional labour costs to compensate for waste in the Value Stream
- o Inaccuracies in the procurement process resulting in unnecessary purchases
- o Complex procurement processes encouraging 'every man for himself' buying patterns.

## Supplier Management

If the procurement process has already been streamlined, cost reduction may lie in the consolidation of suppliers. Consolidation has the potential both to reduce procurement costs and enhance allocation of funds (Bragg, 2010). Concentrating purchases through a smaller number of suppliers creates higher volumes purchased per supplier. This could assist with negotiation for price reductions, rebates, discounts and consignment usage. Consolidation should always accompany a supplier-rating system in which non-performers are warned and, where there is no change in their service, rated 'low' and placed on a 'no-buy' list. Good performers are therefore rewarded with increased orders or ongoing contracts. The organisation benefits from reliable supply for all processes as well as the power of negotiation for better prices through these longer-term relationships.

It is worth it to highlight poorly-performing suppliers in this way. These suppliers often offer excellent prices but the benefits are negated by their late delivery or poor quality. Ultimately the cost of doing business with them far outweighs their cost advantage. The financial benefit of eliminating these suppliers could include eliminating receiving inspections (labour cost), product returns (inventory that cannot be used) and the time necessary to process credits.

To help achieve focus, it is recommended that the bottom 10 percent of suppliers be reviewed over time and that the poor performers be removed one by one. For the purpose of this analysis, consider the total acquisition cost rather than just the product or service cost before making a decision to consolidate:

o List price, less any rebates or discounts
o Freight cost to ship
o Packaging cost
o Tooling and set-up costs
o Warranty details
o Payment terms
o Currency used.

## Spend Management

Analysis of spend can offer significant benefit to an organisation. It requires a team capable of the intensity required by the investigation and led by a process master or Sensei. However, the potential cost savings to be derived can dramatically offset the efforts required. Figure 4.2 illustrates the generic process and phases involved in analysis and improvement of spend management.

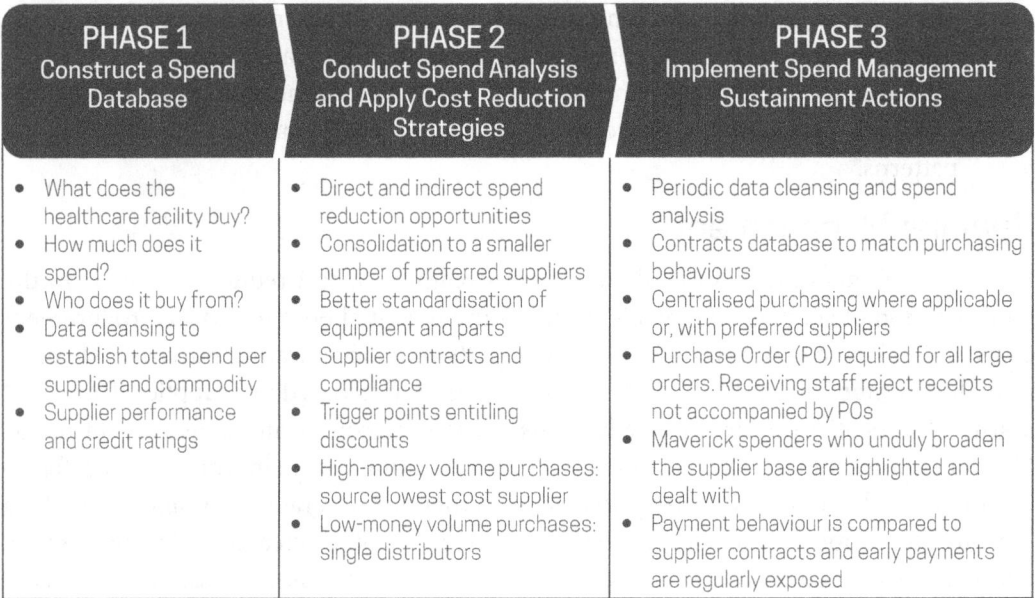

| PHASE 1<br>Construct a Spend Database | PHASE 2<br>Conduct Spend Analysis and Apply Cost Reduction Strategies | PHASE 3<br>Implement Spend Management Sustainment Actions |
|---|---|---|
| • What does the healthcare facility buy?<br>• How much does it spend?<br>• Who does it buy from?<br>• Data cleansing to establish total spend per supplier and commodity<br>• Supplier performance and credit ratings | • Direct and indirect spend reduction opportunities<br>• Consolidation to a smaller number of preferred suppliers<br>• Better standardisation of equipment and parts<br>• Supplier contracts and compliance<br>• Trigger points entitling discounts<br>• High-money volume purchases: source lowest cost supplier<br>• Low-money volume purchases: single distributors | • Periodic data cleansing and spend analysis<br>• Contracts database to match purchasing behaviours<br>• Centralised purchasing where applicable or, with preferred suppliers<br>• Purchase Order (PO) required for all large orders. Receiving staff reject receipts not accompanied by POs<br>• Maverick spenders who unduly broaden the supplier base are highlighted and dealt with<br>• Payment behaviour is compared to supplier contracts and early payments are regularly exposed |

▲ Figure 4.2: Analysis and improvement of Spend Management

# Standardising Equipment and Systems

Standardisation of equipment, machines and systems has the advantage of simplifying operations, training, spares and maintenance tasks. Organisations that have grown organically over the years boast a multitude of varieties in their systems or equipment, which can have far-reaching implications for costs. Evaluate the following and then discuss ways to simplify each:

- o  Costs associated with additional training needs and providers
- o  Differences in maintenance costs between options
- o  Additional costs and holding costs relating to spares.

# Unnecessary Training Costs

At the end of Chapter 2 we discussed the importance of well-focused training and development that is carefully designed to encourage the right behaviours, and therefore the right culture for change. Training that does not deliver the desired results will not realise a return on the investment (ROI) and becomes yet another wasted expense (Brinkerhof, 2010). As is illustrated in Figure 4.3, a proper strategy around the end goal should ensure training that delivers on all fronts.

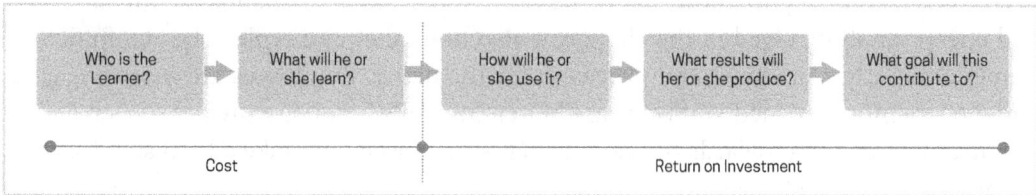

▲ Figure 4.3: Planning around training ensures ROI

Where the steps illustrated above have been ignored, training scrap rates in some sectors have averaged a staggering 85 percent (Figure 4.4). One way to predict a training bout's likelihood to deliver on its promises is to evaluate similar, previous training against the five-step process depicted above. What has been the scrap rate of training in the past and what did this cost? How can this be avoided going forward?

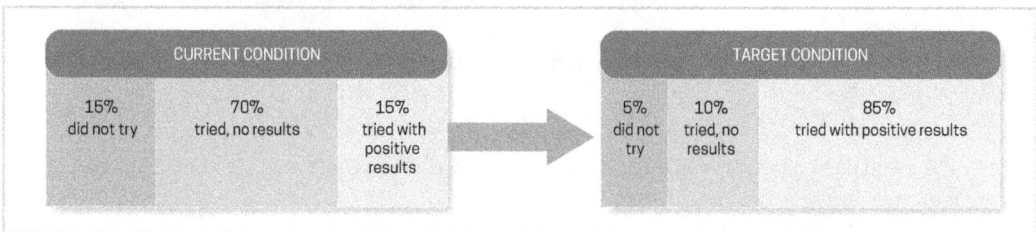

▲ Figure 4.4: Learning from the past decreases training scrap rates in the future

Planning for future training in this way evaluates the costs and estimates the scrap rate (Brinkerhof, 2010). Unless the transition to the Target Condition depicted in Figure 4.4 is achieved, your training will remain a black hole of deficit in your budgets.

# The Manning Planning Advantage

Has your organisation streamlined the manning of key processes to prevent avoidable waste? Excess as a result of careless manning comes in various forms:

- o Total manning levels might be correct. But perhaps the wrong amount of manpower is allocated to various processes causing excess in some areas and shortages in others. Refining manning levels may not necessarily yield an improvement in normal labour costs but benefits will be realised in reduction of both unnecessary overtime and also time and efficiencies lost due to manning shortages.
- o Manning shortages clearly result in lost process time and raise the likelihood of non-compliance to quality standards, both of which bring avoidable associated costs.
- o Manning excesses result in 'built-in-fat' in processes and unproductive use of time. Leaner manning will translate to a saving in labour costs.

These are just a few of many opportunities for improved cost management. The sky is the limit when it comes to further innovation and development and to bespoke solutions that suit your facility's

> Employees are more engaged, patients are more satisfied and costs are better controlled.

needs. It is comforting to know that while Lean Management demands the full attention and energy of all involved in the change, it also nourishes and replenishes tenfold, as it shapes and sculpts practices and processes for the better. Employees are more engaged, patients are more satisfied and costs are better controlled. You are invited to step across the threshold of Lean towards the clear benefits that await, and take a bold step forward towards Operational Excellence.

## PRACTICAL ACTIVITY: Bringing Cost Drivers into the Light

Gather the management team and include representation from the Finance department. Discuss the following:

- ▸ What are the crucial areas identified for cost reduction in the strategic plan?
- ▸ What are the typical losses influencing the crucial areas?
- ▸ What are the cost drivers affecting the losses? Which of these cost drivers will be pursued?
- ▸ What further investigation is required to quantify the potential savings for the selected cost drivers?

Once the team has gained insight into the key areas for change the North Star can be updated to include this focus.

You can access further information on performing a structured Cash Loss Analysis in *Clear Direction* (Heathcote, 2014).

*'The only thing that is constant is change.'*

That was said by Greek philosopher Heraclitus, who lived from 535 BC to 475 BC. He was known for asserting that change was ever-present and fundamental to the essence of the universe. Centuries later, has anything changed?

The extents to which leaders are adaptable to transformation and capable of managing change, have direct bearing on and dramatically influence how employees feel about these events. Even if employees do not at first necessarily support the change, a leader's attitude to change will filter through staff like ink through blotting paper, either exacerbating fears of the new horizons in sight or amplifying buy-in and openness to the change effort.

Leaders must furthermore remember that any planned change effort will need to resonate with, and be carried out by, human beings. It is imperative to design a strategy that proactively addresses people's likely responses to change and provides a structure that makes the change effort as clear as possible.

> A leader's attitude to change will filter through staff like ink through blotting paper.

Finally, linking an emotionally and developmentally intelligent design for change to your organisation's truest values adds heavyweight integrity to the process.

## First Hearts then Heads

'Change has a heart', says John Kotter, New York Times best-selling author and globally renowned authority on leadership and change. Kotter teaches that, 'People change what they do less because they are given analysis that shifts their thinking than because they are shown the truth that influences their feelings' (Kotter, 2002: p1).

So, how do we influence the way people feel and win them over to our change strategy by touching their hearts?

Kotter further explains that we have to help people 'see'. As we aspire to Operational Excellence we need to show people the compelling, eye-catching, dramatic scenarios that visualise the reality we are creating as a collective. Presenting employees with the results of a diagnostic analysis is much like showing them little more than the shadows of what could be. Sure, we use Value Stream Maps and all manner of diagnostic studies to gather data with which to make informed decisions and provide direction. But will this win over employees' hearts? Will these analyses make them buy into the change effort heart, soul and sinker? Change efforts require people to be willing to undertake new behaviours. Both emotion (heart) and thoughts (mind) trigger new behaviours and habits and make them stick. It takes concerted and calculated effort to ensure employees are truly onboard a change effort—mentally and emotionally.

Find a compelling way to explain the need for change. Unconventional methods loaded with shock-value are fantastic when it comes to breaking down organisational complacency. Consider the example of an organisation that piled refuse from their consumables sky-high and in plain sight. As the pile grew, a sign above the heap was updated daily to show the financial loss that the waste generated. Another company piled a mountain of gloves on the boardroom table illustrating cost incurred as a result of buying the very same item through a variety of suppliers.

How might you appeal to people's emotions to fuel change? Consider the following suggestions and devise your own, persuasive approach:

- o Interview patients on camera and show your staff a montage of frustrated and satisfied patients to depict the impact of improvements they make on real people's quality of life and health.
- o Hand out anonymous patient questionnaires about service experience and display the results in the work space for all to read (see Figure 5.1).
- o Invite employees from a division that has successfully undergone a change process to come and talk openly to employees about to embark on one. Open the floor so that people can express their sentiments without fear of condemnation.
- o Create visuals to compare financial losses incurred from *Muda*, *Mura* and *Muri* to the equivalent number of new computers the organisation could have bought, the equivalent cost of building new facilities for staff or patients, the equivalent number of neonatal syringes that could have been acquired, the added number of nurses or doctors who could have been hired with those funds.
- o Give a few employees or patients activity trackers and have them wear them for a few days to log the kilometres walked between processes. If excessive, distances recorded might motivate for change to movement and transportation methods used by staff.
- o Chart and display the number of incorrect prescriptions dispensed, the number of patients who have left without seeing a doctor after waiting all day to drive home the true extent of failings in service.
- o Task volunteer employees to spend a day 'in a patient's shoes'. Give them 24 hours off work during which they are to experience the patient journey from start to finish and report back on the experience first-hand.
- o Task your employees with taking photographs of waste or writing about wasteful processes they encounter and submitting these for display and collation, perhaps even giving a prize to those who have captured the greatest areas for improvement.

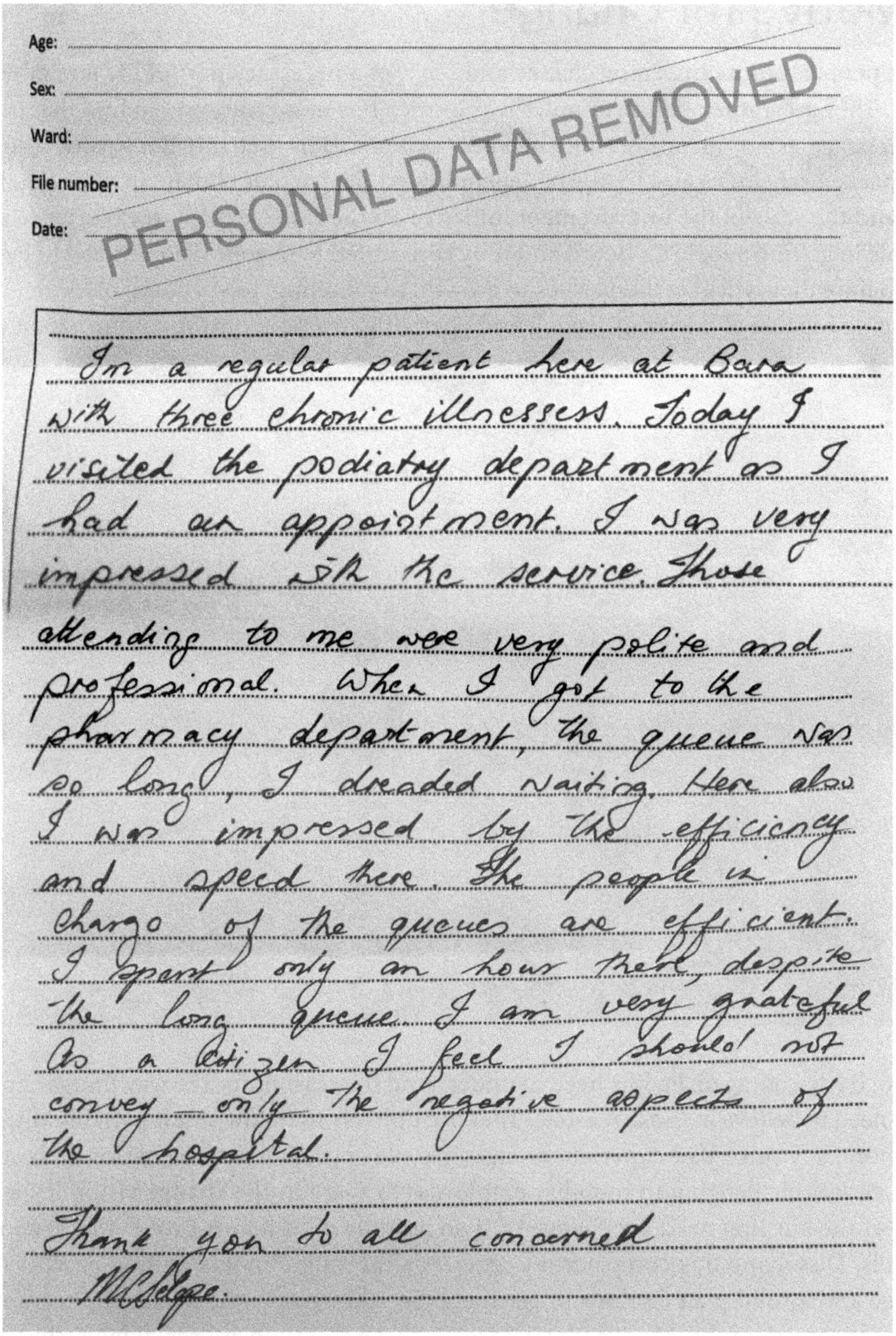

Age:

Sex:

Ward:

File number:

Date:

I'm a regular patient here at Bara
with three chronic illnesses. Today I
visited the podiatry department as I
had an appointment. I was very
impressed with the service. Those
attending to me were very polite and
professional. When I got to the
pharmacy department, the queue was
so long, I dreaded waiting. Here also
I was impressed by the efficiency
and speed here. The people in
charge of the queues are efficient.
I spent only an hour there, despite
the long queue. I am very grateful
as a citizen I feel I should not
convey only the negative aspects of
the hospital.

Thank you to all concerned
M. Sloane.

▲ **Figure 5.1**: A formal compliment received from a patient visiting one of the Cohort 1 hospitals.
This letter was shared with the staff illustrating that their hard work was indeed paying off.

# A Motive for Change

Some people thoroughly enjoy change and see it as a necessary part of life and development. They are, more often than not, the minority. It is more common to find that people view change as an uncomfortable, needless complication that threatens to overburden jam-packed schedules and lives. So, depending on the current climate in your organisation and the scale of the improvement initiative on the cards, expect to experience some trouble in getting people on board and fully committed to change. People need to be won over before they will give themselves to growth, to moulting, to shedding old skin and to emerging capable of thinking, feeling and operating in a new, out-of-comfort zone.

Do not be discouraged. People need to understand the reasons for the way things happen. They need to believe in those reasons. They are unlikely to follow a new path blindly. Furthermore, any prior bad experiences make people approach new scenarios with added caution. It is challenging to mobilise employees to share in the change vision if they do not feel the burning need for change or if an attitude of 'if it ain't broke, why try fix it?' prevails. Dissolving this complacency requires a thorough understanding of what must change and a solid plan for how to get there. To address this the leadership team must reach consensus on the 'Motive for Change', so that a common approach takes shape and becomes the key message and driver for change that is communicated to the rest of the organisation.

Remember: your people are at the oars. A successful change in direction pivots on understanding what makes them tick. What will make them row, as a collective, in a new direction?

Referring to the GDOH initiative, patient complaints of long waiting times in the public health system resulted in both the Minister of Health and the Gauteng MEC for Health prioritising the issue. The Voice of the Patient was taken to heart, and it triggered an improvement initiative in selected Gauteng hospitals. Waiting times is not a new focus area for the GDOH and falls within the six quality priorities detailed in the health strategy. In all communications with the hospitals and their respective improvement teams, this Motive for Change was emphasised and promoted. See Table 5.1 for the Motive for Change developed by the GDOH Steering Committee.

**EXAMPLE**

| A MOTIVE FOR CHANGE |
| --- |
| **WHY ARE WE DOING THIS?** |
| <ul><li>Service delivery is not what it could be</li><li>Improve access and reduce waiting times = service more clients</li><li>Make existing capacity more efficient – work smarter, innovatively to do more with what we have</li><li>Reduce waste and re-allocate the resources</li><li>Happier patients and staff, enhance patient experience and care</li><li>Matching customer needs with how expectations are met</li><li>Improve the image of the public health system</li><li>Better risk management – reduce safety issues for the patients and staff</li><li>Influence organisational culture</li><li>Empower staff to continuously improve through the Daily Management System</li></ul> |
| **WHICH INITIATIVES HAVE BEEN IDENTIFIED?** |
| Reduce patient waiting times for:<ul><li>Folder retrieval and registration</li><li>Out-patient clinics</li><li>Out-patient pharmacies</li></ul> |
| **WHO IS TO BE INVOLVED?** |
| Clusters of facilities (regional and clinics) will be selected and placed into cohorts.<br><br>Cohort 1:<ul><li>Chris Hani Baragwanath Academic Hospital</li><li>Leratong Hospital</li><li>Sebokeng Hospital</li><li>Kopanong Hospital</li></ul>Each cohort will assign:<ul><li>3-4 facility staff</li><li>CEO present for the host project</li><li>Quality management representative to take over from each CEO</li><li>3-5 Provincial / District representatives</li></ul> |

▲ Table 5.1: The GDOH's 'Motive for Change' Map

# A Vision for Change

A Vision for Change statement depicts a striking, bold and ongoing commitment to achieving a desired condition—in a few carefully chosen words. The vision must be clear enough to be articulated

> The vision must be clear enough to be articulated in less than one minute and succinct enough to be written out on a single page.

in less than one minute and succinct enough to be written out on a single page. It is a shared vision. Though the senior leadership team communicates, supports and ultimately achieves the vision, the more employees participate in its creation the more likely their acceptance of, and emotional connection with the vision's ideals.

Figure 5.2 (Faull, 2014) depicts the Vision for Change developed for the GDOH Service Delivery Improvement Initiative. It illustrates the Current Condition, which, although unknown at the time, was based on the experiences of the LIA's facilitators. It therefore included these three model areas:

- o reduce waiting times in the registration and retrieval of patient folders
- o reduce waiting times at out-patient clinics
- o reduce waiting times at out-patient pharmacies.

Once each of the hospitals in Cohort 1 was visited and evaluated in more detail, it became possible to better define the Current Condition.

**EXAMPLE**

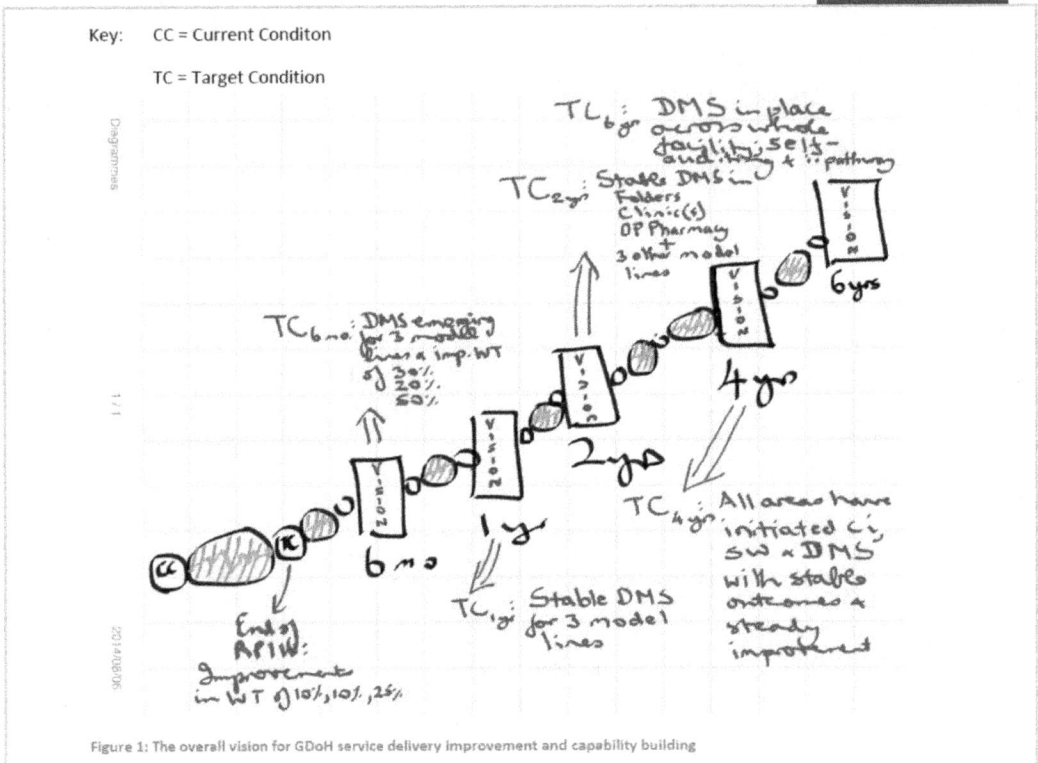

Figure 1: The overall vision for GDoH service delivery improvement and capability building

▲ Figure 5.2: A Vision for Change indicating Current and Target Conditions

Figure 5.2 illustrates the interim Target Conditions (or mini-visions) building up to a six-year Vision for Change. The first Target Condition entailed achieving up to 25 percent improvement in patient waiting times by the end of a five-day Rapid Process Improvement Workshop. Then, a longer-term of six months was allocated to seeing the Daily Management System (DMS) adopted in the model areas along with a corresponding improvement in waiting times of up to 50 percent. Within a year, the DMS was to be stable in the three model areas. Within two years the DMS was to be a sustained feature and three additional model areas would then be targeted. Achieving the four-year Target Condition would see the entire facility initiate Continuous Improvement and Standard Work, with stable DMS and steady and constant improvement in waiting times. Within six years an autonomous, self-auditing system with a stable DMS is expected to function across the entire facility.

Consensus on the level of support that each facility would receive and how this would mature over the six-year period was coupled with the Vision for Change. For the first 12-24 months the LIA facilitator would coach the facility. Thereafter, private sector companies with extensive continuous improvement experience would be invited to 'adopt' each facility and provide ongoing support and guidance. Dovetailing this would be the ongoing development of internal GDOH Lean apprentices who would be coached to take over the support to the facility after two years. Going forward, as the facility develops its own capabilities, external support is to be scaled down so that by the end of the six-year period, in-house capability will sustain the performance improvement without external consultants.

This is an ambitious undertaking, but two years down the line—one third of the way through the six-year initiative—there is evidence of close alignment to the Vision as it was initially communicated in 2014.

# The Structures for Change

Unfortunately desire for change and an improvement plan are not enough to make change happen. People need to undertake the specific activities that move the organisation closer to the change effort's goals. Designing an implementation structure will go a long way to ensuring the right people are involved, doing the right things and in the right way. Figure 5.3 provides a guideline of the recommended structures to be identified for sizable change efforts.

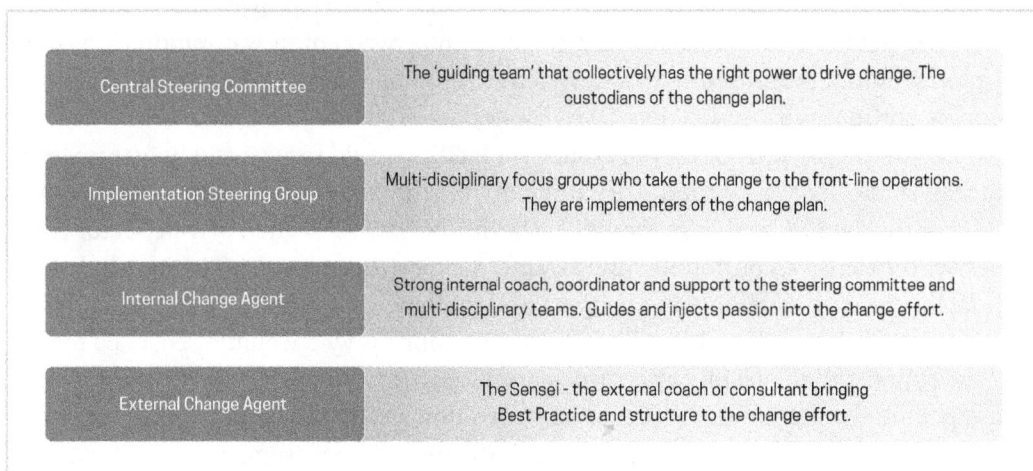

| | |
|---|---|
| Central Steering Committee | The 'guiding team' that collectively has the right power to drive change. The custodians of the change plan. |
| Implementation Steering Group | Multi-disciplinary focus groups who take the change to the front-line operations. They are implementers of the change plan. |
| Internal Change Agent | Strong internal coach, coordinator and support to the steering committee and multi-disciplinary teams. Guides and injects passion into the change effort. |
| External Change Agent | The Sensei - the external coach or consultant bringing Best Practice and structure to the change effort. |

▲ Figure 5.3: Recommended structures to support the change effort

Choose Steering Committee members with these key characteristics (Kotter, 2002):
- o A good mix of interpersonal and professional skills
- o The leadership capacity to create the vision, motivate and drive change
- o Organisational credibility
- o A strong network of contacts within the organisation
- o Relevant knowledge to empower people and remove obstacles to change
- o Formal authority and the managerial skills to plan and organise the change.

Discussions that took place at the GDOH Central Office in Johannesburg, saw a Steering Committee (Steerco) elected to guide and drive the initiative through to completion. The Steerco consisted of senior representation from Quality Assurance, the office of the Gauteng MEC for Health, Hospital Services, District Health, Human Resources, Communications, Strategic Planning, Ops UP (Initiative of the Presidency) and the CEOs of four Gauteng hospitals. All met and defined the way forward to guide the change effort.

The Steerco drafted a change plan containing the basic improvement strategy, the vision and supporting structures. This would form the basis of the communications to the hospitals selected to take part, and also provide a consistent sense of purpose in the leaders' messages to their teams. Although there was initially good progress and involvement, the Steerco later became largely inactive and disconnected from the improvement process. This development was indeed flagged as a risk to thwarting a change effort. It remains a learning point for future drives.

Improvement programmes in the public healthcare system are regularly derailed when those expected to make the changes are pulled onto other initiatives or called out of scheduled meetings and workshops to attend 'more important meetings'. As such, it is important to respect and ring fence such initiatives and protect key individuals from diversions. The Steerco was trained in Lean basics and part of this introduction included an explanation of the 3S Model (Faull, 2014). The model (see Figure 5.4) shows how operations are generically structured into three tiers: Strategic, Systemic and Situational. Recognising these three levels and the role each plays is an important element to planning for change and ensuring that structures compliment the improvement strategy.

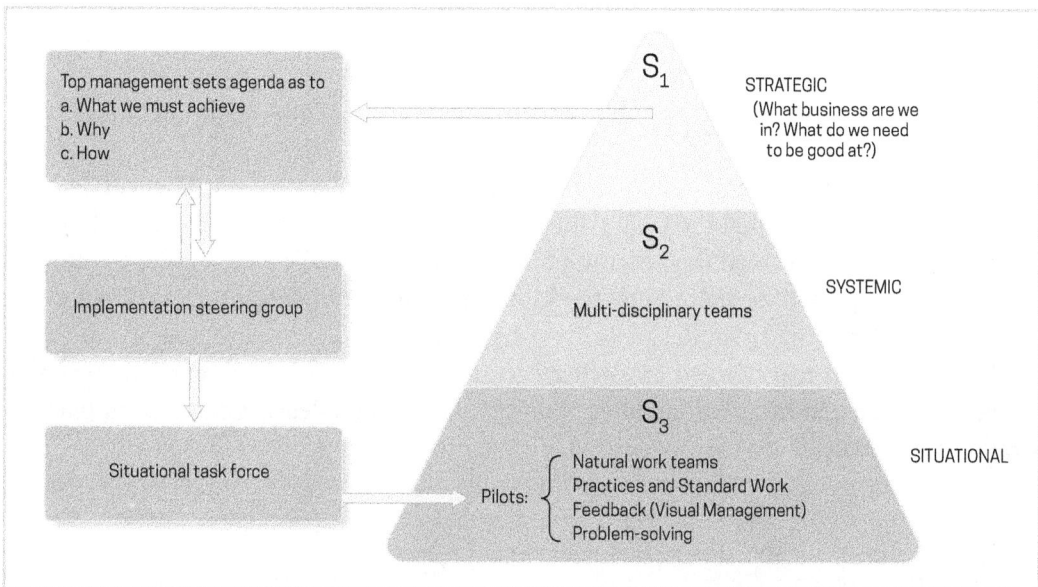

▲ Figure 5.4: The 3S Model presented by Prof. Faull at the introductory Lean workshops

It is up to the senior leadership (the S1 or Strategic tier) to define the strategy and cascade this through the ranks to ensure all levels are on board with the change effort, why it is needed and how it will be executed. They are also responsible for offering necessary support to ensure all levels are enabled and empowered to act on the Vision for Change, so that when barriers are encountered these are swiftly and effectively dealt with.

After initial communication sessions with the labour unions, Senior Management Team, Provincial Health Council, board members, Gauteng Legislature and hospital CEOs, the GDOH Service Delivery Improvement Initiative was finally launched, and teams at the frontline (the S3 or Situational tier) were mobilised. This also meant preparing departmental heads (the S2 or Systemic tier), who steer the change within their respective areas, for inter-departmental collaboration. At this stage the 3S Model for change was developing but still unstable in its performance—common in the early stages of improvement. When the 3S Model is functioning effectively:

- o Purpose and direction are clear
- o Multi-disciplinary teams collaborate and guide the implementation
- o Organic work teams commit to daily problem-solving in areas that matter
- o Communication and feedback filter up and down, from S1 to S2 and S2 to S3 and vice versa, moving the organisation forward towards its North Star goals.

To compensate for the Steerco absence throughout the GDOH process, hospital-level Steering Committees were developed—with varying success. This enabled the CEOs at each hospital to meet regularly with their departmental heads, receive feedback in the form of A3 summaries, and ensure the goal of improvement on patient waiting times was being met. Lean Management practices began to feature as Standard Work for the leaders—a factor critical to success discussed further in Part II.

# The Learning Strategy

We have explored the notion that well-focused training positively influences learner behaviour to the extent that the right habits to stimulate improvement are cultivated. The LIA facilitators constructed the Learning Strategy that would develop employees at each of the 3S tiers, providing them with the knowledge and confidence to take Lean practices to the three primary model areas identified. By implementing the strategy and then reflecting on what had worked and what had not, teams could then refine the process for model areas that came online later. Figure 5.5 details the learning that took place at Cohort 1 hospitals.

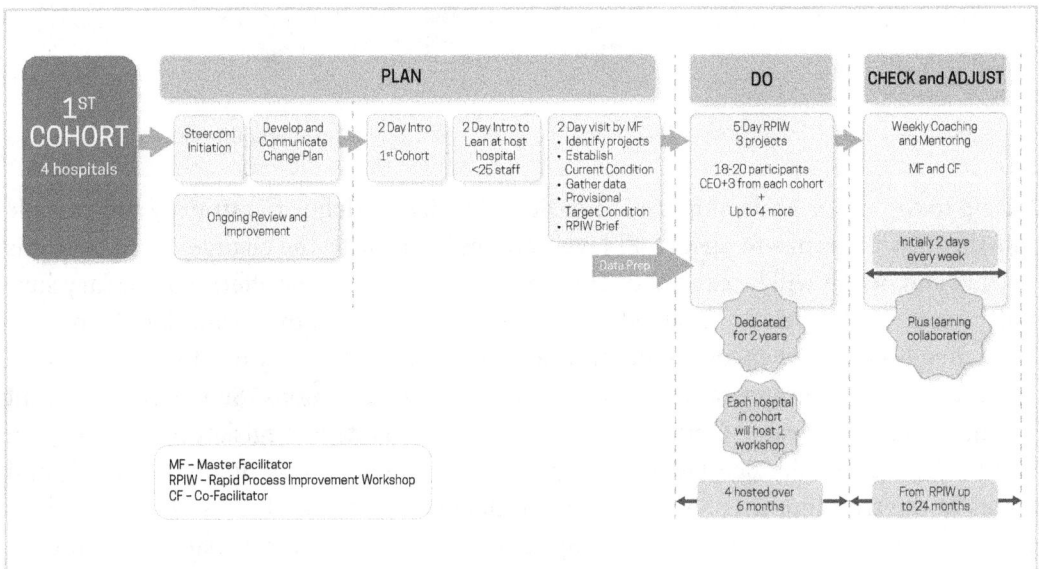

▲ Figure 5.5: Learning approach taken for Cohort 1 hospitals

The model areas initially targeted through this approach were Patient Affairs (registration and filing), Out-patient Clinics and Out-patient Pharmacies. The three model areas selected were tackled through analysis of the Value Stream prevalent at each. Patient waiting times would be the focus point for all improvement teams.

Once the Steerco had been formed and the change plan formulated, Cohort 1 training workshops were launched. Referring back to Figure 5.5, Cohort 1 change teams came together at the first hospital to undergo introductory Lean training.

In Figure 5.6, Cohort 1 partake in a bus accident simulation game to learn process improvement by practically making changes in a contrived emergency setting. Prof. Faull guides the team to capture the Current Condition, identify obstacles observed and to agree as a team on the next Target Condition. This game allowed for true application of desired process improvement principles.

▲ Figure 5.6: Prof Faull guides Cohort 1 teams through a simulation game

The host hospital then identified 25 employees representative of each of the three model areas to undergo the same introductory Lean training a few days later and also to undertake the same bus accident scenario challenge (Figure 5.7). This gave the facilitators the opportunity to engage directly with staff who were given a voice to express first-hand some of the obstacles they deal with everyday. It also gave the participants the opportunity to ask questions about the ensuing changes and the role they were expected to play.

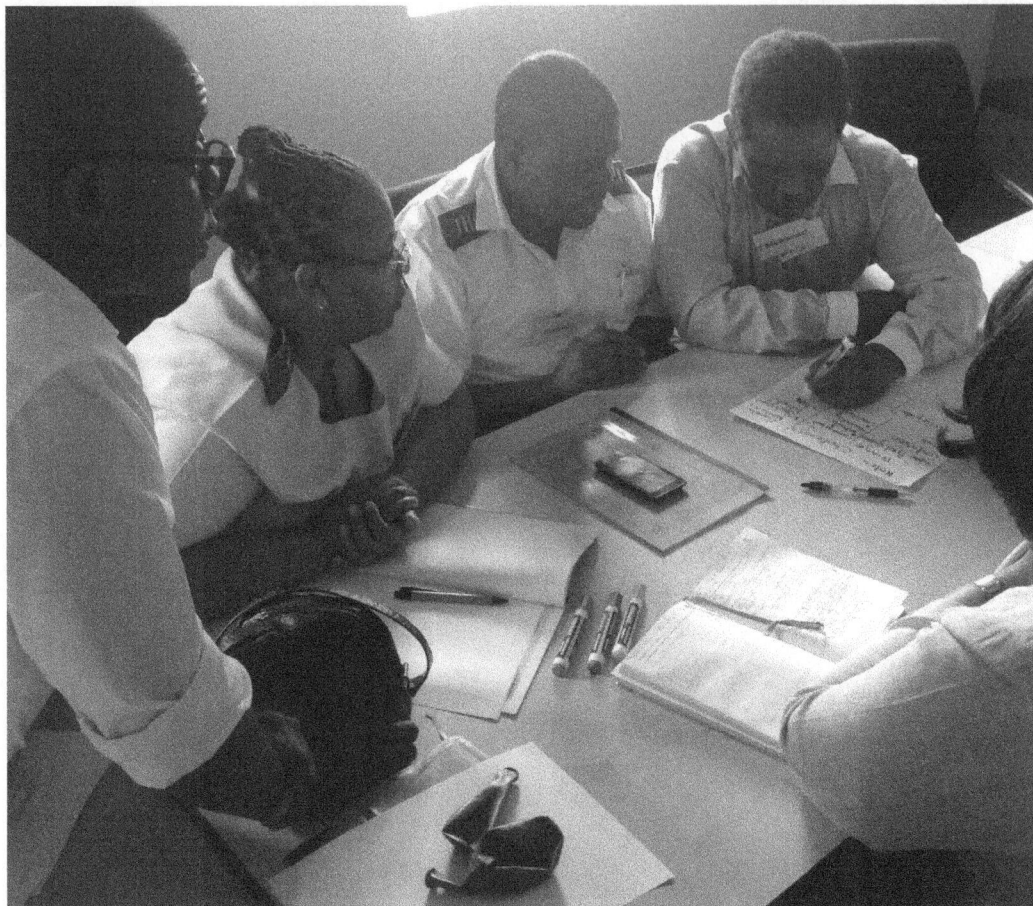

▲ Figure 5.7: Team brainstorming during the bus accident simulation game

Thereafter the LIA facilitators visited the host to prepare for the upcoming Rapid Process Improvement Workshop (RPIW). This entailed visiting the model areas, observing the process and defining the strategy for the RPIW. Facilitators met with area teams and took the time to communicate with all those involved to ensure staff that did not take part in the host introduction event were also up to speed.

The Current Condition was captured and initial thoughts around the Target Condition were displayed. This was shared with the RPIW team who were in turn expected to develop their own version of the Current Condition based on their own personal observations. This preparation served to illustrate the potential for improvement but also to give the LIA facilitators enough background to guide the teams successfully.

Figure 5.8: Prof. Faull talks through a display of the initial findings

After the preparation phase came data-gathering efforts to ensure that, prior to the start of the workshop, there would be data available for the team to work with. The data gathered included detail on patient waiting times, patient arrival rates and other relevant observations.

The RPIW took place one week later and involved each Cohort 1 hospital's change teams, including individuals from the model areas. The teams put their heads down and undertook an intense five-day workshop (illustrated in Figures 5.8 through 5.12).

Figure 5.9: Tshepo Thobejane (LIA) takes teams through a structured agenda of the day's activities

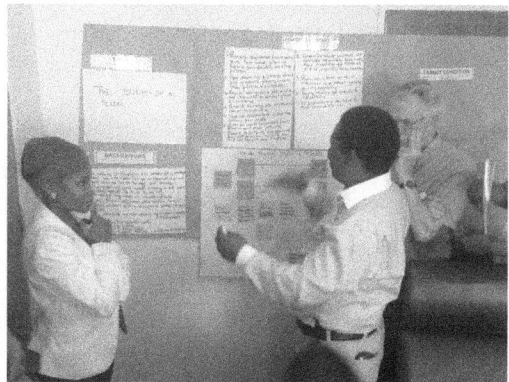

Figure 5.10: Team members tasked with 'Folder and Registration' improvement debate and capture the current process flow

Figure 5.11: The Medical Out-patient Department (MOPD) improvement team documents patient waiting times at each stage in the Value Stream to determine the Total Journey Time and the Service Efficiency

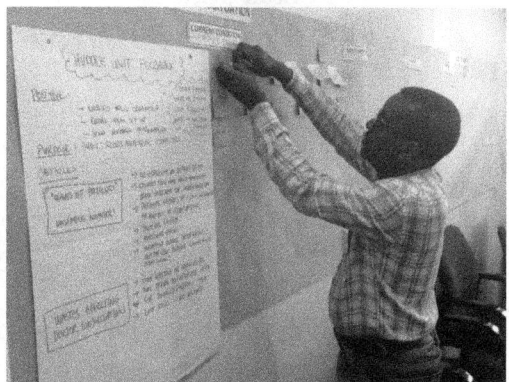

Figure 5.12: As part of 'Grasping the Current Situation' exercise the MOPD improvement team summarises feedback from unit members interviewed and uses it to update their Value Stream Map

Improvement teams spent time at the scene of the proverbial crime, or Gemba (Figures 5.13 and 5.14). There, they observed the work done by queue marshals and pharmacy staff to better understand the Current Condition.

▲ Figure 5.13: At the Gemba where files are issued

▲ Figure 5.14: At the Gemba where scripts are filled

Once the RPIW was complete and once each team could show they had made substantial progress in achieving reduced patient waiting times, the model area team received ongoing coaching and mentoring. The coaching sessions commenced within two weeks from the completion of the RPIW. This support helped to nurture the learning process and encourage the teams in sustaining and continuously improving on the new performance now in place. The Daily Management System was also initiated during these coaching sessions. Support was initially provided on a weekly basis but, over time, was spread out over longer periods as team members' confidence and capabilities grew.

Progress invariably slips after a breakthrough event such as a RPIW. The seeds of newly planted Lean principles remain fragile until they have had time to take root and develop into the saplings of permanent Best Practice. Coaching sessions are therefore mandatory 'fertiliser' and also help to address any areas of concern.

> The seeds of newly planted Lean principles remain fragile until they have had time to take root and develop into the saplings of permanent Best Practice.

Never imagine that lively debate will subside. Even after the RPIW, the Out-patient Pharmacy team was not convinced that moving smaller batches through the process would save time. It was therefore necessary to bring in coaching support—in this case Tshepo Thobejane from LIA (Figure 5.15)—to practically demonstrate to them the true impact that batching can have on patient waiting times.

▲ Figure 5.15: Tshepo Thobejane demonstrates the effect of large batches on patient waiting times at the Out-patient Pharmacy.

# The Three Levels of Learning

While detailed and sophisticated in their approach, when it comes to Operational Excellence the processes described above are only the beginning. Attending a workshop or a lecture (Figure 5.16: Learning Level 1) is not enough to bring about fluency in the language and behaviour of process improvement. Even 'learning-by-doing' (Learning Level 2) will only take your people so far. For learning to truly penetrate into the psyche of an organisation and result in behavioural changes, new skills must be practised repeatedly until they become automatic. Only then will we have reached Learning Level 3 as shown in Figure 5.16 (Faull, 2014).

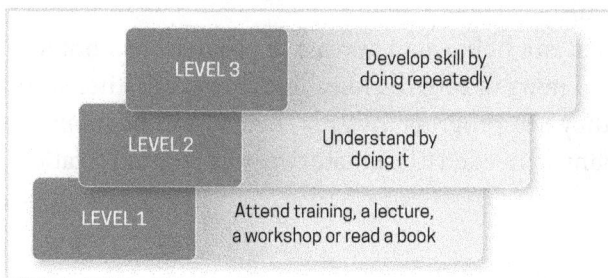

| LEVEL 3 | Develop skill by doing repeatedly |
| LEVEL 2 | Understand by doing it |
| LEVEL 1 | Attend training, a lecture, a workshop or read a book |

◀ Figure 5.16: Three Levels of Learning to strengthen excellence

It was therefore important for Cohort 1 to repeat the process and launch RPIW's in each of the hospitals in succession giving each participant four chances to learn the process and hone their skills. With this experience in hand teams would be more confident when launching future change events in other areas of their hospitals. In this way, people become capable of deploying the learning and results to new departments so taking progress forward. As the saying goes—the proof of the pudding is in the eating. Two of the Cohort 1 hospitals launched improvement efforts in Casualty and the Surgical Outpatient Clinic respectively—under their own steam.

No consultant can guarantee sustained change to an organisation. Developing in-house capability is truly the cornerstone of sustainability. Only through the development of Thinking People capable of delivering sustained value, does a change initiative stand a fighting chance. This comes from practice.

> Developing Thinking People capable of delivering sustained value will give your change initiative a fighting chance.

# Two-Way Communication

Too often, leaders initiate a change effort and hope that front-line staff will make it happen without leaders getting their hands dirty. There is tremendous advantage in a bottom-up approach to change. But without top-down support any change achieved has a predictably short lifespan.

Earlier in this chapter we were introduced to the 3S Model (see Figure 5.4), which describes how operations are structured into *Strategic*, *Systemic* and *Situational* tiers. Expanding on the model, it is recommended that the right escalation and feedback mechanisms be installed to facilitate up-and-down communication through the three tiers. Teams from the Situational tier (S3) should regularly report on their progress to the Systemic tier (S2) who in turn report to the Strategic tier (S1) in free flowing two-way communication between levels. Situational tier (S3) teams should also be empowered to escalate obstacles that fall outside of their control to the Systemic level (S2) so that timeous feedback can be provided to them. The same goes for the Systemic tier (S2) reaching out to the Strategic tier (S1) for support.

Failure to construct the sort of formal system that the 3S Model offers, opens teams (S2 and S3) up to the risk of abandonment when they most need back-up.

> Do not lose out on an opportunity to share the good news of progress!

It also risks senior levels of management not being kept abreast of progress. Do not lose out on an opportunity to share the good news of progress! Leaders (S1) are further stimulated to support their teams when they see progress towards their vision becoming a reality. Figure 5.17 illustrates the mechanism needed to animate two-way communication.

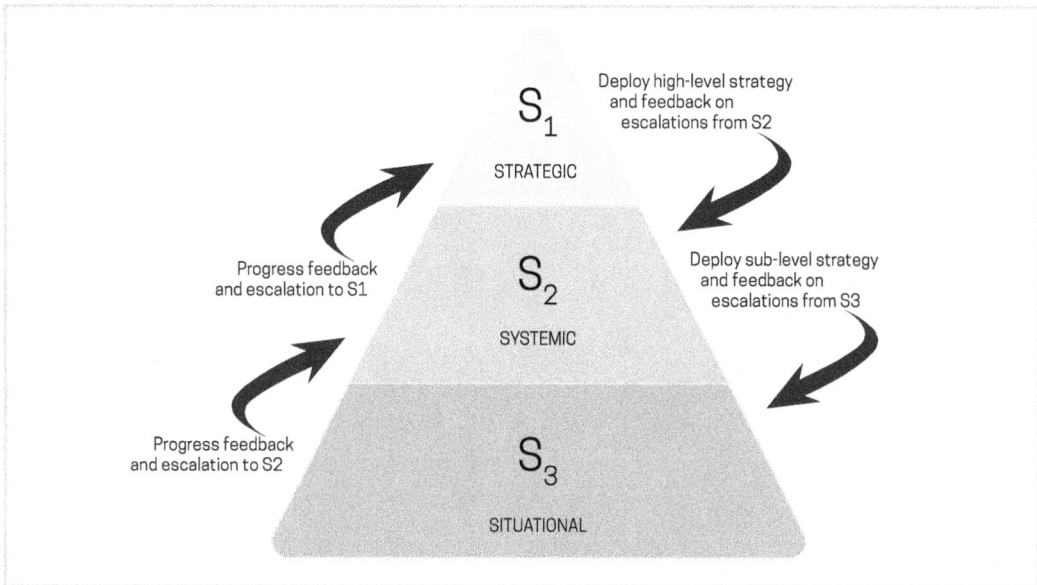

▲ Figure 5.17: Ensuring Two-way Communication between the 3S tiers

# Capitalising on Quick Wins

*'In successful change efforts, empowered people create short-term wins—victories that nourish faith in the change effort, emotionally reward the hard workers, keep the critics at bay, and build momentum. Without sufficient wins that are visible, timely, unambiguous and meaningful to others, change efforts inevitably run into serious problems.'*

*(Kotter 2002: p125)*

It is understandably difficult to garner support for an improvement initiative when it first launches. Very little tangible change has actually taken place at that point in time. The path to employee buy-in is smoother when tangible, upfront benefits are manifested. Strategically and deliberately focus on those all-important short-term gains in the initial stages of a change process. As the results of positive transformation are laid bare you will have your greatest sceptics on your side and prompt the support of all tiers. Remember: people believe in personally tangible, visible benefits that speak to their hearts and minds! This applies whether they sit at S1, S2 or S3.

People typically fall into three response-categories during the so-called DO phase of any change effort (Pascal, 2006):

o *Supporters*: 10 percent of staff is generally supportive of the plan.
o *Watchers*: 80 percent are generally pleased that the organisation is getting its act together, but are waiting to see what happens next.
o *Grumblers*: 10 percent are generally against the change.

Capitalising on Quick Wins can help with backing the supporters and winning over the watchers. There is not much to be done about the grumblers at this stage so do not expend much time on changing the stance of this minority group. They may come around in due course or even move on.

In the case of our GDOH Service Delivery Improvement Initiative, upfront wins were achieved at the first RPIW. The first hospital tackled benefited from the following improvements:

> Back the supporters, win over watchers and do not worry about the grumblers at this stage.

- o Patient registration waiting time was reduced by 63 percent
- o The MOPD Clinic patient waiting time was reduced by 13 percent
- o The Out-patient Pharmacy waiting time was reduced by 23 percent.

These gains were not initially sustained. It took a few rounds of iterating the processes that cut waiting times to stabilise new systems. Most importantly, after the short but intense five-day RPIW effort the team could see that this kind of change was indeed possible—which was highly motivating! Teams were then energised to tackle the same problems at the other Cohort 1 hospitals with equal—if not more—vigour. See Table 5.1 for the actual results achieved after the intensive 5-day workshops. See Chapter 9 for further details on the results.

| HEALTHCARE FACILITY | MODEL AREA | WAITING TIME RESULTS | | |
|---|---|---|---|---|
| | | CURRENT CONDITION BEFORE RPIW (min) | ACTUAL CONDITION AT THE END OF RPIW (min) | PERCENTAGE IMPROVEMENT AFTER 5 DAYS |
| Hospital 1 | Registration | 276 | 102 | 63% |
| | Clinic | 211 | 183 | 13% |
| | Pharmacy | 79 | 61 | 23% |
| Hospital 2 | Registration | 143 | 43 | 70% |
| | Clinic | 112 | 74 | 34% |
| | Pharmacy | 40 | 13 | 68% |
| Hospital 3 | Registration | 77 | 55 | 29% |
| | Clinic | 112 | 83 | 26% |
| | Pharmacy | 15 | 5 | 67% |
| Hospital 4 | Registration | 137 | 86 | 37% |
| | Clinic | 45 | 21 | 53% |
| | Pharmacy | 64 | 41 | 36% |

▲ Table 5.1: Results achieved at each of the hospitals that underwent the RPIW

Leaders might take a page from Gauteng MEC for Health, Ms. Qedani Mahlangu's book. Two Lean apprentices from her office were dedicated to the Cohort 1 project. And, despite the challenges of her schedule, she was present, interested and involved, even attending the RPIW feedback session to offer her support (Figure 5.18).

◄ Figure 5.18: Gauteng Health MEC Qedani Mahlangu attends the RPIW feedback session and offers support and encouragement to team members

## PRACTICAL ACTIVITY: Bringing a Change Plan to Life

Once a Steerco with adequate authority and representation has been elected, develop the following as part of the documented change plan:

▸ The Motive for Change detailing why the initiative is needed for future growth.

▸ A long-term Vision for Change, as well as intermediate mini visions (interim Target Conditions) for smaller step change achievements.

▸ The 3S structures that will be introduced to support and implement the change, including representation from each S1, S2 and S3 tier of the organisation.

▸ The Learning Strategy to guide what the employees will need to learn and apply, to effect changes in performance and habits.

▸ An escalation and feedback mechanism to ensure employees receive the needed support and ensure communication of progress as it is achieved.

▸ A plan to recognise and advertise early improvement gains that motivate teams to continue with the change effort and so maintain its momentum.

▸ Armed with the change plan leaders can commence communication to the rest of the organisation of the exciting developments in store.

For more information on developing a change plan, refer to *Clear Direction* (Heathcote, 2014).

*The first responsibility of a leader is to define reality. The last is to say thank you. In between, the leader is a servant.*

Max De Pree, American businessman and author

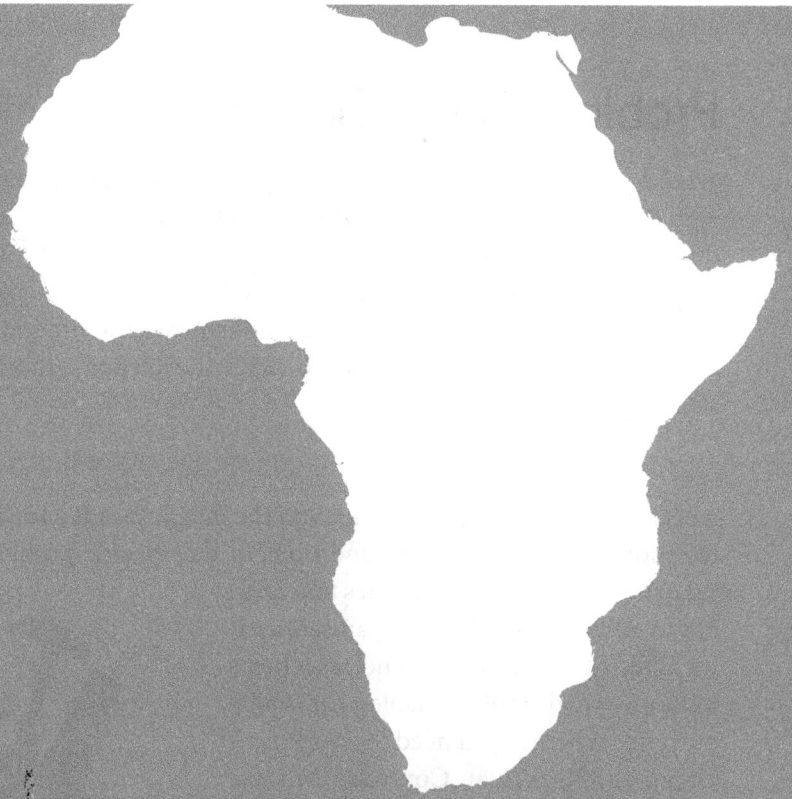

# PART II
EXECUTION

# Problem First, then Tool

Would a mechanic tasked with revamping of a cherished classic randomly select a tool with which to undertake the work? Would they base their selection solely on the fact that other mechanics have found the gadget useful—in other contexts? Would the mechanic hope that the device will somehow 'work' for this unique repair too?

Any mechanic worth their salt first diagnoses the unique elements of the refurbishment needed before deciding how to tackle the job and—most importantly—which tools suit the commission.

*What is the problem that you are trying to solve? What is causing it?*

Answering these questions brings you the insight needed to select the very best option—the tool to apply to the nuts and bolts of the specific problem defined. Selecting from the array of tools and techniques that Lean has to offer, to remodel an organisation, is no different. With so many choices it helps to know which tool is enabled for which purpose. Whether you need 5S Workplace Organisation, Visual Controls, Mistake Proofing, Kanban (signalling system) or some other tool, will largely depend on what needs fixing.

In the words of author and Professor of Lean Enterprise at the University of Buckingham, John Bicheno: 'Don't be a tool head'. Be selective when it comes to the tools and techniques you bring on board to fix a broken process—and first be sure of why they are the right ones for the job.

# Introduction to Visual Management

Visually depicting performance is a powerful tactic for managing the process and exposing opportunities for improvement. Show your people what the desired performance looks like. With the right visual systems in place, teams can quickly discern normal from abnormal, and respond to anomalies to nip them in the bud.

Visual Management makes use of these key tools:
o   5S Workplace Organisation (5S)
o   Visual Control

These two tools work in tandem to create a visual workplace, so making problems transparent and promoting productivity.

To illustrate 5S think of a shed or garage that looks like a graveyard for unwanted items. It is almost impossible to find anything in this space. Applying the principles of 5S to the mess, we begin by clearing everything from the area and sorting the items discovered into those that need to be there, those to get rid of and those that belong elsewhere. The space is tidied from top to bottom and wall-to-wall. Now clean and clear, the necessary items are lovingly reintroduced and located for ease of access. Labels now show where everything goes. The next time someone looks for something, it is predictably easy to locate. Anyone walking into this space can easily define its raison *d'être*. Thanks to the 5S organisation effort, they see the purpose of this space clearly. More on 5S later.

To illustrate Visual Control consider driving along a highway, en route to work. The road surface markings provide visual instructions to drivers as to their space allocation on the road, so visually controlling driver behaviour. Imagine the chaos in their absence? What makes this type of Visual Control interesting is that an experienced driver naturally drives within the demarcated lines without consciously thinking about them. A learner driver will however rely on the lines to ensure they conform to the regulations. Only later, with more experience, does this conscious obedience fade into subconscious reflex. The same applies to employing Visual Controls in daily operations.

Visual Control provides an effective way to govern the management of a process. It offers a way to tap into subconscious thought that drives behaviour, so getting people to react in the right way to everyday, repeatable scenarios without their having to worry about how to respond each time.

5S and Visual Controls are useful tools that can influence the development of Best Practices and therefore improve performance. However, Visual Management goes further than the tool. It helps develop the 'Thinking System'—a system in which the behaviours that drive continuous improvement are regularly triggered in Thinking People.

Visual Management relies on the Improvement Cycle (Figure 6.1). In a process that takes advantage of the right visual elements, abnormalities are quickly spotted and teams have a visual benchmark against which they can compare something atypical. They are empowered to reflect on this information and agree on causes and countermeasures, prompting them to take action. Filtering the action taken through the PDCA phases further stabilises performance until the next abnormality is—again through 5S and Visual Control—identified.

> Abnormalities are quickly spotted and teams have a visual benchmark against which they can compare something atypical.

The Improvement Cycle is clearly a continuous process and not a one-hit wonder. Indeed, it forms the very backbone of the Daily Management System discussed in Chapter 8.

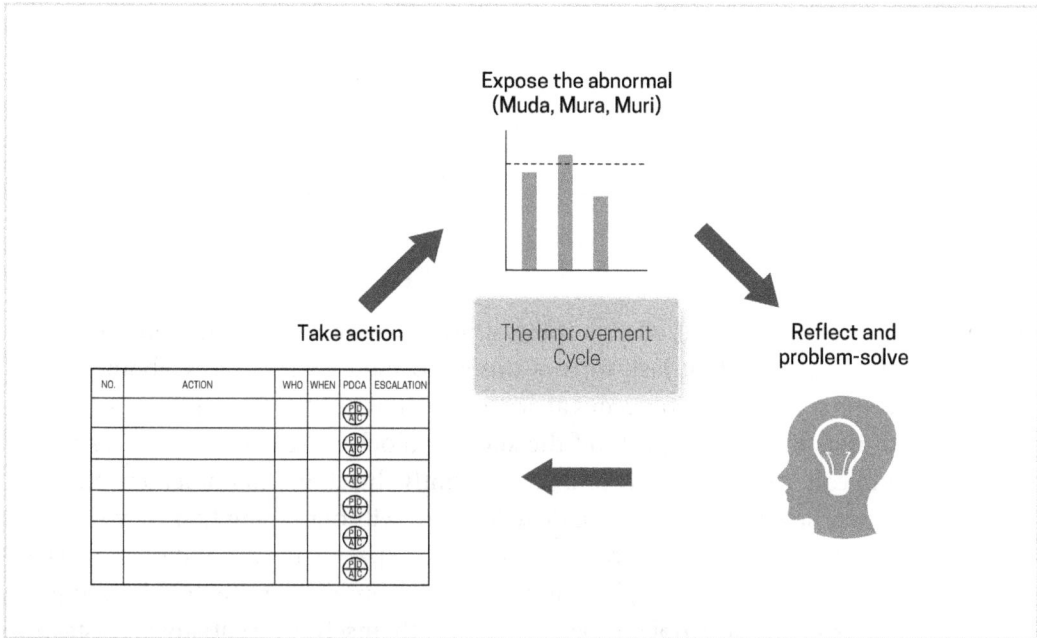

Effective Visual Management has been achieved when:

o The workplace is visual and has become the teacher. Visuals employed clearly illustrate abnormal versus normal conditions. Teams are triggered to act when abnormalities are identified.

o The health of the operation is transparent—visible at a glance.

o The workplace is clean and organised according to 5S guidelines.

o Visuals employed connect employees to disciplined processes and Best Practice.

o Visuals standardise ways of working.

o Visuals display only current and relevant data and information.

o Daily accountability is visual and personal.

An underestimated by-product of these efforts is the way in which a clean, visual and organised workspace boosts staff morale. People often comment on the way the workplace feels once Visual Management has been properly introduced.

# 5S Workplace Organisation

*A Japanese sensei visits a supplier to teach them the Toyota Production System.
Having made a long trip to get there, he first uses the rest room. But, upon emerging
he declares that he is leaving immediately. 'The toilet is a mess!' he says angrily. 'Until
you have the discipline to keep your toilet clean, you are not ready for the Toyota
Production System.'*

*Toyota lore*

5S is a foundational practice. It offers a solid, strategic and consensus-driven floor upon
which to build structures that last, to root out abnormalities and bring about change.
Think of 5S as the training that precedes an athlete's win when the time has come to com-
pete. Think of it as the perfect push off the starting blocks when the start gun fires. Its
absence dramatically affects stability and consequently the ability to implement Kaizen.

Yet, 5S is often neglected. Teams bulldoze forward without seeing that they have not
taken the initial state of the ground into account. It is preparing the ground that forms the
foundation for all the other principles and practices to build upon. By first 'clearing the
window' to the process, the problems begin to reveal themselves essentially kick-starting
the Improvement Cycle into action.

The 5S improvement tool has five key stages. Each begins with the letter 'S'. Together,
the five stages provide a simple yet highly effective structured approach to creating order,
discipline and basic stability in the workplace. Figure 6.2 depicts the 5S Model, illustrating and explaining each of the 5S stages in sequence, starting with SORT:

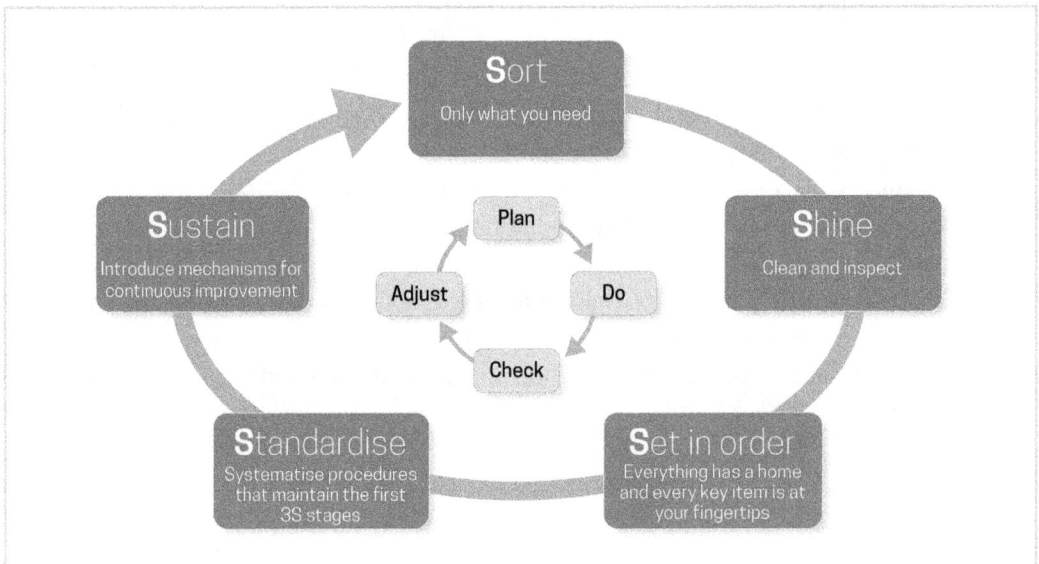

▲ Figure 6.2: The five stages of the 5S Workplace Organisation improvement tool

5S is equally relevant to improving a newsroom, factory, bank, back office, home-office, garage, hospital—indeed any sort of environment in need of streamlining. A well-organised workplace that is conducive to getting the right things done in the right way is simply non-negotiable. It is an absolute must.

> Bringing 5S into the heart of an organisation is like connecting an IV line to a weakened body and supplying it with a needed nutrient or drug compound.

Many have grappled with the 5S paradox: though reasonably easy to understand, 5S is challenging to entrench into the lifeblood of a management system. What is this lifeblood? It is the collective ethos of everyone's daily work habits. It flows through the arteries of an organisation and feeds the heart of change. Bringing 5S into the heart of an organisation is like connecting an IV line to a weakened body and supplying it with a needed nutrient or drug compound. In the same way that the results of a proposed treatment require a decisive doctor and patient adherence, so too does an effective dose of 5S require the drive and support of leadership with the courage of their conviction to bring about change and lead teams that stay the course. 5S will help you reap the following benefits:

o 5S exposes out-of-standard conditions. This is fundamental to problem-solving.
o 5S decreases opportunity for error, inversely boosting the quality of work.
o It encourages disciplined work habits and housekeeping.
o 5S clears the cloud of clutter so reducing excessive transport and motion, waiting, searching and other *Muda, Mura* and *Muri*.
o It cements the basics that sustain a clean and safe workplace.
o It introduces shared responsibility for improving and maintaining the workspace.

## Start with a 5S Baseline

Before making any improvements, first train your team in 5S principles. Then, capture the Current Condition. One way of doing this is to take 'before' photographs and conduct a thorough audit of the model area.

Table 6.1 outlines a useful Audit Sheet used by a Cohort 1 pharmacy team. Be sure to customise the form to suit the particular area you wish to improve. Remember that pharmacies, administration counters and clinics all feature different abnormalities and opportunities. This sheet can be combined with existing safety audits to assist the team in the audit process and simplify the work involved.

Score the sheet in this way:

*Scores: 1: not in place; 2: partially in place; 3: in place*

To avoid capturing vague audit scores on the 5S Audit Sheet, any audit check scoring lower than three must be accompanied by a comment on the concomitant area of improvement required. This will also make it simpler for follow-ups and subsequent audits.

## BASIC 5S AUDIT SHEET

| 5S STAGE | NO. | AUDIT CHECK | IMPROVEMENT AREAS | SCORE | | |
|---|---|---|---|---|---|---|
| | | | | 1 | 2 | 3 |
| SORT | 1 | All equipment, consumables and items necessary to service patients are clearly located and easily accessed. | | | | |
| | 2 | Items of secondary importance are allocated to a holding area or archive. Responsibility has been allocated to ensure its maintenance and upkeep. | | | | |
| | 3 | A clear policy guides the regular discard of unnecessary items. | | | | |
| | 4 | The area is audited weekly for SORT OUT opportunities and these are added to a clearly visible action board | | | | |
| SHINE | 5 | Necessary items are clean and fit for purpose. | | | | |
| | 6 | Cleaning schedules follow regular routines. | | | | |
| | 7 | The floor area is clean and free of dust and litter. Cupboards, storage areas, drawers, keyboard and mouse sets, desks etc., are clean. Walls, windows, lights are clean and in good condition. Tea rooms, rest areas, meeting areas are clean and hygienic. Cables are properly bundled and free of dust. | | | | |
| | 8 | The area is audited weekly for SHINE opportunities and these are added to a visible action board. | | | | |
| SET IN ORDER | 9 | All essential items are: <br> • Located according to frequency of use <br> • Labelled for ease of retrieval <br> • Laid out so as to reduced motion and time waste <br> • Inventory monitored to ensure min and max levels are maintained | | | | |
| | 10 | Working areas are properly demarcated and labelled. | | | | |
| | 11 | There are well-marked storage areas for all items e.g. files, medicines, consumables, archives, waste, kitchen containers etc. The manner of marking chosen highlights a missing item's absence. | | | | |
| | 12 | Regular-use items are kept close to where they are needed. All documentation, standards and procedures are located close to the working area and are clearly demarcated. | | | | |
| | 13 | Containers are safely stacked. | | | | |
| | 14 | Waste containers are clearly marked, stored and segregated. | | | | |
| | 15 | The area is audited weekly for SET IN ORDER opportunities and these are added to a visible action board. | | | | |
| | | | TOTAL SCORE OUT OF 45 AND % | | | |

▲ Table 6.1: Example of a basic 5S Audit Sheet

Figures 6.3 through 6.6 depict a Cohort 1 pharmacy team undergoing 5S training followed by a visit to the Gemba to conduct their 5S audit. They walked the area, opened cupboards and drawers, and took photographs of their findings.

▲ Figure 6.3: Conducting 5S training

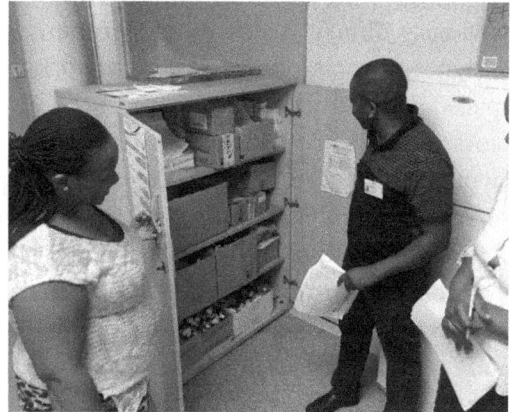

▲ Figure 6.4: Conducting a 5S audit

The 5S process uncovered several areas of *Muda*, *Mura* and *Muri* tucked away behind closed doors, inside drawers and hidden in the wings of daily habits and routines. The team printed their 'before' photographs, labelled each one and pinned them onto a white board so that they could discuss these—now visual—opportunities for improvement.

▲ Figure 6.5: Current Condition 5S photographs and comments displayed

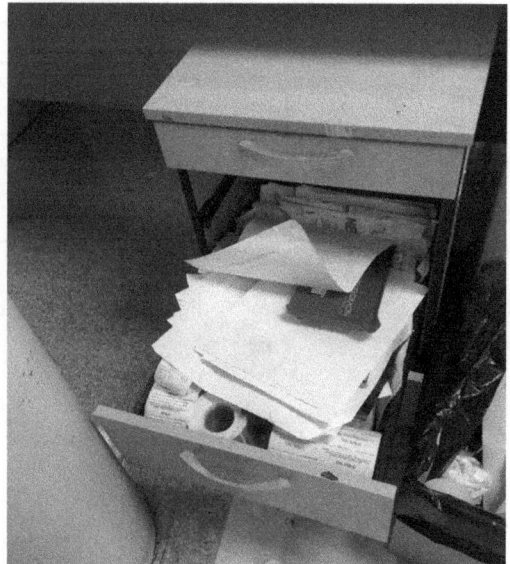

▲ Figure 6.6: A drawer over-burdened with items to be sorted and cleared

The results of the 5S audit, photographs and discussions were used by the team to document their baseline scores and findings. They then clarified which improvement actions would be immediately pursued and those that would need tackling over a longer period of time.

# 5S Stage 1: SORT

Completing the 5S audit lays the ground-work for 5S Stage 1: SORT a work area into a space conducive to excellence. It is obviously difficult to clean and properly designate people and items in a work-space filled with clutter. An area in chaos blurs any vision of ideal inventory and

> Without performing the critical step of SORT in the work area you may end up rearranging one mess into neat piles of smaller, divided messes.

layout. Without performing the critical step of SORT in the work area you may end up rearranging one mess into neat piles of smaller, divided messes, all the while building waste into the so-called 'new and improved design'.

Table 6.2 illustrates the key points that will help you facilitate the SORT stage. If you have not performed 5S before, follow the guidelines presented, but always reflect on and learn from what did and did not work in your specific context. With time, you will develop your own approach to enact alongside the fundamental 5S principles.

| SORT – ONLY WHAT YOU NEED | | |
|---|---|---|
| Key Points | Description of Activity | What you will need |
| 1 | Remove all items that can reasonably be cleared: desks, tools, materials, documentation, shelves etc. Only fixed equipment and immovable items should remain. Create a blank canvas from which to work. | Moving equipment if required |
| 2 NEEDED \| NOT NEEDED | Sort all the cleared items into two piles or sections:<br>• Items essential to the work<br>• Items non-essential to the work<br>Place unneeded items in a temporary holding area to be shortly cleared. | Holding area |
| 3 | Take photographs of :<br>• Essential items<br>• Unnecessary items | Camera |
| 4 STANDARD | Develop a visual one-page document to illustrate the standard for SORT for this area. Display the standard on the team board or at the workstation. | Photographs taken, computer and laminator |
| 5 | Conduct an 'after' audit for SORT. Focus only on progress made—as reflected by scores. List outstanding items on the team action board. | Customised audit, pencils and action board. |

▲ Table 6.2: Steps to follow to carry out a SORT activity

It may be challenging to identify unnecessary items at first. Employees can become attached to items in their workspace and may insist that that everything is necessary! Probe employees with the following questions to help expose non-essential items:

- o  Do you need this item to do your work?
- o  When was the last time you used it?
- o  Do you need it here?
- o  Do you need so much of it?
- o  Could someone else put it to better use?

> Effective change speaks to both the hearts and minds of the people engaged. We cannot make sound and lasting decisions without their involvement.

Figure 6.7 depicts pharmacists, assistants and pickers working together to gather all items in the pharmacy work area and localise them onto one desk to be sorted. This was undeniably an emotional exercise for all involved. It is fundamental to remember that effective change speaks to both the hearts and minds of the people engaged. We cannot make sound and lasting decisions without their involvement.

▲ Figure 6.7: Centralising all items in a workspace to begin the SORT process

In Figure 6.8 the team is discussing and debating each item on the table in front of them. They agree on what is essential to get the work done and divide the items into two piles—what is needed, and what is not needed to perform their work (see Figure 6.9).

It was immediately, visually apparent that non-essential items were taking up a tremendous amount of space on work surfaces and inside drawers. With these items cleared, pharmacy staff could finally see the impact that the clutter of unnecessary items was having on overall performance and morale.

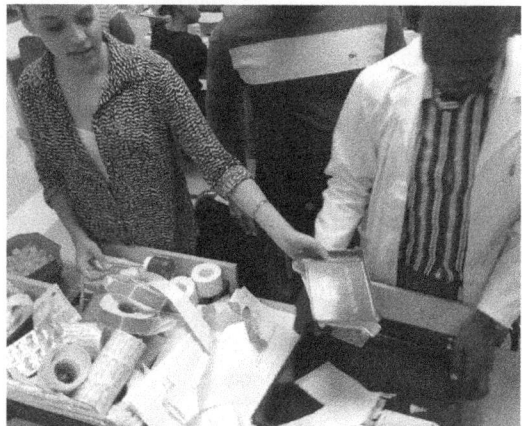

▲ Figure 6.8: SORT items into two piles to separate the essential from the non-essential

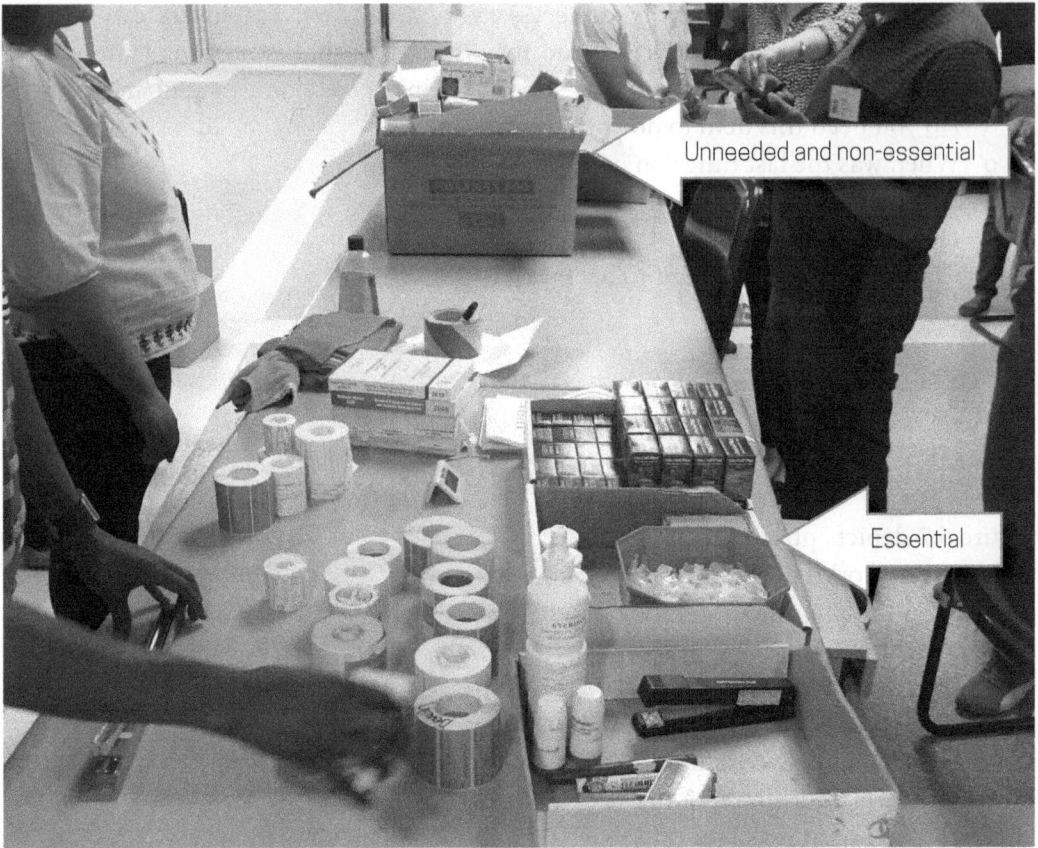

Figure 6.9: Sorted, unneeded items are ready for 'archive', 'reallocate' or 'discard' decisions

Help your team to make decisions regarding discarding and relocating items unnecessary items:

- o Obsolete items: sell, depreciate, give away or discard
- o Defective items: return to supplier or discard
- o Garbage: recycle or throw away
- o Non-essential items: move to another area where they are needed or discard
- o Daily-use essential items: staff to carry on their person where possible; alternatively, locate at point of use
- o Items used weekly: keep close to point of use
- o Items used monthly: store where accessible and easy to find
- o Items seldom used but essential: store out of the way but where they are easy to find.

# 5S Stage 2: SHINE

The second stage of 5S is your opportunity to improve the look and feel of a work area by unleashing a thorough bout of cleaning. Everything gets a scrub, scour and polish—from top to bottom. This means removing all dirt, grime and dust and thoroughly cleaning equipment, floors, walls, ceilings and lighting. Ensure that you take a three-dimensional view of the work area to prevent concentrating on surfaces alone. If you are cleaning equipment, make sure to tackle all six sides of the machinery and not just the front parts or areas in plain view.

> 'Clean with meaning' and visually 'sweep with your eyes' so that you uncover problems that are quietly begging to be resolved.

Consider a dirty car that needs a wash. Looking more closely at the detail of the engine, body and interior as you clean, allows you to learn more about the condition of your vehicle. Not only does a full-house car wash result in a pristine vehicle, it also provides an opportunity to inspect the car for damage, scratches or areas needing repair.

Cleaning is therefore only one aspect of SHINE. A much more important principle is to 'clean with meaning' and visually 'sweep with your eyes' so that you uncover problems that are quietly begging to be resolved. Once problems have been identified, the next step is to get at the root causes, to prevent their recurrence going forward. Table 6.3 illustrates key processes and equipment to consider when undertaking a SHINE exercise.

| SHINE – CLEAN AND INSPECT | | |
|---|---|---|
| Key Points | Description of Activity | What you will need |
| 1 | Clean the work area from top to bottom: floors, walls, ceilings, lights, equipment (all sides). | Cleaning materials, cleaning guidelines, 'Cleaning in Progress' sign—if applicable. |
| 2 | Visually inspect for problems:<br>• Sources of dirt, contamination, dust or leaks<br>• Damaged or faulty items needing repair or replacement<br>Tag items to be addressed and place them in a temporary holding area. | Tags, pens, string, holding area |
| 3 ? | Use basic problem-solving techniques to understand the causes of the problems picked up and allocate actions to resolve them. Identify reasons for dirt, contamination, dust or leaks and agree on ways to make cleaning easier. | Fishbones and 5 Whys |
| 4 | Take photographs of the newly cleaned area. | Camera |
| 5 STANDARD | Develop cleaning and inspection schedules to prevent problems recurring and to maintain the condition of the work area and equipment. Make sure the schedule covers who, what, where, how and why for each point. | Computer, laminator |
| | Develop a visual one-page guide to illustrate the standard for SHINE. Display the standard on the team board. Be sure to also allocate the correct storage of cleaning materials. | Photographs taken, computer and laminator |
| 6 | Conduct an 'after' audit for SHINE. Focus only on progress made—as reflected by scores. List outstanding items on the team action board. | Customised audit, pencils and action board. |

▲ Table 6.3: Steps to follow to carry out a SHINE activity

Have you ever considered the network of cleaning activities that sustain cleanliness at a busy shopping centre, airport or entertainment facility? Ironically, the better this 'behind-the-scenes' work is carried out, the more likely that it will be taken for granted by visitors. This work, driven by specific systems, procedures and practices, ensures key areas look and feels so clean that visitors never stop to think about hygiene levels.

The cleaning and inspection schedules referred to in Table 6.3 need to clarify who does what to maintain the cleanliness of a workspace. Without this sort of structure and accountability, employees may not fully take on the responsibilities of cleaning. It should be noted that cleaning should not fall squarely on the shoulders of contractors such as cleaning companies. Team members must take responsibility for how they treat their workspace and how they hand it over to other shifts.

Table 6.4 presents an example of a Cleaning Schedule that can be adapted to suit a particular area. It could even include audit checks from the 5S Audit Sheet that each person must perform in their area of responsibility. During SHINE's problem-solving steps, you may have identified various sources of dirt. Apply the schedule to seek and address these.

**EXAMPLE**

| DAILY CLEANING SCHEDULE | | | | | | | | |
|---|---|---|---|---|---|---|---|---|
| AREA: | OUT-PATIENT PHARMACY | | | | | | | |
| LEADER: | BILLY | | | | | | | |
| AREA OF RESPONSIBILITY | REST AREA | MEETING AREA | TABLE 1 | TABLE 2 | TABLE 3 | TABLE 4 | STORAGE 1-4 | STORAGE 5-8 |
| JOHN | ■ | | | | | | | |
| VUSI | | ■ | | | | | | ■ |
| ANGELO | | | ■ | | | | ■ | |
| JOHAN | | | | ■ | | | | |
| THABO | | | | | ■ | | | |
| GINA | | | | | | ■ | | |
| ANGUS | | | | | | | ■ | |
| BENJAMIN | | | | | | | | ■ |
| THABASENG | ■ | | | | | | | |

▲ Table 6.4: Example of a Cleaning Schedule

When undertaking cleaning activities, always remember:

o Safety first. Before cleaning and inspecting, equipment must be properly switched off and guaranteed safe for handling. Request a formal lockout procedure from the maintenance or technical department if needed.

o Seek guidance from maintenance or technical personnel to ensure proper cleaning procedures are followed when:

- Cleaning electrical components and motors
- Selecting suitable cleaning materials (especially to avoid potentially corrosive chemicals)

o Choose methods that do not just move the dirt or dust to other areas, but remove it altogether and prevent recurrence.

o If applicable, engage an equipment start-up plan to ensure all equipment is tested and running to standard, safely.

Figure 6.10 and 6.11 show the pharmacy team at a Cohort 1 hospital cleaning the area's walls, floors, work surfaces and windows. In the end, the space was spotless and, although a tough job, all took pride in the outcome.

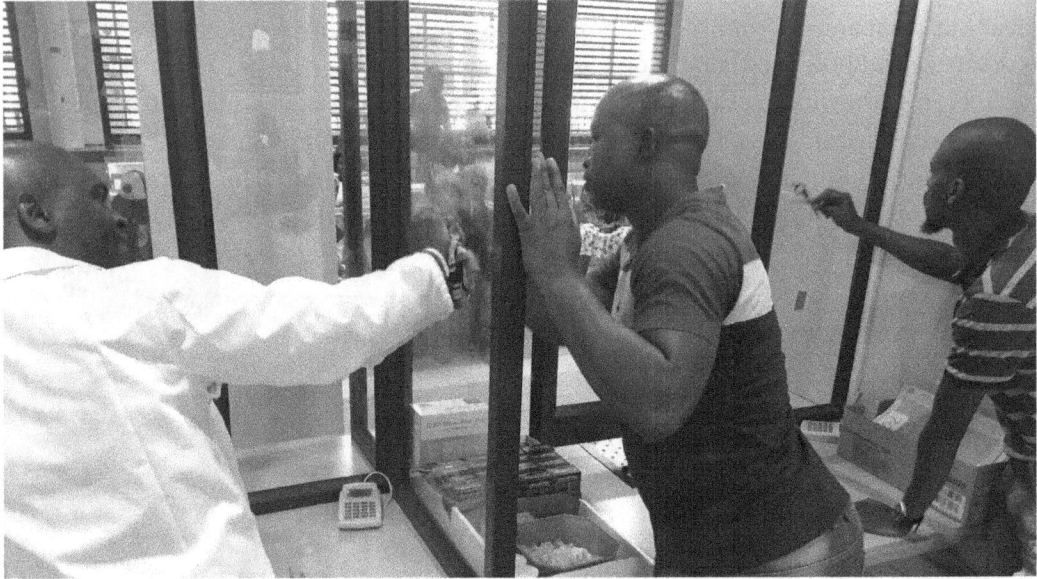

▲ Figure 6.10: Cleaning the workspace at a pharmacy counter

▲ Figure 6.11: Cleaning the pharmacist's worktable

# 5S Stage 3: SET IN ORDER

The next stage of 5S, SET IN ORDER, aims to arrange every essential item in a way that optimises employee performance. In this way, SET IN ORDER connects people to their workspace. Having already used SORT and SHINE to de-clutter the area and clean the workspace, we now turn our attention to finding the ideal location for each item necessary to the work. We establish the ideal position for easy retrieval and easy return, so fuelling workspace ergonomics. Table 6.5 provides guidance on how to undertake the SET IN ORDER 5S stage.

> Having already used SORT and SHINE to de-clutter the area and clean the workspace, we now turn our attention to finding the ideal location for each item necessary to the work.

| SET IN ORDER – WHAT YOU NEED AT YOUR FINGERTIPS | | |
|---|---|---|
| Key Points | Description of Activity | What you will need |
| 1 — Every essential item is allocated a 'home' | Review the workspace and surrounding areas and identify the ideal motion or movement needed to retrieve items. Consider:<br>• Where essential, frequently-used items should be located and in what volumes<br>• Where essential but seldom-used items should be located and in what volumes<br>• Where walkways, equipment, infrastructure and storage should ideally be located<br>• Ensure every essential item is allocated a 'home'. | Spaghetti Diagram of the employee motion pattern and the standard procedure for performing the work. |
| 2 — Name | Make labels for each 'home' to ensure that when an item is removed, it is easy to see the place to which it needs to be returned. | Computer, laminator, yellow tape, pens, Prestik adhesive or wire/cord on which to hang signs. |
| 3 | Take 'after' photographs capturing properly demarcated areas and correctly located items. | Camera |
| 4 — STANDARD | Develop a visual one-page document to illustrate the standard for SET IN ORDER for this area. Display the standard on the team board or at the workstation. | Photographs taken, computer and laminator. |
| 5 | Conduct an 'after' audit for SET IN ORDER. Focus only on progress made—as reflected by scores. List outstanding items on the team action board. | Customised audit, pencils and action board. |

▲ Table 6.5: Steps to follow to carry out a SET IN ORDER activity

When deciding on the ideal location for needed items and the surrounding layout, use the following guidelines:

- o Where possible, locate frequently used items at employee's fingertips or even on their person.
- o Locate seldom-used items out of the way, but ensure they are accessible when needed.
- o Locate heavy items at a height that will not cause harm when lowering or lifting them.
- o Reduce employee motion by reducing unnecessary walking, turning, stretching and bending (see Figure 6.12).

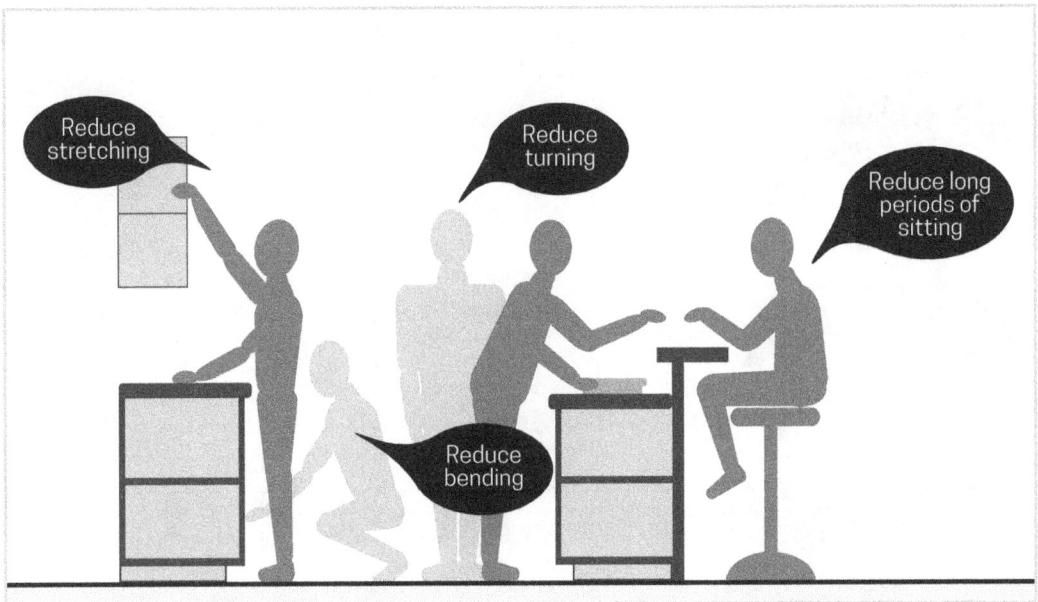

▲ Figure 6.12: Considering workspace ergonomics when deciding on the location of essential items

As mentioned earlier in this chapter, the improvement team should remain cautious and curious when making improvements. It is always wise to seek input and involvement from those actually performing the work when deciding on changes to optimum flow and item location. The Spaghetti Diagrams discussed in Chapter 3 are invaluable when deciding on layout and location. Also refer to Figure 6.13 for a useful guideline as to the ideal distances to use when locating key items in an immediate workspace.

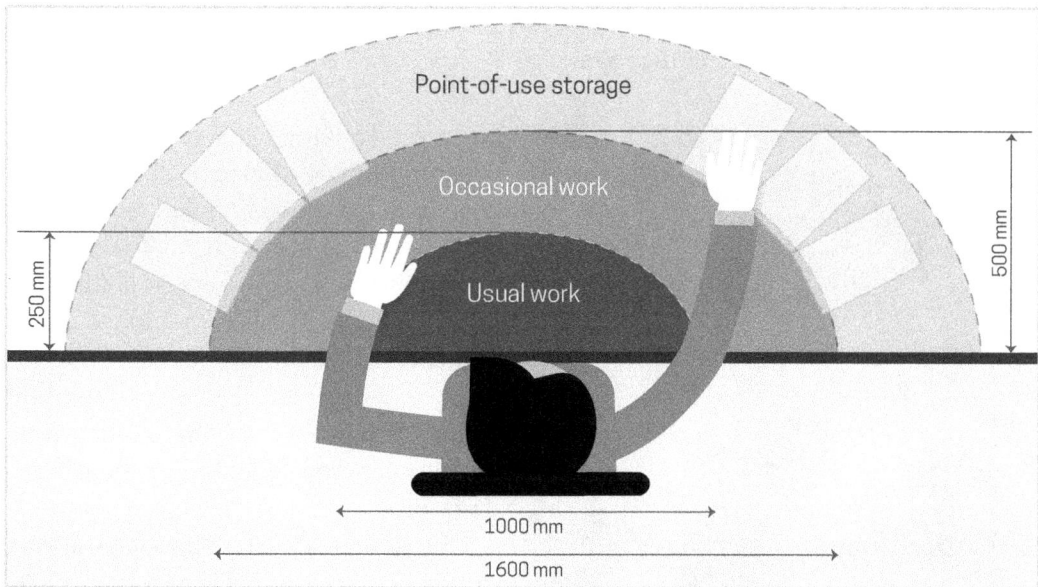

▲ Figure 6.13: Distance guideline for locating items for optimum access

At the Cohort 1 pharmacy referred to in this chapter, every essential item was localised to a logical 'home' and properly labelled. Frequently-used labels were positioned next to each pharmacist and the equipment needed to complete the script was conveniently placed in front of them and demarcated. The new workspace design included a Visual Control to limit the number of bins allowed into the workspace. Teams had experienced difficulty in controlling patient file batch sizes brought into the pharmacy. Demarcating a grid of rectangular blocks on the surface of worktables using adhesive tape (see

▲ Figure 6.14: Every needed item has a location and a Visual Control sets the maximum volume

Figure 6.14) not only kept scripts neat and easily retrievable, but also controlled the numbers of patient files released into the system. When the blocks were full and a patient file was clearly allocated to each rectangle on the worktable, no more patient files were brought in. When blocks emptied, this triggered team members to pull more files in or to provide support in areas where there was more congestion.

This is an effective means of using 5S and Visual Controls to manage process flows. The outcome is improved productivity, better work-in-progress control, better management of quality—ultimately

Making the process visual also makes it easier to introduce and train new staff and show them the ropes.

improving waiting time. Making the process visual also makes it easier to introduce and train new staff and show them the ropes.

▲ Figure 6.15: Innovative storage systems for script labels

▲ Figure 6.16: Locating consumables and limiting the volume placed at the dispensing counter

Figure 6.15 shows the simple yet ingenious system developed by pharmacists at a Cohort 1 hospital to hold labels—using cost-effective broomstick handles. This nifty system made access, visibility and replenishment of labels that much easier. Patients reaped the benefits of staff beginning a shift with all essential items in place. This spoke to the fundamental Cohort 1 mandate: cutting patient waiting times.

5S ensures the workstation is always ready for business. Dispensing times will suffer when pharmacists waste their time searching for items or waiting for an item not speedily replenished when it has run out. At the pharmacy in the previous example, essential dispensing counter items were located for ease of access and in agreed volumes corresponding to the rate at which they were spent (see Figure 6.16). A counter that looks professional also instils confidence in patients. Think of a well-organised, clean and tidy workspace as a visual message to patients: 'Welcome! We are prepared for excellent service!'

Once you have consensus on the placement of essential items, teams will need to visually maintain the new location. Failure to do this may result in items slowly migrating to old locations and the area regressing to the 'before' Current Condition. Use yellow paint, labels, tape and markers and, where appropriate, mark the location of each needed item so that the employees responsible for returning or replenishing those items do not waver from the standards.

# 5S Stage 4: STANDARDISE

Remember that it is fundamental to fertilise the fragile sapling of any new improvement with entrenched consensus-driven procedures that preserve the best new methods. Ultimately, we want to entrench the new practices and allow them to take root so that they become permanent, automatic features of the management system.

When we implement 5S, we are in fact implementing a Kaizen event. Kaizen in turn assumes the corresponding implementation of formal standards to support the new performance as part of PDCA. With 5S in place, we need standards that will define the rules and serve as a benchmark or sounding board against which to measure performance. The standard is a subtle coach continually coaxing team members to improve.

Though the 5 stages of 5S as depicted in Figure 6.2 show STANDARDISE as a fourth step, it is in fact a step we pursue after completion of each of the first 3 stages of 5S (Figure 6.17). This key fourth step is integral to each of the first three stages of 5S. We can only proceed to stage five when STANDARDISE has been applied to each of the first three stages. STANDARDISE can therefore be thought of a watershed 5S stage.

> Fertilise the fragile sapling of any new improvement with entrenched consensus-driven procedures that preserve the best new methods.

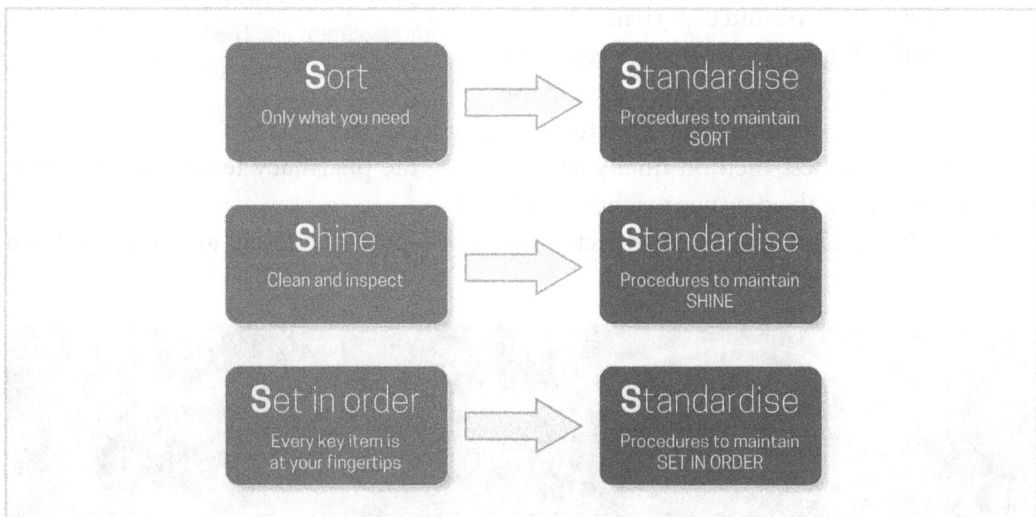

| Sort | | Standardise |
|------|--|-------------|
| Only what you need | ⇨ | Procedures to maintain SORT |
| Shine | | Standardise |
| Clean and inspect | ⇨ | Procedures to maintain SHINE |
| Set in order | | Standardise |
| Every key item is at your fingertips | ⇨ | Procedures to maintain SET IN ORDER |

▲ Figure 6.17: STANDARDISE after each of the first three stages of 5S

Standardising after each of the first three stages (SORT, SHINE, and SET IN ORDER) ensures that gains made do not deteriorate as we advance to further steps in the improvement process. To STANDARDISE also helps a team to comprehend the learning gleaned after each cycle of change.

When the pharmacy team at the Cohort 1 hospital referred to in this Chapter established a new 5S condition, they discovered that—despite heartfelt attempts to SORT,

> It is quite common for certain initial improvements to fail the first few days of testing and scrutiny.

SHINE and SET IN ORDER—some elements of their process were still problematic. For example, as labels ran out and new ones needed to be loaded, it would take time to complete the replenishment. In another example some of the rolls would unravel and need to be rolled up again, again wasting time. It is quite common for certain initial improvements to fail the first few days of testing and scrutiny. The team moved to support the new, slightly flawed, label process by discussing options to make replenishment easier and to prevent the rolls from unravelling. Simple changes could address the problems such as positioning more frequently-use rolls on the outside of the holder and by holding the rolls in place with a clip. Most importantly, the team could see that this experience had not reflected a failure on their part, but rather a normal element of continuous improvement and the PDCA cycle.

This example clearly shows that the stamp of approval that is to STANDARDISE should only be given to new best-methods deemed successful—tried and tested! Otherwise the team may unwittingly let undesirable elements and standards seep into the soil around the sapling of a new process.

Another useful exercise to undertake is to invite team members from other units or lines to try out the changes implemented. The pharmacy in our example invited colleagues from other tables to sit-in on and experience the new systems so that impartial, outsider perspectives could be taken into account. This is a great way to solicit buy-in and input before institutionalising a change.

> The team could see that this experience had not reflected a failure on their part, but rather a normal element of continuous improvement and the PDCA cycle.

With the new best-method finally agreed upon, the pharmacy team could proceed with standardising the new approaches developed.

A new 5S standard can be constructed into a one-page document and displayed at a workstation (Figure 6.18).

| 5S STANDARD | |
|---|---|
| Area | Table 1 |
| Date | 16 June 2016 |

Picking Station:
- Only bins, files and measurement sheets to be located here.
- Sanitise table at end of each shift.
- One patient per block in sequence.
- No stacking of bins on top of each other.

Scribing Station:
- Only regulations, pens, calculators, staplers, labels, bins, scripts and files to be located here.
- Pharmacists see one patient at a time.
- Sanitise table at end of each shift.
- Replenish labels at the end of shift

Dispensing Station:
- Only bins, files and scripts to be located here.
- One patient per block in sequence.
- No stacking of bins on top of each other.
- Dispense to one patient at a time.
- Sanitise table at end of each shift.

▲ Figure 6.18: Example of a 5S standard

Treat your standard as a living, breathing mentor, a live document that is actively used. Ensure it does not become another piece of paper cluttering the walls. Teams and their supervisors should frequently compare the Current Condition to this vibrant document, so that performance is at all times maintained at desired levels.

# 5S Stage 5: SUSTAIN

The final and most challenging stage of 5S is to sustain new Best Practices established. Remember that leaders must be relentless in sustaining a change effort and new habit. Also important, is ongoing team commitment to upholding and prolonging new behaviours. Let us come back to the analogy of a brilliant doctor (leader) presenting an excellent treatment regimen to a sick patient. The patient (team member) plays their part when they adhere to the protocol knowing it is the only way to become well again. The standards (treatments and protocols) put in place will help your team practice the right behaviours (adherence). Over time these habits will develop into second nature. Figure 6.19 illustrates this progression.

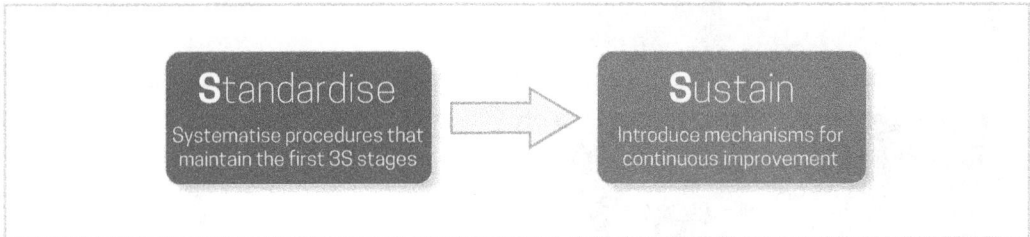

**Standardise**
Systematise procedures that maintain the first 3S stages

**Sustain**
Introduce mechanisms for continuous improvement

▲ Figure 6.19: Progressing from the fourth to the fifth stage of 5S

## Weapons for Change: 5S Audit and the Daily Management System

You have powerful tools in your arsenal of change—certain select mechanisms that push your teams to improve on the Current Condition. While motivating people they also nurture the newly planted seeds of 5S excellence to create roots and stems, leaves and shoots and, one day soon, the fruit of your team's labours. In other words, these mechanisms give extraordinary longevity to 5S.

The first mechanism is the powerful 5S audit. By customising the audit to a work area and then auditing the area at regular intervals, the team will trigger ongoing improvement in that space. The second recommended mechanism—the Daily Management System serves as a visual dashboard depicting the team's 5S performance. Together these mechanisms give you a double-barrelled aim at improvement results.

The Daily Management System is discussed in more detail in Chapter 8. For now, let us touch briefly on the fact that incorporating results of the 5S audit into the Daily Management System allows teams both to track their 5S condition and update their action boards to deal with slips in performance, or with new ideas for better ways of working. In this way 5S joins the other *Muda*, *Mura* and *Muri* exposed in the measurement system of the Improvement Cycle. Figure 6.20 provides an example of a visual so that 5S can form part of the Daily Management System.

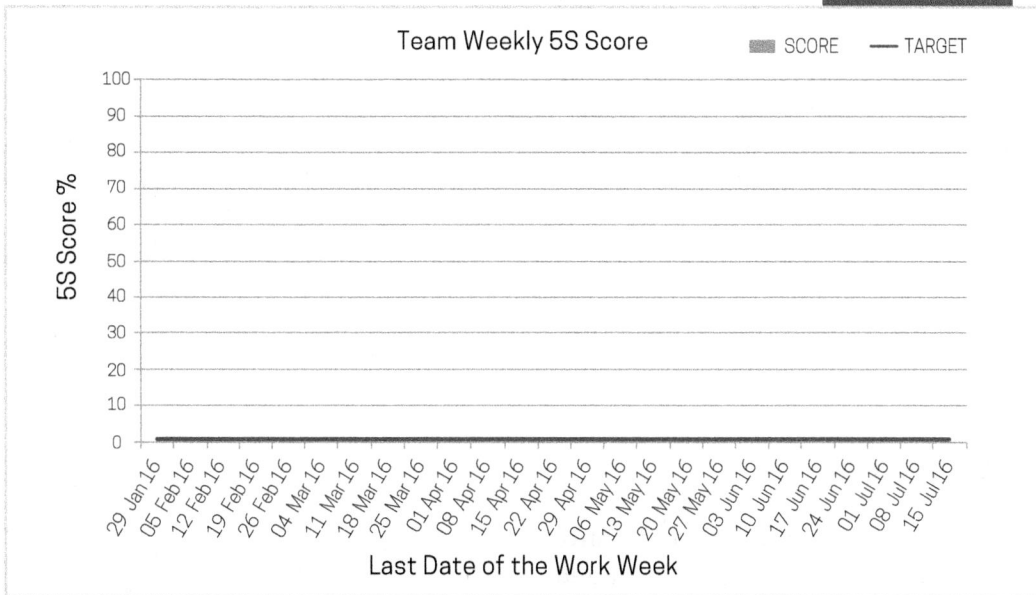

Figure 6.20: Implementing a 5S tracking mechanism in the Daily Management System

## PRACTICAL ACTIVITY: Making 5S a Reality in your Work Area

The 5S activity is best led by an experienced facilitator and the following steps provide guidance to the process:

▸ Select a model area to take part in the 5S Kaizen. Invite staff from the area (up to 10 people) to participate in the activity.

▸ Select a quiet day or a weekend day on which to undertake the 5S initiative so that patient service is not detrimentally affected.

▸ Cordon off the area for the duration of the exercise.

▸ Arrange all necessary cleaning materials and consumables such as tape, pens, laminator etc. and plan the procedures you will follow.

▸ Provide the participating members with basic 5S training. This should be done by an experienced internal person or, if possible, an outside training facilitator.

▸ Customise the 5S audit so that it is easy for the team to understand. The audit items must relate to their specific area whilst preserving the fundamentals of 5S.

▸ Conduct the 5S audit and take photographs of offending items and processes.

▸ Summarise and display the audit score on a graph. Display the photographs taken and write comments on each photo clarifying the issue visually identified and which 5S stage (SORT, SHINE or SET IN ORDER) the abnormality relates to.

▸ Return to the model area and conduct the SORT, SHINE and SET IN ORDER activities, strictly adhering to the guidelines. Ensure each phase is complete before moving on to the next.

▸ Test the new system for a time and to work through initial (expected) teething problems. Fine-tune the system and ask team members from other areas to 'test drive' it. Finalise the design and update the 5S standard. Display the new standard and make sure team members can see it from their workstations.

- Coach the team members to adhere to the new standard, assisting them to eliminate any additional obstacles. Bear in mind this could take days, if not weeks, to become effective. Do not abandon the team at this time, as the system is fragile.
- Schedule regular audits (at first weekly and later monthly once performance has stabilised). Add the results onto the 5S Score and include results in the Daily Management System.

Once the 5S condition is stable, reflect on what was learned. Consider whether the learning could be deployed to other lines and areas. Once more staff are engaged in 5S, so the workload to maintain it will lessen.

# Visual Control

As the name suggests, Visual Control makes use of tools that people can see and that elicit both a head and heart response. It brings the process alive by providing ongoing feedback that is visual and that

> Quite simply, visual cues control behaviour and subsequently the outcome of processes carried out by people.

helps teams to make decisions about their daily work. It can, in some cases, remove the need for decision-making entirely—a powerful ally to Standard Work. Quite simply, visual cues control behaviour and subsequently the outcome of processes carried out by people.

Think about some examples of Visual Control:

- o When you drive towards an intersection, it is not necessary for you to think about whether to stop or proceed through it. The colour of the traffic light tells you exactly what to do.
- o At the supermarket, the light above a teller's counter indicates an opening and you automatically proceed to pay there.
- o If clear signage properly demarcates a waiting area, a nurse will be able to locate the pensioners or paying patients when she is looking for them and quickly know who to service first.
- o At triage, a visual board or cards can manage prioritising of patients, so ensuring the most critical cases get the most immediate attention.
- o When a pharmacy assistant walks the isles scanning shelves for stock that is running low, clearly indicated minimum, maximum and re-order levels provide immediate clarity and save time

When deciding on a Visual Control cue, teams should consider their model area's unique input and output measures—as discussed in Chapter 3—as well as the nature of the process they want to manage. There may also be an overlap with some of the 5S innovations identified. In most cases, teams find it better to innovate and design a tool that will serve their particular needs rather than copy a device used elsewhere. Some ideas to spark your creativity might include:

- o Graphs showing key targets and that trigger a response when the target is missed:
  - Patient waiting time at a particular process
  - Employee productivity in the pharmacy (scripts per person per hour)
  - Clinic start times
  - Registration cycle times
- o Demarcation controls:
  - Lines depicting walkways
  - Equipment to control queues
  - Visuals to define areas
  - Visuals governing the amount of work-in-progress permitted
  - Location and limit lines for essential items
- o Labour planning mechanisms:
  - Attendance matrix to manage labour allocation and workload
  - Skills development matrix to address flexibility and succession planning
  - Labour rotation plan to facilitate cross-skilling and flexibility
- o Signal controls:
  - *Andon*, such as a lighting system that indicates a machine has malfunctioned
  - *Kanban*, such as a signal triggering the process into action (e.g. a series of patient files arrive at a pharmacy window, triggering the pharmacist into action to process corresponding scripts in the same order in which the patient files arrived)
- o Daily Management board to manage short-interval control and problem-solving:
  - Display boards show Target Condition, Current Condition, obstacles, problem-solving activities, countermeasures to fall back on and performance targets

Figure 6.21 gives an example of a nifty Visual Control tool used to track and respond to employee attendance patterns. The supervisor in charge is able to capture an employee's attendance for each day of the month using this template. It is also displayed on the Daily Management board. Data capture happens prior to a shift starting, so that if an employee is absent the supervisor can move staff around or request support from another department. This Visual Control mechanism removes attacks of variation and ensures the team numbers remain stable so that processes are able to function as they are designed to, with little or no impact on patient service. It also facilitates spreading leave out over certain periods to ensure there is always enough staff to service patients with excellence. Supervisors can also use the chart to track serial absentees and manage their behaviour or institute disciplinary action accordingly.

## ATTENDANCE VISUALS
### AVAILABLE ▪ FLEXIBLE ▪ SKILLED

| MONTH | AUGUST 2014 |
| --- | --- |
| AREA | CELL 15 PROCESSING |
| LEADER: | BILLY |

| EMPLOYEE | 1 | 2 | 3 | 4 | 5 | 6 | 7 | 8 | 9 | 10 | 11 | 12 | 13 | 14 | 15 | 16 | 17 | 18 | 19 | 20 | 21 | 22 | 23 | 24 | 25 | 26 | 27 | 28 | 29 | 30 | 31 |
| --- | --- | --- | --- | --- | --- | --- | --- | --- | --- | --- | --- | --- | --- | --- | --- | --- | --- | --- | --- | --- | --- | --- | --- | --- | --- | --- | --- | --- | --- | --- | --- |
| JOHN | | | | | | | | | | | | | | | | | | | | | | | | | | | | | | | |
| VUSI | | | | | | | | | | | | | | | | | | | | | | | | | | | | | | | |
| ANGELO | | | | | | | | | | | | | | | | | | | | | | | | | | | | | | | |
| JOHAN | | | | | | | | | | | | | | | | | | | | | | | | | | | | | | | |
| THABO | | | | | | | | | | | | | | | | | | | | | | | | | | | | | | | |
| GINA | | | | | | | | | | | | | | | | | | | | | | | | | | | | | | | |
| ANGUS | | | | | | | | | | | | | | | | | | | | | | | | | | | | | | | |
| BENJAMIN | | | | | | | | | | | | | | | | | | | | | | | | | | | | | | | |
| THABASENG | | | | | | | | | | | | | | | | | | | | | | | | | | | | | | | |
| COLOUR CODES: | PLANNED LEAVE | | | | | | LOANED OUT | | | | | | | SICK LEAVE | | | | | | | | | AVAILABLE | | | | | | | | |
| | AWOL | | | | | | LATE | | | | | | | | | | | | | | | | | | | | | | | | |

▲ Figure 6.21: Example of a Visual Control to track staff attendance and absenteeism and manage staff leave patterns

# Plan Do Check Adjust

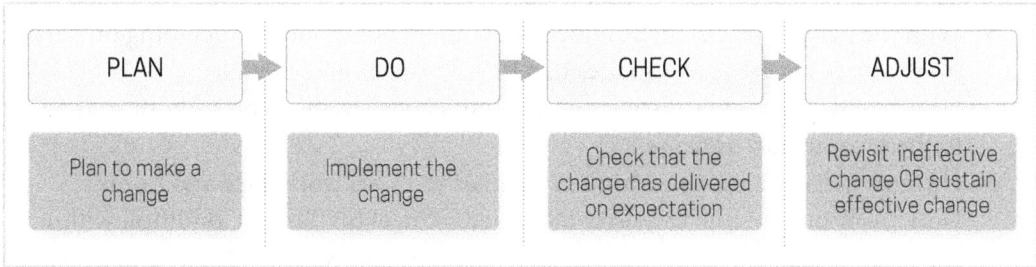

| PLAN | DO | CHECK | ADJUST |
|------|-----|-------|--------|
| Plan to make a change | Implement the change | Check that the change has delivered on expectation | Revisit ineffective change OR sustain effective change |

▲ Figure 6.22: The PDCA cycle

We will always come back to the PDCA cycle (depicted in Figure 6.22) as it provides a structured framework through which to drive change towards the Target Condition, and then sustain the new performance. To illustrate this principle, think about an amateur golfer wishing to improve his game. If a golfer regularly shoots over 105 (Current Condition) and he wishes to shoot in the 90s within 12 months (Target Condition) our golfer must evaluate his current performance to realise the following obstacles are hindering progress towards the Target Condition goals:

o   Excessive distance to reach the driving range undermines the frequency of practice sessions
o   Once at the range, not enough time is spent on practicing
o   Uncertainty over which areas to target for improvement.

Analysing the root causes blocking performance and designing a PLAN that tackles these three areas of concern gives our golfer key insight into what must change. He also sees that improvement is not just about monitoring the results on his scorecard, but rather about managing the work to achieve the Target Condition score:

o   Driving less distance allowing more time for practice
o   Allocating enough time to practice and adhering to it
o   Spending time with a coach / mentor to target specific improvements.

These input measures drive the ultimate output measure of the Target Condition handicap. With a PLAN in place, our golfer moves on to DO, CHECK and ADJUST what is planned:

- o With the help of his coach, he allocates 20 hours per month to focussing on particular areas of his game and makes this PLAN part of his schedule.
- o He schedules coaching sessions every Thursday afternoon for an hour and sticks to them come rain or shine.
- o He finds a driving range within ten kilometres of his workplace and home.
- o He actively pursues the activities identified to meet his Target Condition within 12 months through a weekly CHECK. He ensures that what is required to meet the goal, is in fact taking place.
- o His CHECK shows that while he is meeting the target for hours spent practicing, now at a nearby driving range, he is still cancelling 50 percent of his coaching sessions as they clash with business meetings.
- o He sees the need to ADJUST and moves the coaching from a Thursday to a Friday.
- o After two months he re-evaluates to find he has stuck to the PLAN and there is evidence of steady improvement in his game.
- o As part of ADJUST he concludes his improved methods are working, and sticks to them, so standardising them.

This is a simple example of PDCA in action. But, its principles apply both in linear scenarios like the situation faced by our golfer as much as to complex change efforts. It is common to see improvement strategies derailed by PDCA that is half-heartedly applied. Figure 6.23 shows the relationship between performance and PDCA cycles. Busy schedules often mean we PLAN and DO a fair amount, but do not take the time to CHECK and ADJUST. As such, many change processes are started, but only a few yield the expected results. Commit to rigorously working through PDCA every time there is an opportunity to run the cycle. This will take you closer to the Target Condition you aspire towards— your North Star.

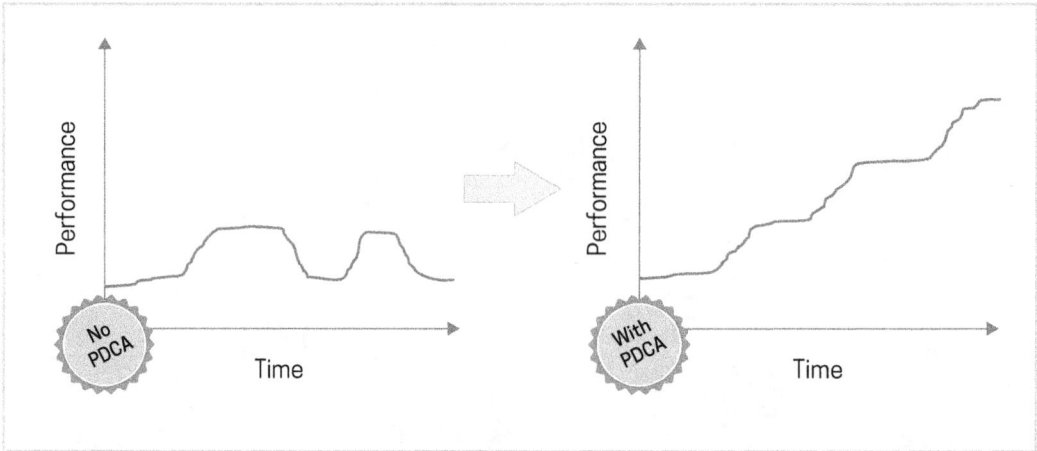

▲ Figure 6.23: The relationship between performance and PDCA

It is normal that some countermeasures will not produce the expected results. Always remind teams that this is not a sign of failure but an opportunity for learning. By following PDCA the team can comfortably evaluate the learning and proceed to better countermeasures, all the while gaining insight into the inner workings of the process they are engaged in improving. When a scientist carries out an experiment, it may take several attempts to get ratios, chemicals and formulas right. Each 'failure' is a step forward that maximises learning and minimises 'failure' for the next round. That is wonderful! Embrace the process!

Declare with confidence:

*'I might not have the answer yet, but I now know ten ways of how not to get at it!'*

PDCA cycles have the capacity to develop your team into a 'community of scientists' who routinely compare what they think will happen to the actual results, and who learn from the difference. (Rother, 2011). This is further explored in Chapter 8.

# Basic Problem-Solving

Problem-solving tools help link an effect to a particular cause. Often there will be several causes to wade through to seek out the root cause—the fundamental reason/s for a problem's existence. Although they can be quite rewarding when used in isolation, problem-solving tools should ideally combine with the PDCA cycle. Following-through on all of the PDCA stages will set the team up for success.

Organisations of all sorts face a massive variety of challenges. These are adequately overcome by an equal plethora of problem-solving methodologies at your disposal. Figure 6.24 illustrates a typical array of challenges faced and typical philosophies and tools engaged at each level. It also shows that the number of problems increases towards the lower levels but increases in complexity towards the upper levels.

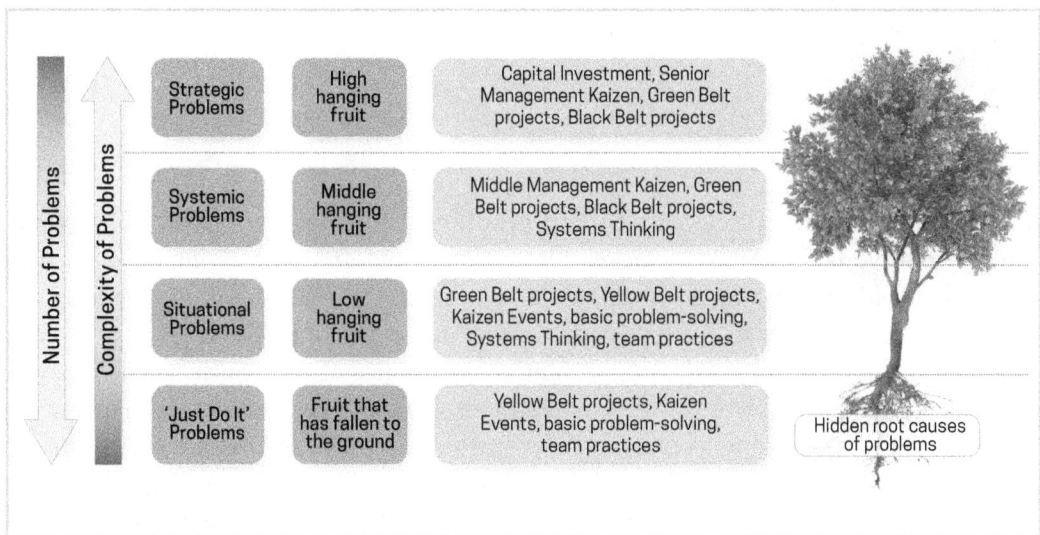

| Strategic Problems | High hanging fruit | Capital Investment, Senior Management Kaizen, Green Belt projects, Black Belt projects |
|---|---|---|
| Systemic Problems | Middle hanging fruit | Middle Management Kaizen, Green Belt projects, Black Belt projects, Systems Thinking |
| Situational Problems | Low hanging fruit | Green Belt projects, Yellow Belt projects, Kaizen Events, basic problem-solving, Systems Thinking, team practices |
| 'Just Do It' Problems | Fruit that has fallen to the ground | Yellow Belt projects, Kaizen Events, basic problem-solving, team practices |

Hidden root causes of problems

▲ Figure 6.24: Challenges faced at different organisational tiers

Cohort 1 tackled many of the 'just do it' and situational problem types and scratched the surface on some of the systemic issues that crossed borders affecting more than one model area or department.

Teams came together to brainstorm the problems using the 5 Whys technique and Fishbone Diagrams since these methods were perfect for the level of problems. Both are fresh and simple approaches to quickly uncovering the root causes of problems.

# Fishbone Diagrams

Aptly named, Fishbone Diagrams offer a brainstorming tool drawn in the shape of a fishbone. They are a remarkably simple, visual means of generating ideas in a team. The head of the fish represents the obstacle, problem or effect under discussion. The fish's bones are in turn populated with possible causes of what has been captured at the fish head. This technique encourages broad thinking about the 'bones' or causes of challenges faced, so narrowing down root causes. Figure 6.25 shows a theoretical Fishbone Diagram. Here we will focus the question: Why does a driver keep stalling his vehicle?

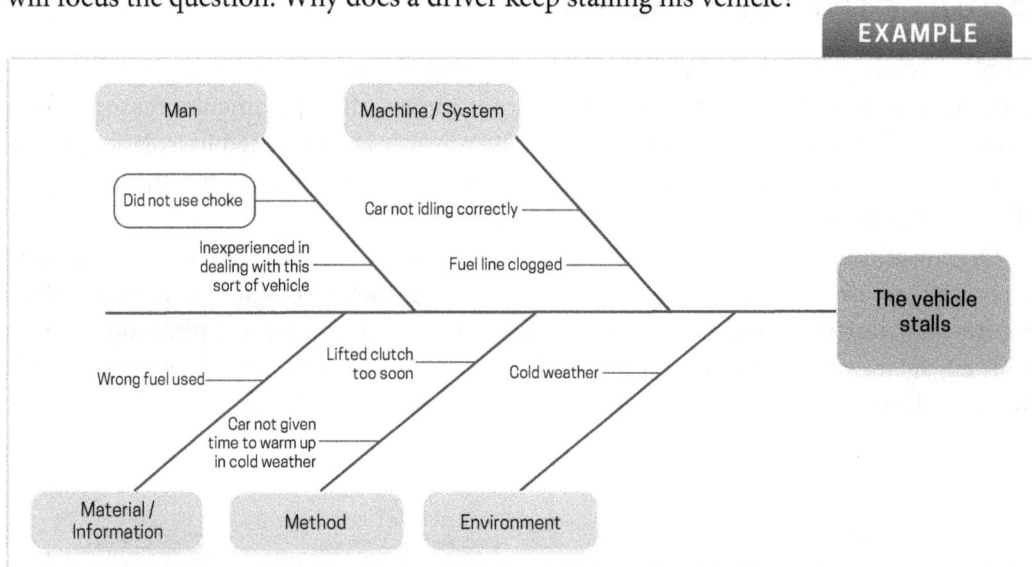

▲ Figure 6.25: Example of a Fishbone Diagram

The Fishbone Diagram includes standard headings to help categorise possible causes. These also serve as a reminder to the team as to the elements to think about. In some cases the cause could be listed under more than one heading, and the team can decide under which category to place it. As this is a brainstorming process, all causes should be captured but teams must refine ideas by seeking true evidence of each cause listed. This will filter out sources of problems that are not relevant. Figure 6.25 sees the most likely cause circled. This is how we single out a factor for further investigation of underlying dynamics. It is important that the team consider these sub-causes before proceeding to remedial actions that treat the symptom rather than the cause. Where the ultimate cause circled is more complex in nature, it may be worth developing a Fishbone Diagram just for this theme. Alternatively, where more straightforward, we could proceed using the 5 Whys.

# 5 Whys

A child's affinity for problem-solving is both wonderful and natural. When children ask questions, they are never satisfied with superficial answers. They invariably probe further with yet another 'why?'. Somehow, as we get older, this ability wanes and we stop asking as many questions as we once did. We become less curious. Perhaps we believe we have seen so much that we do not need to wonder more deeply? But, that is an oversight. The 5 Whys takes us back to a childlike penchant for asking smart questions. In the context of Operational Excellence this basic technique digs deeply at the root cause of a problem through a series of 'why?' questions. The tool offers a quick, focused and easy way through which anyone in the organisation can probe a problem.

When you initiate a 5 Whys process, you may discover that there are many answers to a question and the process could descend into a labyrinth of causes. This makes root cause identification nearly impossible and team members risk losing faith in the process. Let us reiterate—be vigilant about having evidence for each answer that is accepted as an option. When a possible root cause is put forward, have the team hold it up to the light of factual evidence. This will clean up the information captured so that the next level of questioning is more elegant.

You may be wondering about the name, '5 Whys'? The tool is so named as it encourages you to ask the question five times. In some cases the root cause of problem is revealed in less than five 'Why?' questions. In others it takes more than this. So, think of the number five as a guideline and alter the 5 Whys to suit the situation you are exploring.

Once your team gets at the root cause then test the countermeasure suggested by running it through a PDCA cycle. This process will expose any causes not properly interrogated and take them back a step in the analysis.

# 5 Whys and the Fishbone Diagram in Tandem

Coming back to the problem explored in our Fishbone Diagram example, Figure 6.26 breaks down the most likely causes even further to uncover the deeper, hidden root causes. The team is then in a better position to explore possible countermeasures and actions to address the root of the problem.

**EXAMPLE**

Why is the driver not using the choke?

He is not aware that a choke is to be used.

How do we know this?

The driver provided this information when questioned about repeated stalling.

Why is he not aware?

It is not mentioned in his training.

How do we know this?

Checks with both the training manual and trainer have revealed that this information is not included in the driver induction course.

Why is this not in his training?

Training only deals with fuel-injected models.

How do we know this?

A training manager has verified the contents of the training manual.

Why is the training limited to fuel-injected models?

Carbureted models are not listed in the asset register.

How do we know this?

Only vehicles listed on the asset register have corresponding driver training and development schedules. This has been verified by the Finance Manager.

Why are carbureted models not listed in the asset register?

They have been omitted accidentally.

How do we know this?

The administrator responsible has been questioned and confirms this.

**Possible Countermeasure:**
- Ensure each driver receives the correct training

**Possible actions to test:**
- Update asset register
- Update standard and provide administrator with training
- Rectify training manual
- Refresh training for drivers
- Conduct assessments and coach accordingly

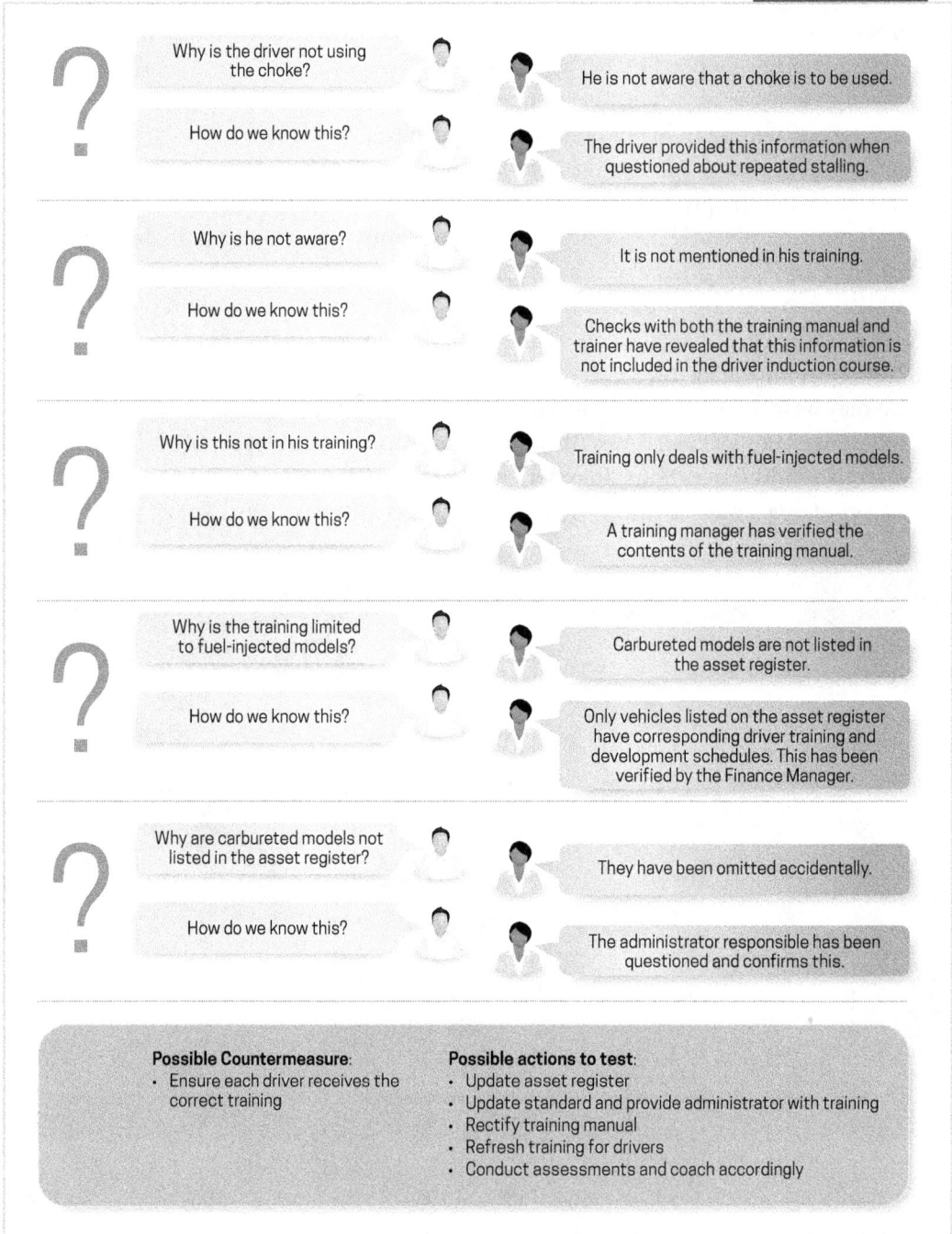

▲ Figure 6.26: Example of the 5 Whys the process: asking 'Why?' five times

The 5 Whys method is also highly effective when used on its own. Remember that if the problem at hand seems quite straightforward, the team can move to 5 Whys to uncover the cause. If the team is finding that getting at the heart of a problem is more complicated, they may need first to construct a Fishbone Diagram to narrow down their focus.

Any sub-causes established can be added to our Fishbone Diagram to show the team's thinking but also to keep a record of the decisions made (Figure 6.27).

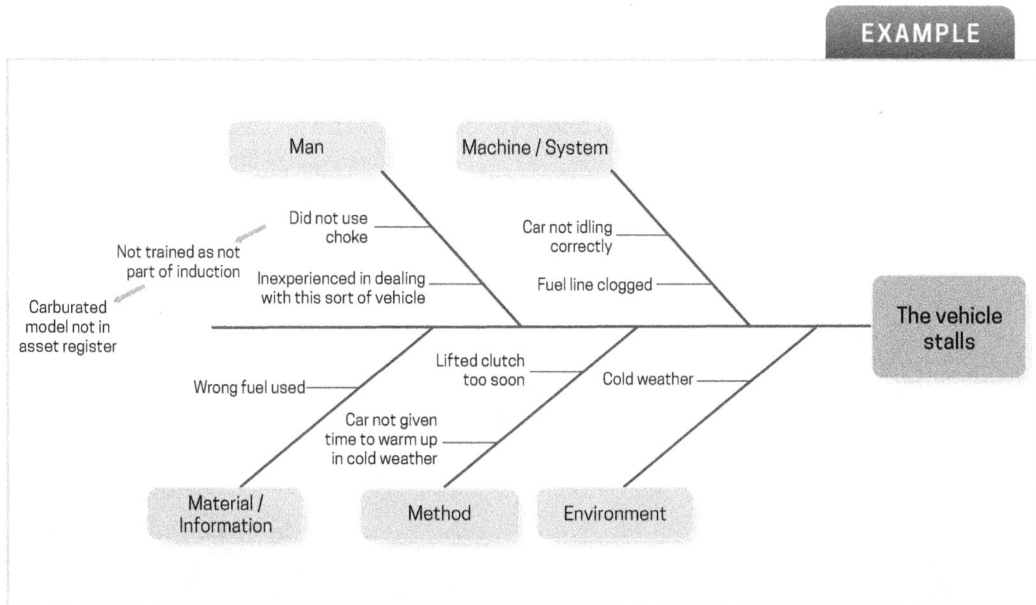

▲ Figure 6.27: Adding sub-causes to the Fishbone Diagram

# Countermeasures and Plans

A countermeasure is a solution to or buffer against the cause of a problem or undesirable situation. The countermeasures are then further broken down into individual action items. Every time we implement an action, we are experimenting and several rounds of trial and error may be required to deal properly with a problem's root cause. In some cases more than one root cause may exist and the team can pursue more than one countermeasure to alleviate these. It is good advice to implement one action at a time, so that the PDCA cycle can be properly applied. Implementing too many remedial actions at once can leave a team struggling to pinpoint the change that actually worked best and standardising incorrect practices or introducing a process that has no real impact on the problem.

> Implement one action at a time, so that the PDCA cycle can be properly applied.

Coming back to the scenario of excessive patient waiting time faced in a public healthcare space let us refer to Table 6.6 for an example of possible countermeasures to the issue of escalating waiting times. In this context the CHECK stage of PDCA will be about comparing the Current to the Target Condition, and the Actual Result will either be a pattern of work which can be observed, or a measureable activity.

| OBJECTIVE | COUNTER-MEASURE | CURRENT CONDITION | TARGET CONDITION | ACTUAL RESULT |
|---|---|---|---|---|
| Visualise performance to trigger problem solving. | Implement a Daily Management System with focus on patient waiting times. | Employees are not aware of current waiting times and therefore take no action to improve them. | Performance is visual, up to date and managed by the team. Obstacles are solved in daily team meetings and countermeasures initiated. | The Daily Management board is installed but daily meetings are not taking place yet. Manager to investigate how time will be made available for these meetings to be made a priority. |

▲ **Table 6.6**: Using the CHECK stage of a PDCA cycle to interrogate countermeasures to excessive patient waiting times

The countermeasures listed above are not detailed enough for effective implementation. We must clearly define who will do what and by when. An implementation plan pinpoints these details and tracks a team's progress using PDCA for each action (Table 6.7).

| NO. | ACTION | WHO | WHEN | PDCA | ESCALATION |
|---|---|---|---|---|---|
| 1 | Install display board | Vusi | 8 Jun 16 | P D / A C | Budget required (George 2 Jun) |
| 2 | Implement display items as per template provided | Sylvia | 9 Jun 16 | P D / A C | |
| 3 | Initiate daily meetings at the board at 7am | Tshepo | 12 Jun 16 | P D / A C | Inform staff of 7am meeting (George 9 Jun) |

▲ **Table 6.7**: Example of an implementation plan that incorporates PDCA tracking

Once an action is activated, the PDCA cycle kicks in and each process is tracked so that when the plan is complete, the 'P' is coloured in, when the action is finished, the 'D' is coloured in and so on. This drives an execution culture among the team. It also improves the quality of processes implemented.

The sum of the actions taken in the implementation plan should lead to an effective countermeasure and the achievement of the Target Condition. Evaluating the success of the countermeasure is then captured in the Actual Result (Table 6.6) allowing the team to CHECK if the Target Condition was indeed met or not.

# Process Standard Work

There is a difference between having a *standard* and achieving *Standard Work*. A *standard* is a rule or example that provides clear guidance—an unambiguous specification of how we define quality and how defects can be avoided. It is precise and documented.

Standard Work on the other hand, refers to the Current Condition of work carried out—how well the process conforms to the standard's ideals. It is the daily practice of achieving the standard.

To evaluate *Standard Work*, go to Gemba, look for the standard and scan through it. It should be a visual, one-page document, visibly located somewhere close to the operation. Then stand and observe the process for a few cycles and assess how well it conforms to the standard. Quite often, the process deviates from the norm. This is the first opportunity for improvement. Once the process has been stabilised and Standard Work accomplished, the process can be further improved and new standards set.

Lean practitioners often say, 'without standards there can be no Kaizen'. In other words, work to standard first, and then seek to change for the better. This is not always a simple matter. Often standards are not available, poorly written or hidden in drawers. It remains important to nevertheless conduct this exercise. Figure 6.28 (adapted from LIA ITL, 2014) illustrates the way in which the improvement approach considers the standard and improves with the help of repeated PDCA cycles.

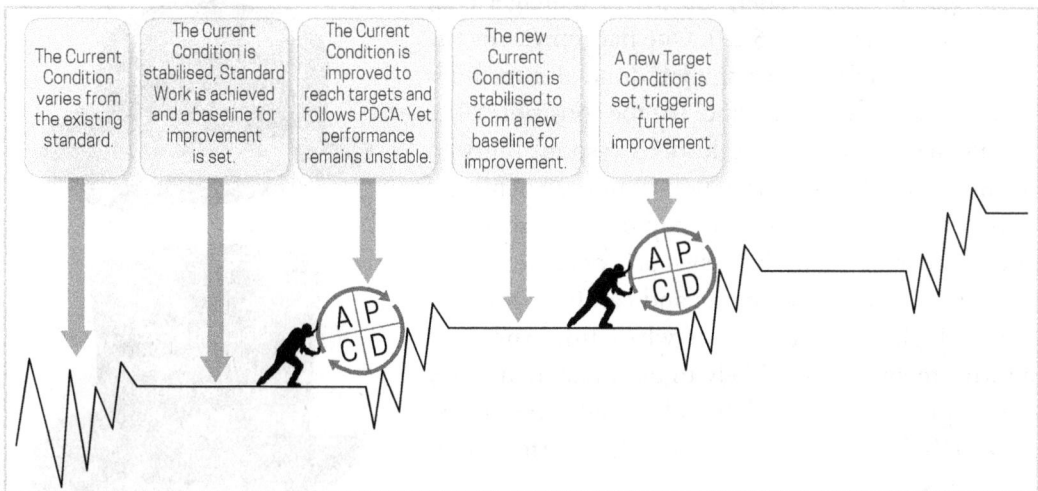

▲ Figure 6.28: Iterating towards the Target Condition by putting Standard Work and Current Condition through repeat PDCA cycles

How is the standard used?
- o Team members refers to the standard to give guidance to work.
- o The team leader or supervisor compares the Current Condition performance to the standard and coaches the employee accordingly.
- o When a new employee is trained, the standard is used to train them in the correct methods to assure the quality required. Later, when compliance is assessed, this is assessed against the standard.

The concept of Standard Work may at first appear rigid. Yet it sets the very benchmarks that make flexibility possible. The management mantra, '*We cannot change what we do not measure*', applies. If standards are in place, teams carry out their Standard Work always adjusting to meet the standard's ideals. Once the baseline is stable, the team is empowered to improve on the standard through cycles of PDCA. Over time and with experience, an organisation can even permit employees to develop their own process standards (always complying with regulations)—a desirable outcome of striving towards excellent Standard Work. Armed with good standards and basic problem-solving training, everyone can run controlled experiments, every day, to improve towards the Target Condition. In this way, employees are empowered and equipped to define and improve processes but always under the guidance and support of their leaders.

What should the standard include?

o The content of the work to be performed is specified line-by-line
o The sequence in which the work is completed is clear
o The timing indicates how long each element of work should be, or how long the task should optimally take
o The outcome is specific so that the quality of the work can be established.

# Leader Standard Work

Every leader (team leader, supervisor manager etc.) wears two hats (Figure 6.29). One hat represents the daily work needed to get the job done and includes basic requirements specific to the position. The second hat represents the leader's responsibility to nurture a culture of continuous improvement and lead by example in all that they do. Improvement efforts are woven into the very fabric of leader's daily activities, seen as must-haves and carefully guarded during high-pressure periods when time spent on improvements is most likely to be threatened. They are integral to their mandate and should to be written into a job description or contract's key performance indicators.

Even the most ingenious new ways of doing things or the most useful improvement to a process can fall away if not deliberately and stubbornly protected. Whether intentional or not, people easily slip back into old ways of working. Until such time as improvements are innate to team members, leaders must dedicate daily or weekly time to evaluating the performance of a new system, and guiding the team to sustain it and feed its longevity. Here, Leader Standard Work can have a major influence on the sustainability of change and ultimately the preservation of a Lean culture.

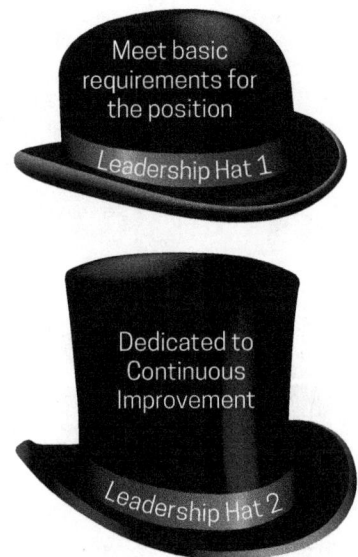

Meet basic requirements for the position

Leadership Hat 1

Dedicated to Continuous Improvement

Leadership Hat 2

▲ Figure 6.29: The two hats worn by all leaders

To some, the concept of Leader Standard Work may appear unconventional. Leaders may argue that their work varies from day to day and that the idea of 'standardising' it will only stifle their ability to perform. But we urge leaders to consider the portion of their day actually spent on work that varies. They are likely to find a

large proportion of what they do is in fact repetitive—and so perfect for standardisation. Furthermore, it is often inconsistent decision-making that introduces errors and other forms of variability. Of course we cannot standardise the entire spectrum of a leader's work. There will always be a portion that requires creativity, innovation and flexibility.

One of the pharmacy teams in Cohort 1 (Figure 6.30) redesigned their lines and replaced uncontrolled batch sizes with a four-piece-flow—only four patient files allowed into the process at any one time. Team roles were carefully designed around this preferred flow. The outcome? Four-piece-flow, coupled with other changes, slashed patient waiting times by up to 68 percent within a few days.

▲ Figure 6.30: A Cohort 1 pharmacy team implements four-piece-flow to replace uncontrolled batching of files and cut waiting times

The incredible impact on patients convinced the team of the benefits of the new approach. Even so, it did not take long for the improvements experienced to waiver as only the team directly involved in the switch to four-piece-flow understood the change. Other lines were still performing in the old way, using uncontrolled batch sizes. In time, even the model team's performance started slipping.

This is exactly the sort of scenario that Leader Standard Work can control. If a supervisor and area manager regularly visit the line and compare the Current Condition to the new standard developed, they will observe the obstacles to

> Leader Standard Work offers routine support and guidance when the team is struggling to maintain momentum and stimulates further improvement.

sustaining the change and be able to support and coach team members. This is what leaders at the pharmacy in question did. After a few weeks, the performance of all teams stabilised to the new standard. But, not without resilience on the part of the leadership who were utterly determined to safeguard the new conditions.

Remember that the Daily Management System and Visual Controls clearly communicate the health of your organisation or work area's Current Condition. Daily Accountability processes (meetings and problem-solving exercises) ensure performance is always being scrutinised through the lens of PDCA. Leader Standard Work offers routine support and guidance when the team is struggling to maintain momentum and stimulates further improvement.

What does it take to develop Leader Standard Work? Figure 6.31 includes elements of Hat 1: processes specific to the job and of Hat 2: the promotion of continuous improvement. These key ingredients develop Leader Standard Work or, a leader's standard routines. A useful tool that many leaders use to keep their work on track is the old-fashioned checklist. A word of caution to leaders: where possible, keep checklists simple. Lengthy checklists lose their impact and become yet another laborious document.

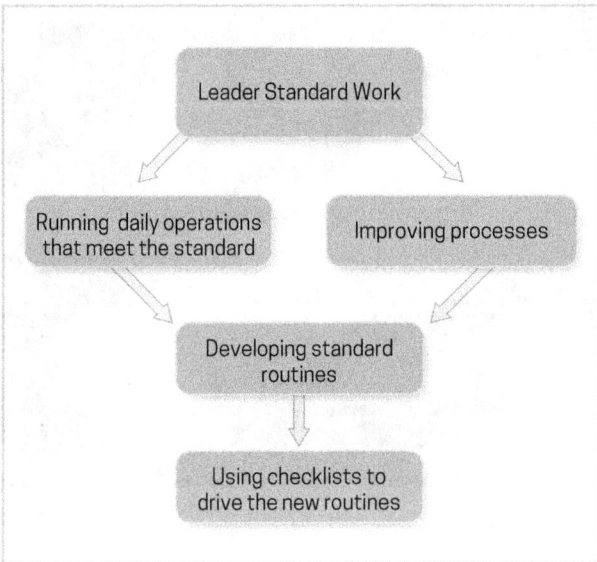

What does a good checklist entail? Table 6.8 provides a starting point for an effective checklist. It contains the routines a leader will need to drive continuous improvement. Leaders need to add elements from Hat 1 to this and then customise it to deliver on the habits required.

◄ Figure 6.31: The process of developing Leader Standard Work

**LEADER STANDARD WORK CHECKLIST**

| FOCUS | TIME | TEAM LEADER | TIME | SUPERVISOR | TIME | MANAGER |
|---|---|---|---|---|---|---|
| GEMBA WALK | 07h00 to 07h30 | • Walk floor as per agenda<br>• Review performance to standard, 5S condition, progress with actions<br>• Use Kata questions and provide guidance | 07h00 to 07h30 | • Walk selected floor as per agenda<br>• Review performance to standard, 5S condition, progress with actions<br>• Use Kata questions and provide guidance | 07h00 to 07h30 | • Walk selected floor as per agenda<br>• Review performance to standard, 5S condition, progress with actions<br>• Use Kata questions and provide guidance |
| MEETING PLANNING | 07h30 to 07h50 | • Summarise Gemba Walk findings<br>• Review priorities<br>• Review labour availability | 07h30 to 07h50 | • Summarise Gemba Walk findings<br>• Plan agenda | 07h30 to 07h50 | • Summarise Gemba Walk findings<br>• Plan agenda |
| S3 MEETING | 08h00 to 08h15 | • Leads S3 meeting as per agenda<br>• Problem solving initiated where needed for 5S and performance<br>• Action list updated as per PDCA | 08h00 to 08h15 | • Attend one S3 Meeting per week | | |
| S2 MEETING | 08h30 to 08h45 | | 08h30 to 08h45 | • Leads S2 meeting as per agenda<br>• Problem solving initiated for escalated items<br>• Action list updated as per PDCA | 08h30 to 08h45 | • Attend one S2 meeting per week |
| S1 MEETING | | | | | 09h00 to 09h30 | • Leads S1 meeting as per agenda<br>• Problem solving initiated for escalated items<br>• Action list updated as per PDCA |
| 5S | Weekly (Tuesday) | • Conduct 5S audit and update Daily Management System<br>• Guide daily actions to address weekly findings | Weekly (Monday) | • Conduct 5S audit rotating between areas<br>• Discuss findings with S1 leaders | Monthly | • Conduct 5S audit rotating between areas<br>• Discuss findings with S2 leaders |

◂ Table 6.8: Example of a Leader Standard Work checklist for continuous improvement elements

# Merger of Breakthrough and Incremental Change

It is common for a team to make leaps in performance when members come together and focus intensely on a particular problem. Taking the time to solve a problem in a structured way usually brings about immediate, tangible and positive change. The Quick Wins discussed in

> A team's fingertips must remain sensitive to the pulse of a new approach, to ensure the heart of change continues to beat.

Chapter 5—that have the capacity to dramatically and quickly improve on a process and win doubters over to the change effort—also illustrate this notion. But, when teams return to the grind of normal schedules after this sort of high-energy episode, they become embroiled in daily challenges. Often, the breakthrough event and its results soon become a distant memory. Measurable declines in performance affirm this.

*Breakthrough Change* refers to highly focused improvement events, usually triggered by long-term tracking, and addressed at the systemic (S2) or strategic (S1) level. The five-day Rapid Process Improvement Workshops attended by Cohort 1 hospital teams are an example of a breakthrough event that, in this case, resulted in dramatically reduced patient waiting times.

*Incremental Change* refers to day-to-day continuous improvement, usually triggered by short-term tracking, and addressed at process level. The Daily Management System installed in each of the model areas drives ongoing team involvement and helps in maintaining the performance achieved at the breakthrough events.

A team's fingertips must remain sensitive to the pulse of a new approach, to ensure the heart of change continues to beat. Breakthrough Change episodes alone are not enough. They are like open-heart surgery to unclog the arteries of a system in need of drastic and urgent change. Once theatre-time is over, a monitor must read and report on the systematic, incremental improvement in the beat of the fragile heart of change. After the breakthrough surgery, incremental healing shows the heart is daily stronger and able to pump lifeblood into processes that are evolving. Breakthrough events are also similar to the way in which the cardiac surgeon operates during an intense procedure over a few hours. Surgery would be pointless were it not for the incremental monitoring that follows, in which the ICU nurses change bandages, administer drugs and respond to changes in blood pressure and pulse until a patient has reached a new Target Condition and can be discharged.

Figure 6.32 depicts the way in which Breakthrough Change and Incremental Change are both critical to successful 'surgery' or intervention in work areas striving for Operational Excellence.

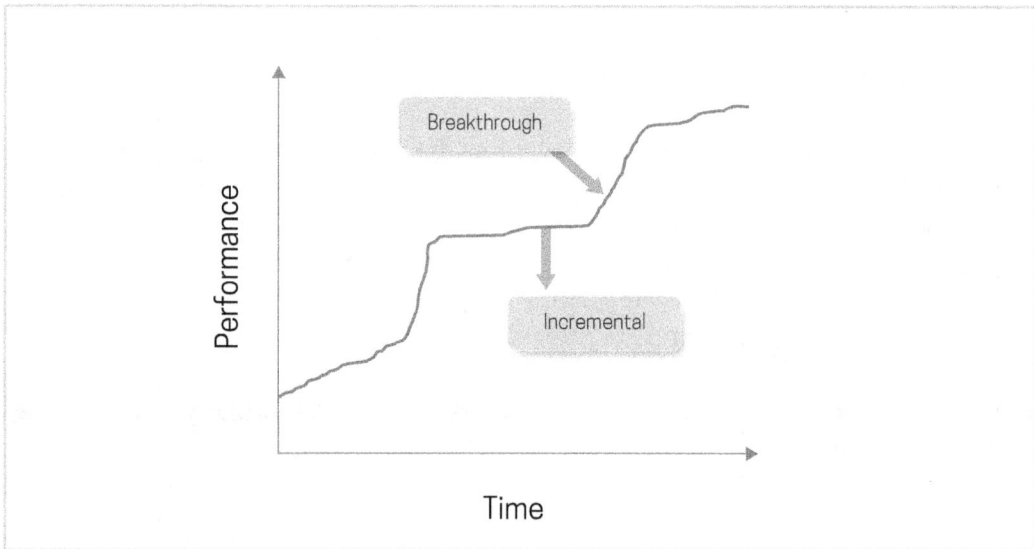

▲ Figure 6.32: The impact of Incremental and Breakthrough Change on performance

Avoid the trap of aiming only at large-scale, dramatic, impressive Breakthrough Change. Give your team a chance to monitor the pulse of smaller everyday Incremental Change with the support of a Daily Management System (further discussed in Chapters 7 and 8).

# Coaching for Performance

The role of the leader is to set Target Conditions. The role of the Target Condition is to create problems and put them squarely between the crosshairs of carefully selected change weapons. The role of problems is to create Thinking People who tirelessly fire at obstacles and waste.

Where does coaching come in to the picture? It is often assumed that once people are trained in better ways of working, that they will simply get on with the job and do things in the new way—and with excellence to boot. In some cases, teams do just this. They implement what they have learned, they meet Target Conditions and everyone benefits. It all goes forward without a hitch.

> The role of the leader is to set Target Conditions. The role of the Target Condition is to create problems. The role of problems is to create Thinking People.

We cannot, however, accurately predict the likelihood of this sort of seamless transition. The reality most teams face is one in which it takes time to grow the skills needed to achieve Lean process management. Books and training take us only so far. For most people, the real learning happens on the frontlines of trying and failing, only to pick up and try again.

It is here that a good coach, with experience in improvement processes and Operational Excellence, can guide a team through these 'failures'—better known as opportunities for learning—and towards the Target Condition. An efficient coach does this through a structured conversation that coaxes ideas from the learner as opposed to simply providing answers. It is better for learners to achieve half the improvement sought through their own efforts than to achieve all of the improvement sought by a cut-and-paste of someone else's ideas. The latter simply robs them of the opportunity to think.

Two coaching methods typically support both Breakthrough and Incremental Change:

- o A3 Thinking (using the A3 reporting tool)
- o Coaching Kata (using the Kata cards)

Figure 6.33 (adapted from LIA ITL, 2014) shows a typical A3 format which is further explained in Chapter 7.

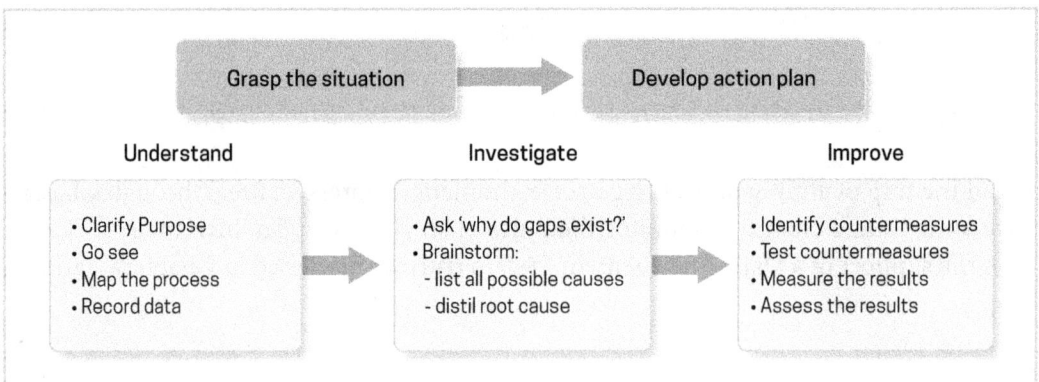

▲ Figure 6.33: The A3 Thinking process

For now, let us focus on the so-called A3 report as depicted in the template shown in Figure 6.34. A coach will refer to an A3 report and ask pertinent questions before offering guidance where needed. This report is a powerful tool for coaching, reporting feedback and knowledge management. It summarises a team's thinking process (also outlined in Figure 6.33) to show how they have grasped a situation and how they have developed the plan of action that will bring about Breakthrough Change in that situation.

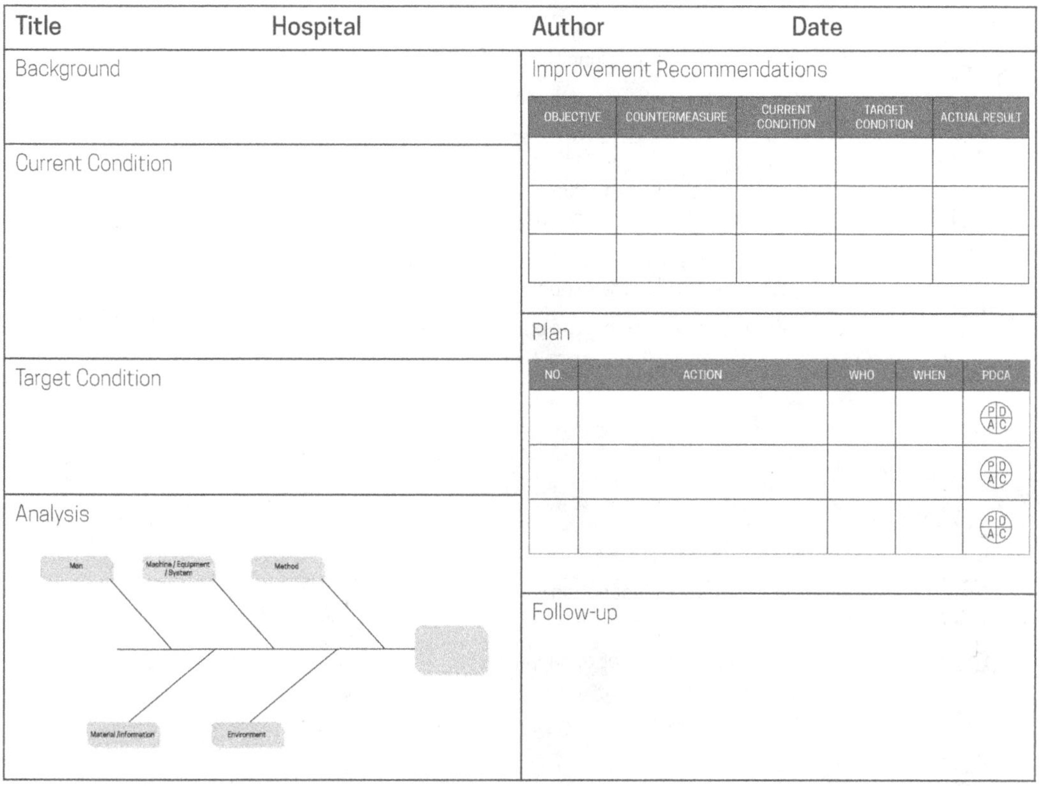

| Title | Hospital | Author | Date | | | |
|-------|----------|--------|------|--|--|--|
| **Background** | | **Improvement Recommendations** | | | | |

| OBJECTIVE | COUNTERMEASURE | CURRENT CONDITION | TARGET CONDITION | ACTUAL RESULT |
|-----------|----------------|-------------------|------------------|---------------|
| | | | | |
| | | | | |
| | | | | |

**Current Condition**

**Plan**

| NO. | ACTION | WHO | WHEN | PDCA |
|-----|--------|-----|------|------|
| | | | | P D A C |
| | | | | P D A C |
| | | | | P D A C |

**Target Condition**

**Analysis**

Men | Machine / Equipment / System | Method

Material /Information | Environment

**Follow-up**

▲ Figure 6.34: A3 report template

A coach uses Kata cards to structure the conversation with the learner or team leader and team. The cards allow for a specific pattern of thinking and are highly effective when it comes to making Incremental Changes.

Figure 6.35 (adapted from Rother, 2011) shows what the front and the back of a Kata card typically look like. To better understand a team's thinking, a coach follows the sequence of questioning depicted.

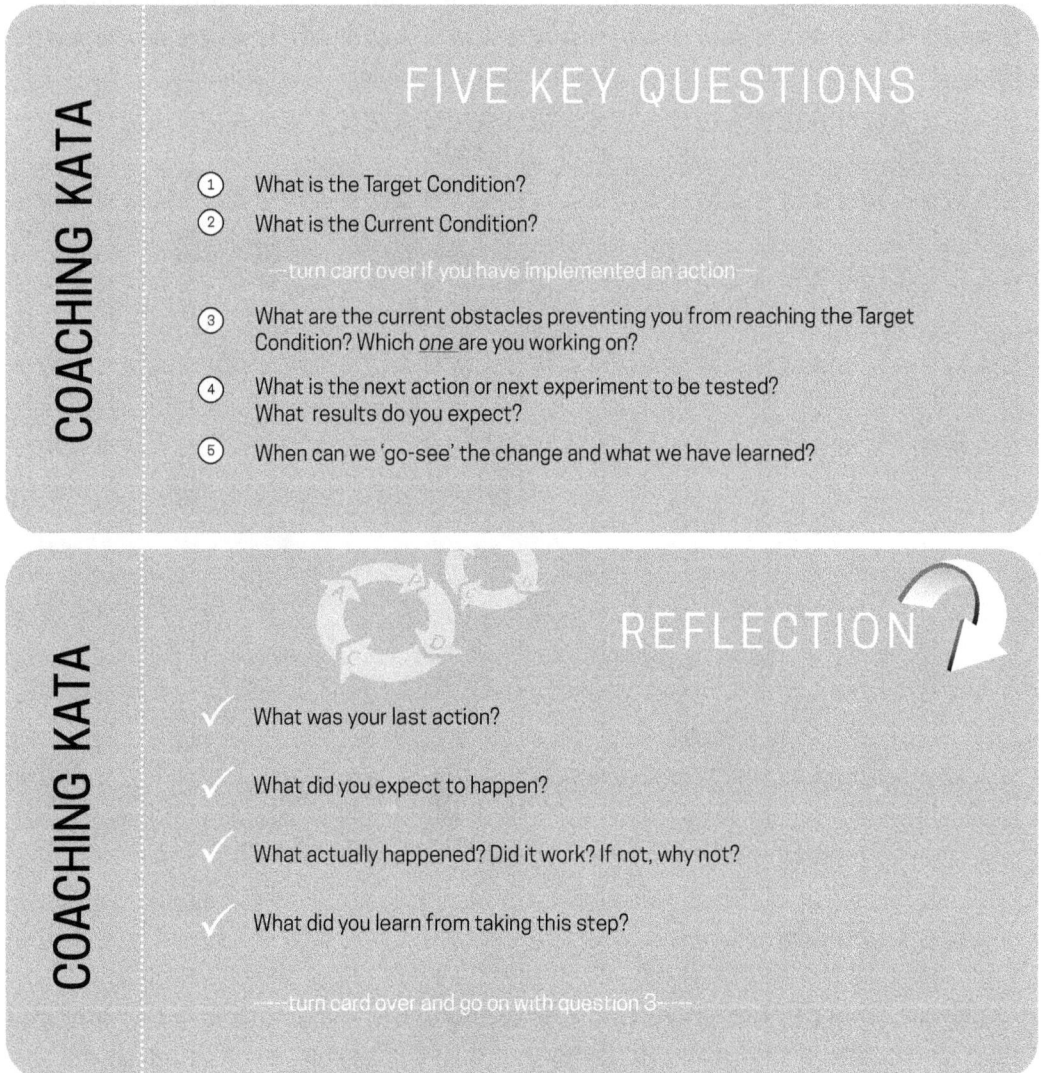

## FIVE KEY QUESTIONS

COACHING KATA

① What is the Target Condition?
② What is the Current Condition?

— turn card over if you have implemented an action —

③ What are the current obstacles preventing you from reaching the Target Condition? Which *one* are you working on?
④ What is the next action or next experiment to be tested? What results do you expect?
⑤ When can we 'go-see' the change and what we have learned?

## REFLECTION

COACHING KATA

✓ What was your last action?

✓ What did you expect to happen?

✓ What actually happened? Did it work? If not, why not?

✓ What did you learn from taking this step?

— turn card over and go on with question 3 —

▲ Figure 6.35: Front and back views of a Coaching Kata card

The Kata card structure also assists learners to give insightful feedback. This process allows for any leader to arrive at the Daily Management board, follow this or a similar set of standard questions and digest the answers in a structured way. The leader or coach is then in a position to support learners and offer guidance where needed. Chapter 8 further explains the power of Coaching Kata.

# The Rapid Process Improvement Workshop

Think of the RPIW Kaizen event as the Lean equivalent of a stick of dynamite. It comes in a small package (it lasts only a few days) and is an intense, high-energy, focused detonation that usually results in earth-shifting, routine-shattering, radically positive Breakthrough Change. This sort of Kaizen event affords each participant a first-hand opportunity to experience the potential for and power of significant transformation.

> Think of the RPIW Kaizen event as the Lean equivalent of a stick of dynamite.

It also targets an element fundamental to change that lasts: winning over people's hearts to the improvement process. Once the RPIW ends, teams are usually elated with the achievements they have managed within a short space of time. This inspires and prompts members towards further learning and action—fundamental to sustaining the changes made. Most importantly, in the context of a public healthcare facility, patients quickly experience the benefits of the Breakthrough Changes reflected in reduced patient waiting times and streamlining of hospital processes.

The RPIW is deliberately structured to guide a team from grasping the Current Condition to reaching the Target Condition and making improvements that last. Figure 7.1 illustrates the path followed during the RPIW—the 10-step Kaizen event. The cyclical process gives stellar, reach-for-the-North Star results when repeatedly implemented over intervals specific to an organisation's needs. Each run will show signs of improvement and growth in the team, until everyone in the organisation is equally engaged in structured improvement in every work area. You are ultimately creating a Kaizen spirit that permeates and seeps into the organiszational culture. You start with Purpose and the North Star and conclude with an improved way of work—that we then choose to standardise.

> Kaizen targets an element fundamental to change that lasts: winning over people's hearts to the improvement process.

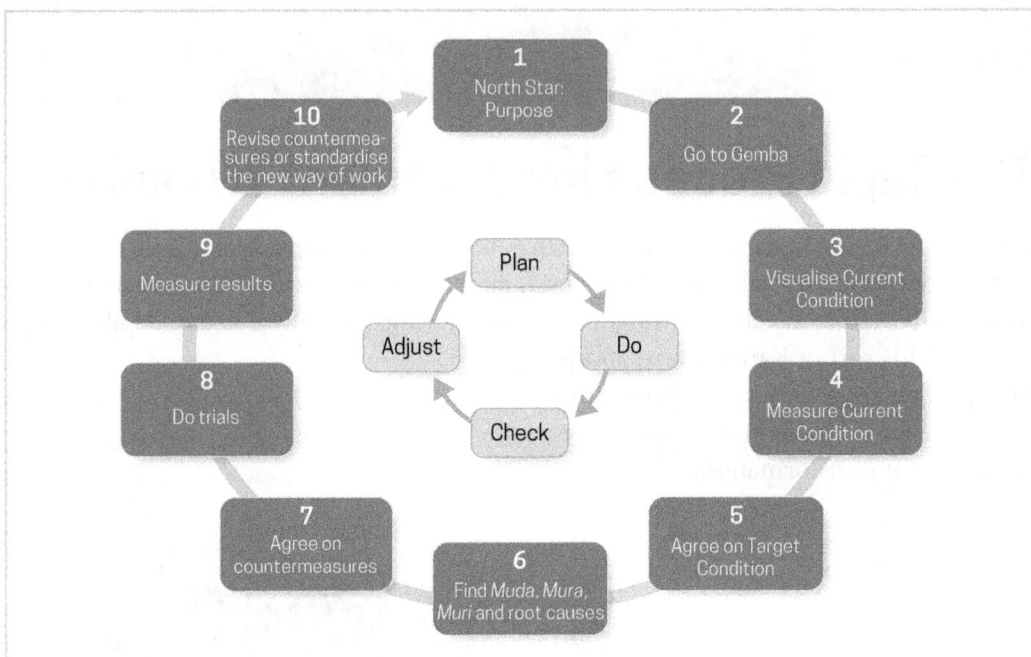

▲ Figure 7.1: The 10-step cycle, designed to be repeated at intervals, during a RPIW Kaizen event

The 10 steps illustrated in Figure 7.1 are spread between each of the five days of the RPIW (Figure 7.2). Does five days sound brief to you? If so, trust that they will be a time of intense and highly rewarding opportunity for leaders and teams alike. At the start of a RPIW there will be uncertainty and reservation. But, by the end of the week, this will be replaced by a palpable energy carrying confidence, excitement and trepidation ahead of teams' final feedback and presentations.

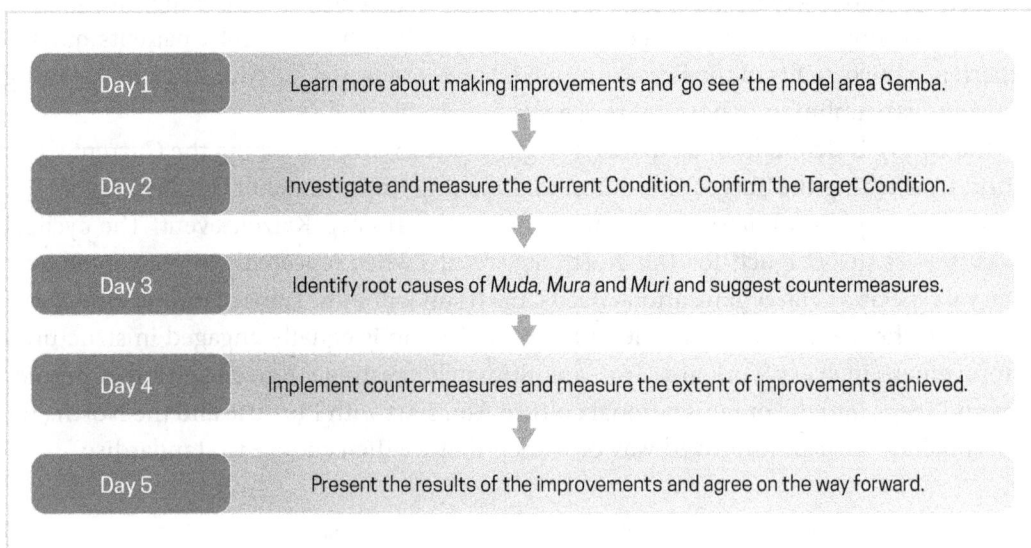

| Day 1 | Learn more about making improvements and 'go see' the model area Gemba. |
| Day 2 | Investigate and measure the Current Condition. Confirm the Target Condition. |
| Day 3 | Identify root causes of *Muda*, *Mura* and *Muri* and suggest countermeasures. |
| Day 4 | Implement countermeasures and measure the extent of improvements achieved. |
| Day 5 | Present the results of the improvements and agree on the way forward. |

▲ Figure 7.2: The five-day structure of the RPIW Kaizen event

Each of the four hospitals hosted three RPIWs—one for each of the three model areas identified for improvement at each hospital—so twelve projects were initiated in total. Teams from every hospital were invited to each workshop so, all in all, each of the teams were able to personally attend four RPIW rounds. The workshop followed the structure outlined in Figure 7.2 each time it was facilitated to encourage repeated practice of the principles. Members of the teams also rotated between model areas exposing them to each process type, meaning that pharmacists had a chance to assist in clinics, clerks in pharmacies, doctors in administrative offices and so on. By the fourth hospital everyone had gained experience in each model area allowing them to see the entire journey of the out-patient and not just their individual departments. With each RPIW attended, teams from all four hospitals showed marked progress in their understanding and application of the RPIW process.

## Are all improvements what they seem?

Shy away from improvement that delivers temporal spikes on the chart of positive change, only to make management or consultants happy but with little impact on healthcare or the patient. A Kaizen event could result in all manner of outwardly positive changes. But are they what they seem? Even though they might all look good, always run any improvements that you wish to preserve as a new 'normal' through the PDCA cycle. To ensure that this happens, the RPIW forces scientific thinking through the 10-step cycle. Figure 7.3 depicts the way in which the ten elements of the Kaizen event are divided into each phase of the PDCA cycle to illustrate how each element builds on the next. It becomes clear that much of the work to be carried out happens during the PLAN stage.

*'Decide slowly and by consensus. But implement quickly.'*

Lean mantra (Liker and Meier, 2006)

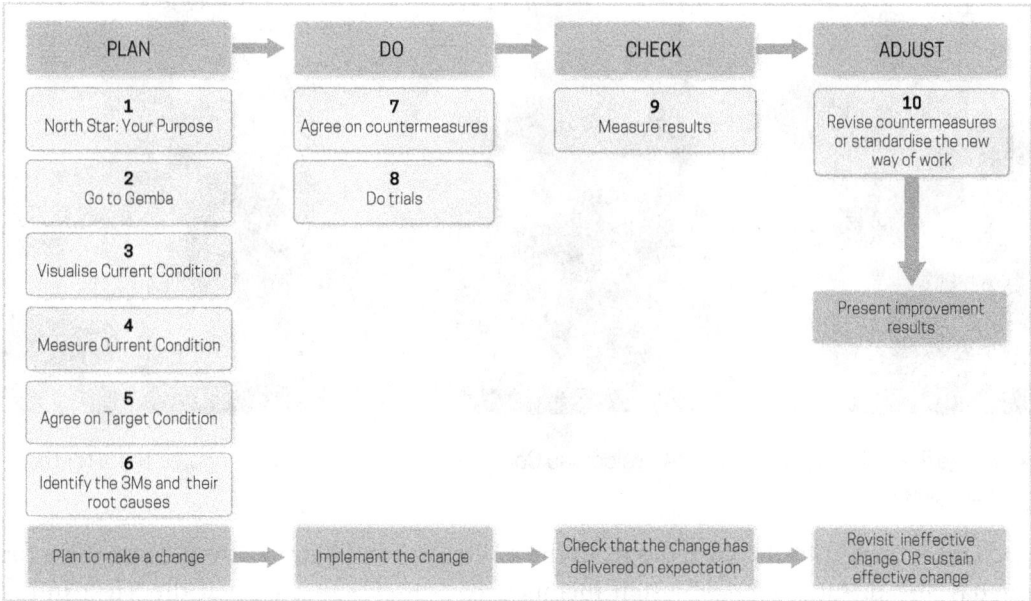

▲ Figure 7.3: Alignment between the PDCA cycle and the 10-step RPIW Kaizen event

# Day 1 of the RPIW

*Directive: Improve staff efficiency, eliminate waste and reduce patient waiting times*

Team members trickled into the training room and aimed for the coffee station. With refreshments in hand, they found a seat and caught up with colleagues from other participating units. The air was thick with both excitement and trepidation. Guided by the directives of the GDOH Service Delivery Improvement Initiative, the Kaizen event kicked off!

As mentioned, teams from Cohort 1 hospitals had four opportunities to take part in RPIWs. At the time of the first workshop, they had already been through the 'Introduction to Lean' and so were prepared for the next step but unsure of what to expect. Generally, at this point teams seldom comprehend the amount of work about to come their way.

Skilled facilitators were brought in by LIA, such as Tshepo Thobejane in Figure 7.4, to guide Cohort 1 teams through each RPIW. The LIA facilitator typically first sets the tone and communicates the agenda for the day, then dives into an overview presentation that refreshes the memory on elements learned in the build-up to the RPIW. This is also an opportunity to focus team attention onto the improvement tools chosen for the workshop day in question.

▲ Figure 7.4: Tshepo Thobejane (LIA) welcomes Cohort 1 hospital teams and prepares them for the week ahead

Each team then briefed colleagues from the model area in Figure 7.5 to prepare them for the day ahead. Although some staff members had received training at the 'Host Introduction to Lean' (see Chapter 5), it was necessary to repeat some of the details of this prior learning to ensure all participants were equally well prepared. Team members were reminded of why they were about to undertake a RPIW, what teams hoped to achieve and how each person could play their part. Individuals were also asked to share any questions they may still have been grappling with.

▲ Figure 7.5: Briefing the pharmacy team to remind them of prior learning carried out in preparation for the RPIW and to cover outstanding questions

Next, LIA facilitators presented work they had carried out prior to the RPIW (Figure 7.6). This gave teams an overview of what the independent LIA observers had discovered on their visit to the model areas and how their findings fitted into the bigger picture North Star goals. This presentation included the draft Value Stream Map, measurements of patient waiting time and relevant observations, all depicted on a brown-paper story-board. In Figure 7.6 Prof. Faull can be seen explaining what he observed at the registration and folder retrieval area and lists key questions for teams to answer. Though teams were expected to create their own brown paper storyboard and produce an updated Current Condition, this quick overview helped them to focus their attention onto the right details and gave them the confidence to get going.

▲ Figure 7.6: Prof. Faull presents the initial findings captured by the LIA facilitators for the registration and folder retrieval model area

Before any mapping or measurement could be done, teams first made their way to each of the model areas for a few hours of observation depicted (Figure 7.7 and 7.8). They were coached to 'go-see', ask questions and show respect at the Gemba.

'Go-see', ask questions and show respect.

▲ Figure 7.7: Teams 'go-see' at the Gemba where files are retrieved

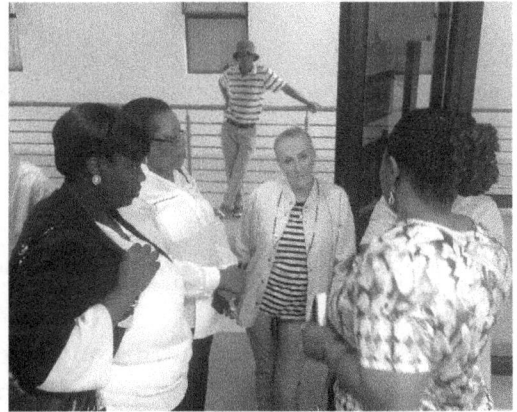

▲ Figure 7.8: Teams 'go-see' at the MOPD Clinic Gemba

In this way, they began to grasp the Current Condition and ensure they have gathered enough material to use later in the week when devising countermeasures to the obstacles identified. It took several hours to complete this 'go-see' activity. To their credit Cohort 1 teams ignored their breaks in favour of tracking a patient's experience down to the smallest detail. With enough observation and data-gathering under their belts, team members then returned to the training room, debriefed and agreed on the plan for the following day's activities.

# Day 2 of the RPIW

It took time for participants to get into the swing of the second day. Once the LIA facilitators had set the scene, teams moved off, again to the model areas visited on Day 1, but now to refine their information-gathering and observe activities they may have missed. When satisfied they had seen enough to develop an accurate Current Condition, they filtered back into the training room and prepared their own storyboard. They documented their findings using tools such as:

- o Value Stream Maps
- o Spaghetti Diagrams
- o Date sheets and graphs
- o Current work patterns.

In Figure 7.9 obstacles observed were captured and they discussed the Target Condition they needed to meet to reduce patient waiting time. This took up a full day.

▲ Figure 7.9: Capturing the observations so that the Current Condition could be defined

Once teams had a semblance of the Current Condition and clarity on a desired Target Condition, they invited staff from the model area in question to a presentation of their findings shown in Figure 7.10. This gave teams a chance to answer staff questions and adjust any errors in their approach.

▲ Figure 7.10: With the storyboard in progress, the team updates the Current Condition and prepares to give feedback to the model area staff

At this stage it was important for the LIA facilitator to remind the model area staff—who were not part of the RPIW but are key to implementing countermeasures that result from the workshop—that this is a learning process, and that their colleagues taking part in the RPIW need and appreciate their input. With the Current Condition complete, the team then debriefed and planned for the following day.

# Day 3 of the RPIW

It is often the case that when teams are let loose on model areas for the first time, there is a burning desire to solve all problems there and then. But, premature problem-solving

> Premature problem-solving leads to vague root cause identification.

leads to vague root cause identification and ineffective countermeasure deployment. LIA facilitators therefore frequently reigned teams in over the first few days and redirected participants solely towards completing their analysis and capturing the Current Condition. Only once a team is truly confident of the way in which they have understood and depicted the Current Condition, can they proceed with earned conviction to root cause analysis and to experimenting with countermeasures.

Preparation of the Current Condition is usually complete by Day 3 leaving teams ready to interpret their findings and problem-solve. Only then are they unleashed and allowed to tackle the obstacles exposed by their 'go-see' and investigations of the Current Condition. The LIA facilitator first coached participants to seek out obstacles that could be resolved within a short period of time and so have a significant impact on patient waiting times—so-called 'low hanging fruit'. Teams made use of Fishbone Diagrams and the 5 Whys technique (see Chapter 6) to dig deeper into 3M obstacles and their root causes (Figure 7.11).

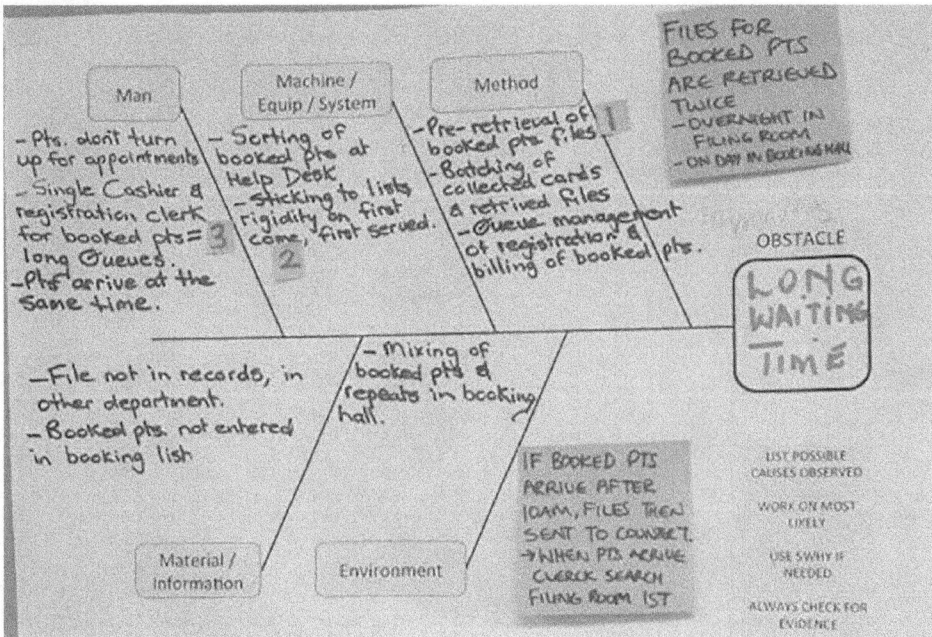

▲ Figure 7.11: A Fishbone Diagram and 5 Whys technique allow the team to capture possible root causes of excessive patient waiting time

With reference to the Fishbone Diagram depicted in Figure 7.11, the team numbered the possible causes using Post-It notes. This identified and prioritised the most likely contributors to extended patient waiting times—pre-retrieval of files, batching, queue management, patient billing etc.—and allowed the team to interrogate these top process offenders. Many of the root causes added to the Fishbone Diagram required verification and the LIA facilitator probed the team for clarification—for evidence. Once the team felt sure that they had properly extracted the most relevant root causes, they discussed countermeasures to each (Figure 7.12). This always seems to be the part that teams most enjoy. The planning stage of the RPIW, although crucial, can admittedly be quite laborious. Once the team begins to talk solutions, their interest in the process piques and they quickly move towards implementation.

> Just as days of hiking rugged terrain are the only way to reach a glorious and undiscovered summit, so too is the rigid and laborious upfront planning needed to lead teams to achieving an unprecedented quality of discussion around obstacles and countermeasures.

| OBJECTIVE | COUNTERMEASURE | CURRENT PERFORMANCE | TARGET PERFORMANCE | ACTUAL RESULT |
|---|---|---|---|---|
| PRE RETRIEVAL Reduce workload & duplication of retrieved files | Retrieve files as patients arrive. | Files retrieved night before 30% of pts. don't honour appointment or arrive late | Files retrieved for patients who dont pitch up equals 0% | 0% |
| BATCHING Reduce numbers in batch to increase the flow | Retrieve 5 files per batch instead of 10. | 10 or more files in batch for retrieval 12-26 min | Less than 10 minutes | 4.56 min |
| PAYPOINT Improve patient flow from retrieval to registration | Re distribute the patients to less congested pay points | Long queues at booking hall for payment & registration 74 min | Less than 30 minutes | 18.5 min |

▲ Figure 7.12: Linking countermeasures to clear objectives keeps focus on the Target Condition

With an approach to improving on patient waiting times now firmly in hand, teams were able to develop detailed action plans in preparation for RPIW Day 4 as shown in Figure 7.13. Often this required several brainstorming sessions with model area staff to gather their input and pre-empt success factors during trials (Figure 7.14).

| NO. | ACTION | WHO | WHEN | PDCA |
|---|---|---|---|---|
| 1 | ALL CONTROL LISTS TO GO THROUGH THE LIFTS FOR RETRIEVAL OF PATIENTS FILES | 2 CLERKS | 22.1.2015 | P D / A C |
| 2 | COMPILE BATCHES OF FIVE | 2 CLERKS | 22.1.2015 | P D / A C |
| 3 | DISTRIBUTE PATIENTS FOR REGISTRATION & PAYMENT TO OTHER PAYPOINTS NOT BUSY. | CLERKS | 22.1.2015 | P D / A C |
| 4 | COURTESY MANAGERS TO MONITER PATIENTS WAITING FOR REGISTRATION & PAYMENT | QUEUE MANAGER | 22.1.2015 | P D / A C |

▲ Figure 7.13: Plan of action to achieve desired countermeasures and interrogate them through PDCA tracking

▲ Figure 7.14: RPIW team members, decision-makers and model area staff brainstorm possible countermeasures to ensure implementation runs smoothly

The team updated the Target Condition with specific details of what needed to change and to what extent. This guide was necessary ahead of Day 4, the day on which

> Many countermeasures do fail initial implementation.

trials would reveal which countermeasures produced the expected results and which needed adjustment. At this stage the team was reminded that many countermeasures do fail initial implementation. Success hinges on the manner in which teams take on these key learning opportunities, recalibrate and try again. In Figure 7.15 one of the teams captures their expectations for improvement over a specific period of time.

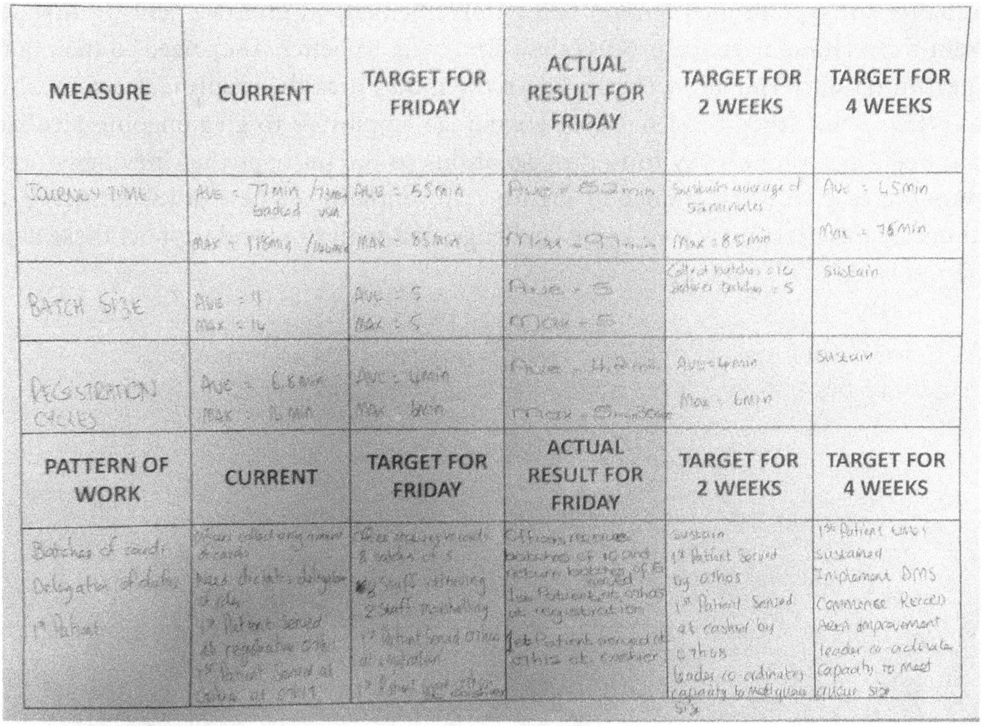

| MEASURE | CURRENT | TARGET FOR FRIDAY | ACTUAL RESULT FOR FRIDAY | TARGET FOR 2 WEEKS | TARGET FOR 4 WEEKS |
|---|---|---|---|---|---|
| JOURNEY TIME | Ave = 77min / based van<br>Max = 115min / based | Ave = 55min<br>Max = 85min | Ave = 65.2min<br>Max = 97min | Sustain average of 55 minutes<br>Max = 85min | Ave = 45min<br>Max = 75min |
| BATCH SIZE | Ave = 9<br>Max = 14 | Ave = 5<br>Max = 5 | Ave = 5<br>Max = 5 | Collect batches of 5<br>Deliver batches = 5 | Sustain |
| REGISTRATION CYCLES | Ave = 6.8min<br>Max = 16min | Ave = 4min<br>Max = 6min | Ave = 4.2min<br>Max = 5min | Ave = 4min<br>Max = 6min | Sustain |

| PATTERN OF WORK | CURRENT | TARGET FOR FRIDAY | ACTUAL RESULT FOR FRIDAY | TARGET FOR 2 WEEKS | TARGET FOR 4 WEEKS |
|---|---|---|---|---|---|
| Batches of counts<br>Delegation of duties<br>1st Patient | *(handwritten, illegible)* | *(handwritten, illegible)* | *(handwritten, illegible)* | *(handwritten, illegible)* | *(handwritten, illegible)* |

▲ Figure 7.15: Phased Target Conditions to reach by the end of the RPIW, within two and four weeks

The end of RPIW Day 3 brought teams back to the training room to debrief and share the plan for Day 4. Colleagues from the model area were again invited to hear what had been accomplished by the team and to offer input and support. It was clear that participants were making excellent progress as they coached model area staff about changes that would be implemented the following day and trained the necessary people in the new processes. Staff concerns and questions were resolved before close of day.

# Day 4 of the RPIW

With the PLAN stage of PDCA now behind teams, Day 4's mandate was to DO, CHECK and ADJUST. The early morning found an apprehensive but enthusiastic team convened in each model area. Despite their mounting uncertainty participants were ready for action. Team members were reminded that real-life implementation might deviate from Day 3's theoretical plan. It was therefore vital for teams to keenly observe the impact that countermeasures would have and help staff adjust where necessary. In theory, a team member should be armed with a diagram or written process allocated to each area earmarked for countermeasures, for example monitoring queue marshal duties, dispensing and picking processes etc. These individuals should act as observers or coaches. Where a countermeasure is not working, an investigation can be triggered and the team brought together to discuss alternatives.

No matter the type of intervention being implemented, an improvement team should refrain from taking over the process they are trying to better. They need to maintain a respectful distance and allow employees of the model area the requisite space in which to do their work. They must however encourage employees to give ongoing feedback. Employee input is often key to finding solutions to the mishaps that inevitably occur, as was the case with the trainee in Figure 7.16. Initially her new tasks, formerly carried out by the clerk, presented some challenges but with time and support these issues were resolved.

> Refrain from taking over the process you are trying to better. Maintain a respectful distance and allow employees the requisite space in which to do their work.

▲ Figure 7.16: The improvement team observed the results of the countermeasure in which a trainee took over some of the work of a clerk, to ensure that the intervention was as effective as envisioned

With the first round of trials over, teams returned to the training room to reflect on what had been observed, capture actual results and revise some of the countermeasures. Where necessary they returned to the model area to test any adjustments made and further refine them. The teams debriefed, prepared for Day 5–the last day of the RPIW—and again shared what had been learned with the staff from the model area. Taking input from staff seriously is a critical element of this stage of the RPIW as it ensures countermeasures can be finalised and updated in the new standards that we are moving toward capturing.

# Day 5 of the RPIW

By RPIW Day 5 almost everyone involved commented on how remarkable the changes made had felt. The way people feel after a brief 5-day engagement is fundamental to sustaining changes made, going forward. If they feel and believe in the change, then we have managed to speak to team members' hearts and secure their buy-in for the evolution that lies ahead.

Brown paper storyboards were updated with trial results and the team agreed on the way forward, capturing decisions made as in Figure 7.17. They decided on activities

> Prior uncertainty and trepidation had morphed into pride and excitement.

ahead of the first follow-up visit from the LIA facilitator, and updated the plan accordingly. The project was summarised into an A3 report (Figure 7.18) and the storyboard cleaned up. Once the team had pinned relevant details to the storyboard they prepared for their afternoon presentations to the hospital staff and central office attendees.

## FOLLOW UP TIME IN 2 WEEKS

| OBJECTIVE | COUNTERMEASURE | CURRENT PERFORMANCE | TARGET PERFORMANCE | ACTUAL RESULT |
|---|---|---|---|---|
| TO REDUCE TRACING TIME | INSTALL COMPUTER IN RECORDS DEPARTMENT. | AVERAGE TIME TO TRACE FILE. 3 min 52 sec | AVERAGE TIME TO TRACE FILE 1 min 30 sec. | |

▲ Figure 7.17: Activity plan leading up to first follow-up visit from the LIA facilitator

**Title:** WAITING TIMES IN MOPD                                    19 - 23 JANUARY 2015

## Background
- Waiting times is one of the six strategic priorities
- Patients wait longer than 3 hours at MOPD

## Current Condition
- Average waiting time at MOPD is 186 minutes
- Doctor arrival times range from 10h05 to 13h00 directly affecting the long waiting time.
- Retrieval of results : There was no waiting time, Computers installed in all 11 consulting rooms. NHLS installed, lab results accessible.
- Lack of booking visibility. Bookings on MEDICOM done by OPD clerk. Total booked 277. Adhered to booking 142. Those who did not attend 135. Total visits 1885.
- Defaulters for the week were 89 (came on wrong date).
- Nurse staff complement shared between MOPD and neuro clinic.
- Patient journey influenced by long waiting time experienced due to delay caused by cleaning in the morning.

## Target Condition
- Average waiting time at MOPD under 120min
- Stable doctor arrival times (09h30 to start), dedicated doctor to start at 08h00, to attend to any patient
- Encourage MEDICOM booking system by all departments referring to MOPD
- Activity based staffing, to enable nurses to assist doctors and patients during consultation
- Data capturer to enter patients in register works in MOPD and another clinic.
- Visual patient journey

## Analysis

| No real change in waiting time, but expected to continue until January 2015 | Impact of new computers visible. Service time for doctors reduced. | Unscheduled ward activity had impact on patient journey |
|---|---|---|
| Doctor start times remain unstable. No accountability for starting late | Nurses, Clerk, Courtesy Manager compliant in their roles | Obstacles this week |

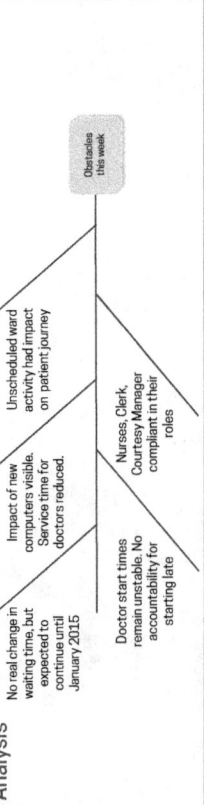

## Improvement Recommendations

| OBJECTIVE | COUNTERMEASURE | EXPECTED RESULT |
|---|---|---|
| Visualize performance | • Make accountability for measurement clear<br>• Capture daily performance | • Measurement sheet correctly filled, daily<br>• Use to expose obstacles |
| Stabilise process | • Right people, right place, ready to start<br>• Registration clerks and courtesy staff follow a standard process<br>• Nurses focus to nursing functions<br>• To ask for relief staff: Clerk & Courtesy Manager<br>• Data capturer in place/ Relief for clerk | • Process runs same way every day |
| Improve booking visibility | • Nurse managers and IT to monitor MEDICOM bookings in the ward/OPD | • Centralized booking system for MOPD and all medical wards & referring departments. |

## Plan

| NO. | ACTION | ACTUAL RESULT |
|---|---|---|
| 1 | Centralize booking system | 51% compliance |
| 2 | Review outcomes of research registrar starting January. CEO to intervene | Discuss with Dr Tsitsi & Prof Huddle |
| 3 | Discourage consultation of OPD patients in the wards | Book patients for MOPD |
| 4 | To reduce/eradicate defaulters – Nurses to do Health Education, CEO to write memo, Hospital Board to inform public | Compliance to clinic attendance |
| 5 | Down-referral process – provide carbonated forms | Expedite down referral of patients |
| 6 | Monitor MOPD activities daily | Staff perform duties |

## Follow-up
Next visit 30 January 2015

> The A3 report was created at the RPIW and then periodically updated thereafter. See Part 3 for a recommended template.

▲ **Figure 7.18:** Example of an actual A3 report as constructed by the team member. The report summarises the thought processes aimed at cutting patient waiting times at an MOPD Clinic

It is no mean feat to present RPIW findings and conclusions. The task was shared and each team member assigned a different part of the storyboard to present. The teams followed the storyboard in the same sequence, beginning with the background, Current Condition, Target Condition, analysis of root causes, recommendations and the results achieved during the trials. The day included time for a mock presentation to the LIA facilitators who provided guidance on content and presentation structure as shown in Figure 7.19.

▲ Figure 7.19: The team practices its presentation prior to guests arriving for final feedback in the afternoon

At last the teams had reached the summit of the mountain they had climbed for five days. It was time to share the RPIW experience as shown in Figure 7.20. Each team presented their storyboard and guests were given a chance to ask questions and seek clarity. It is deeply encouraging to witness the predictable outpouring of positive feedback that guests give to the teams during the presentations.

At this point the magnitude of what teams have achieved—in only a few days— becomes apparent. This stimulates tremendous energy and fuels excitement toward bold, future possibilities.

▲ **Figure 7.20:** Visitors from the hospital and central office attend the feedback presentation for each RPIW

The teams deserve a well-earned rest. Yet, they should not rest on their laurels as they are only at the beginning of the improvement journey. Though the RPIW has run its course, teams have to keep a foot firmly on the gas and capitalise on the visible and temporary energy flowing from the Breakthrough Change process. Teams must use their achievements as platforms from which to launch further improvement. The RPIW should never be seen as a training session to archive, an experience once attended but which had little impact going forward. On the contrary! The RPIW is dynamite, rocket fuel capable of shooting a team towards the North Star goals.

> The RPIW is dynamite, rocket fuel capable of shooting a team towards the North Star goals.

# Coaching through A3 Thinking

Chapter 6 introduced you to the A3 report and underlying thought processes behind effective problem-solving. Let us now turn to the way in which teams and leaders can use this tool to their advantage for improvement. It is useful to remember that A3 Thinking is the problem-solving thought-process guided through coaching (Figure 6.33) and the A3 report is the tool in which you capture the relevant information (Figure 6.34) for use as a talking point. The report is excellent for facilitating communication as it gives simple insight and points for discussion during coaching and feedback sessions.

The A3 report has its origins in Japan. Tradition saw the report compiled by hand—using a pencil and eraser—on a sheet of A3 paper that could be sent out using a fax machine. Though a good Sensei will still encourage the hand-written version, today many people prefer the efficiency of a computer-generated document. Provided the report still achieves its purpose and drives the right behaviour, a typed and printed version is equally acceptable. If the author of the report does not have access to a word processor, then the hand-written version is ideal (see Figure 7.21).

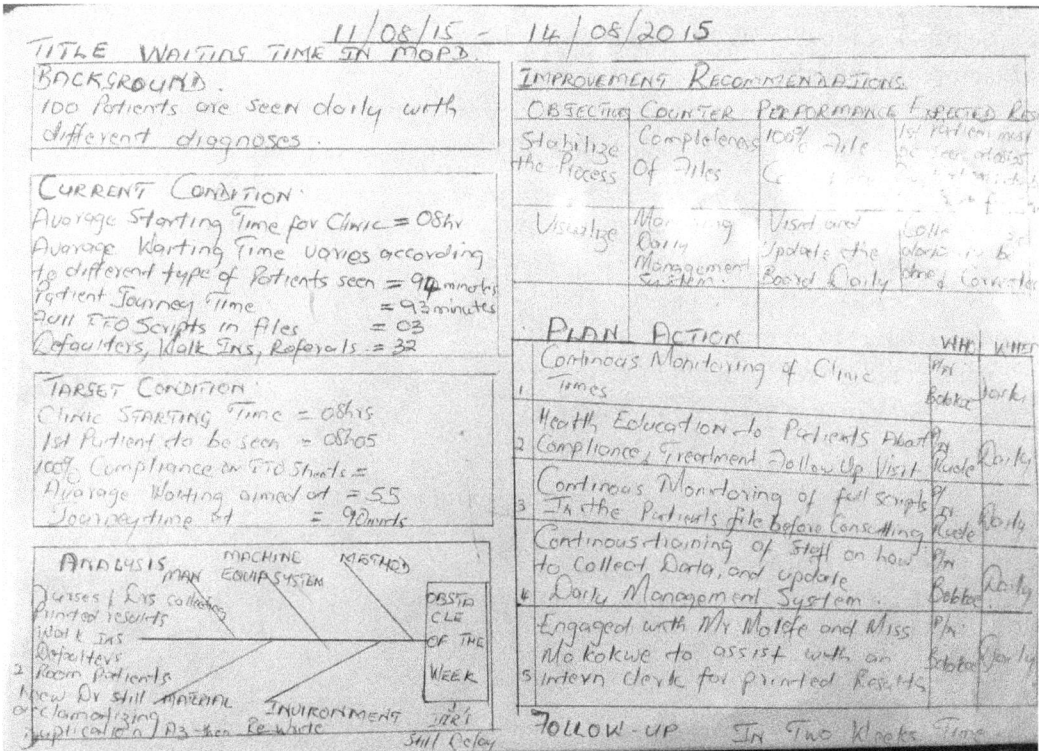

▲ Figure 7.21: Example of a hand-written A3 report for a MOPD Clinic

The A3 report is widely applicable to proposals, status reports and policy deployment documents. Although the A3 report could in theory be used for just about any level of problem, it is most effective where a problem has sufficient depth to warrant it, but also is not so complicated that the report cannot cope with the complexity.

For the purposes of this book, think of the A3 report as telling the story of how we solved a problem, tracing our journey toward Breakthrough Change from start to sequel—on a single sheet of A3 paper. It is the place where you write down your thinking so that you can:

- o Sort your thoughts regarding the problematic situation and countermeasures found to be effective
- o Document key information
- o Capture the decisions taken at each stage of the journey
- o Share it with others and benefit from their input
- o Use a common language as you talk about the journey
- o Optimise feedback sessions so that reporting is quick (ideally under three minutes), efficient and to the point
- o Preserve the learning and manage the knowledge gained for future reflection.

> Think of the A3 report as telling the story of how we solved a problem from start to sequel—on a single sheet of A3 paper.

Participants in the GDOH Service Delivery Improvement Initiative used the A3 report to capture the thought processes that brought about the Breakthrough Changes achieved in each RPIW and also to facilitate ongoing reporting at the Systemic tier (S2) as shown in Figure 7.22. This meant that after the RPIW the managers in each of the model areas reported on their progress weekly or fortnightly, also receiving coaching at these sessions. Two years later, these A3 reports are still used to reflect on past learning in some of the Cohort 1 hospitals.

The A3 report does not house every bit of detail relating to an improvement project. This would make it difficult to extract the key thought processes and weaken the report's keen ability to distil the concentrated essence of an improvement journey. Figure 7.23 presents a detailed explanation of central areas of focus in the A3 report. The idea is not to reduce font size so to squeeze everything in. Rather, we aim to capture only the most essential elements in a way that is visually pleasing and easy to digest.

> If you cannot tell your story on only one page, you probably do not yet understand your journey well enough to share it succinctly.

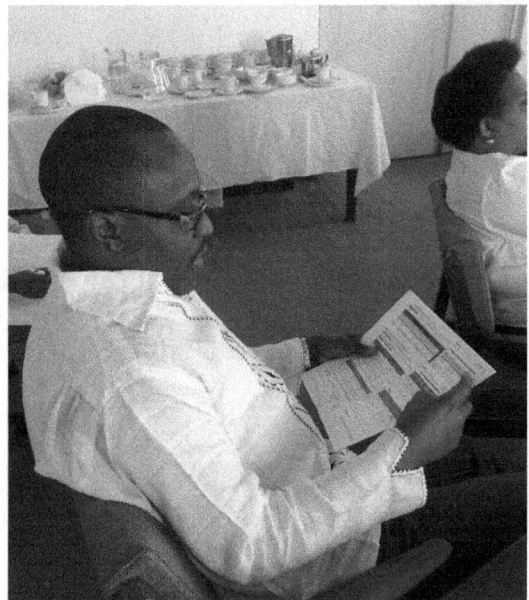

▲ **Figure 7.22**: A doctor gives feedback on a MOPD clinic's improvement journey as documented on a typed and printed A3 report

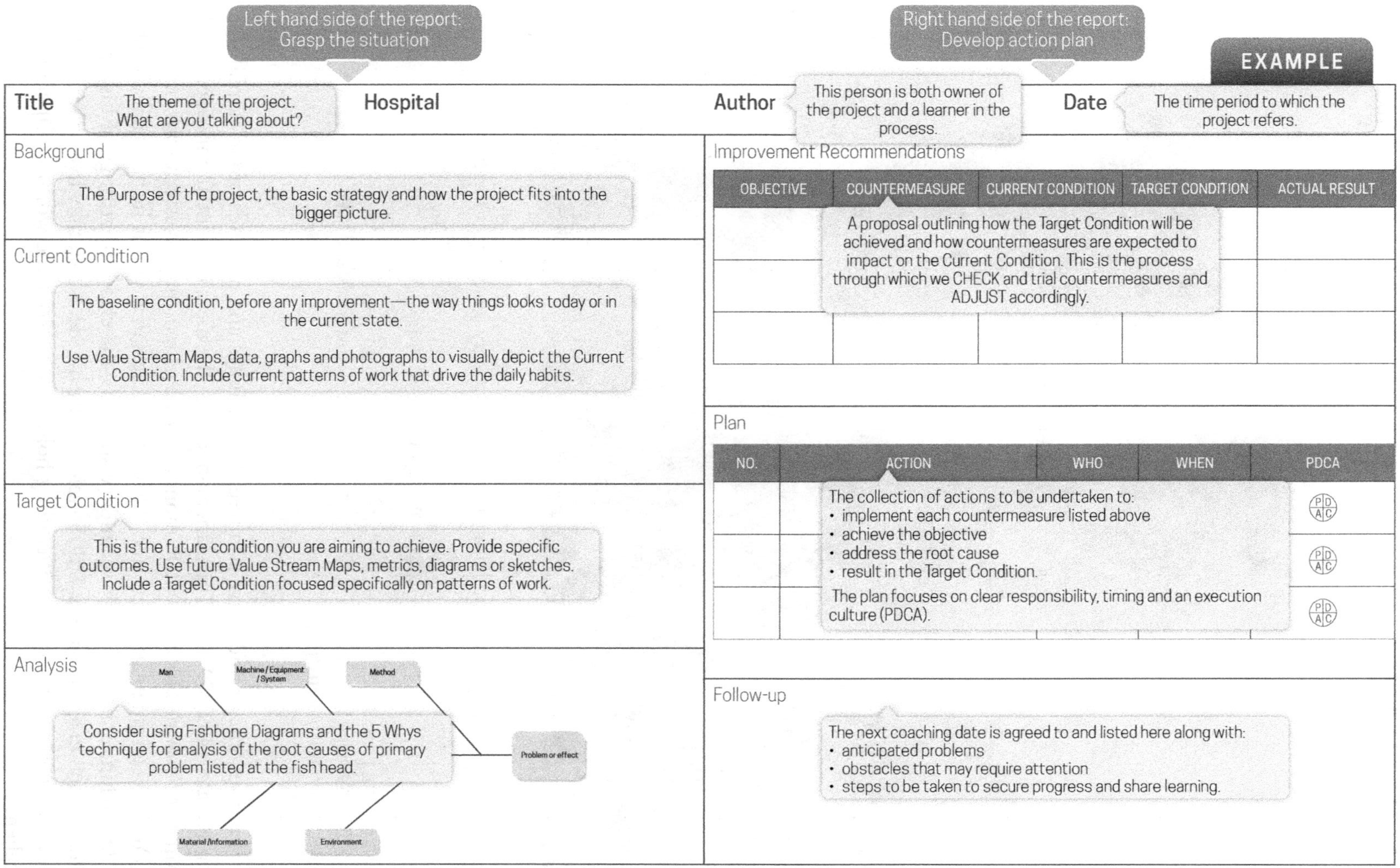

Left hand side of the report: Grasp the situation

Right hand side of the report: Develop action plan

| Title | Author | Date |
|---|---|---|

The theme of the project. What are you talking about?

**Hospital**

This person is both owner of the project and a learner in the process.

The time period to which the project refers.

**Background**

The Purpose of the project, the basic strategy and how the project fits into the bigger picture.

**Current Condition**

The baseline condition, before any improvement—the way things looks today or in the current state.

Use Value Stream Maps, data, graphs and photographs to visually depict the Current Condition. Include current patterns of work that drive the daily habits.

**Target Condition**

This is the future condition you are aiming to achieve. Provide specific outcomes. Use future Value Stream Maps, metrics, diagrams or sketches. Include a Target Condition focused specifically on patterns of work.

**Analysis**

Consider using Fishbone Diagrams and the 5 Whys technique for analysis of the root causes of primary problem listed at the fish head

- Men
- Machine / Equipment / System
- Method
- Material / Information
- Environment
- Problem or effect

**Improvement Recommendations**

| OBJECTIVE | COUNTERMEASURE | CURRENT CONDITION | TARGET CONDITION | ACTUAL RESULT |
|---|---|---|---|---|
| | A proposal outlining how the Target Condition will be achieved and how countermeasures are expected to impact on the Current Condition. This is the process through which we CHECK and trial countermeasures and ADJUST accordingly. | | | |

**Plan**

| NO. | ACTION | WHO | WHEN | PDCA |
|---|---|---|---|---|
| | The collection of actions to be undertaken to: implement each countermeasure listed above • achieve the objective • address the root cause • result in the Target Condition. The plan focuses on clear responsibility, timing and an execution culture (PDCA). | | | P D / A C |
| | | | | P D / A C |
| | | | | P D / A C |

**Follow-up**

The next coaching date is agreed to and listed here along with:
- anticipated problems
- obstacles that may require attention
- steps to be taken to secure progress and share learning.

▲ **Figure 7.23:** The A3 report format showing the thought process behind a problem-solving exercise and a description of the key elements to include.

# Ask. Don't Tell.

*'I cannot teach anybody anything. I can only make them think.'*

—quote attributed to Socrates

> Socratic teaching focuses on ensuring learners are thinking critically and asking more questions than they are fed answers.

For centuries, great minds have admired the teachings and methods of Greek philosopher Socrates (469-399 BC). This Athenian, one of the most influential philosophers of all time, is renowned for his contributions to the development of Western ways of thinking. Yet, he is an enigmatic character. We have no access to anything he personally wrote. We know him chiefly through secondary sources—the classical writings of his pupils Plato, Xenophon and of others. Still, so relevant are his ideals that they live on today and influence us in many spheres—including holding sway over the world of Operational Excellence.

During process improvement, coaches reference the so-called *Socratic Approach*. Socratic teaching focuses on ensuring learners are thinking critically and asking more questions than they are fed answers. Japanese culture also pursues the inquiring, probing mindset that discovers its own answers. It is therefore not surprising that Japanese-derived A3 Thinking relies on a questioning process to truly achieve lasting improvement results.

Your A3 report is a powerful tool through which to structure the conversation between the coach and the learner—in a Socratic way. With an A3 report as a reference for learner and coach:

o   A learner first explains the thinking process that led to grasping the Current Condition and the action plan developed thereafter.

o   The coach spends this time listening and allowing the learner to state their case entirely before beginning the questioning that follows (see Figure 7.24).

A coach cannot know or understand all the details of the problem at hand. Yet, they should have a reasonable sense of how to possibly tackle the problem and use this insight in their probing. Conducting a Gemba Walk prior to coaching is crucial to this understanding. Coaching can even take place at the Gemba if noise levels do not inhibit the conversation. The coach's questions must steer the learner towards the desired outcome to avoid deadlock and simultaneously build their confidence and understanding of the problem. Often, as the learner discovers his or her own path and develops keen insight, they might come up with more creative solutions than a coach had expected and so exceed the desired learning result. In this way, a coach and learner navigate in tandem, as captain and first mate, towards the North Star vision.

> The RPIW is less effective without the mental muscle of a strong, long-term partner for change—A3 Thinking.

The RPIW is less effective without the mental muscle of a strong, long-term partner for change—A3 Thinking. Coupling the RPIW with A3 Thinking offers a powerful alliance that facilitates delivering on and sustaining Breakthrough Change. The RPIW boosts performance over a short period of time. Coaching helps to stabilise improvements made so that we continue to build capability and boost performance further.

A3 Thinking could also extend to the Strategic tier (S1) where CEOs might benefit from capturing the deployment of change into a one-page A3 document—under marginally different headings but following a similar line of thinking. For more information on using the A3 report and its use in the context of Strategy Deployment, refer to *Clear Direction* (Heathcote, 2014).

| Title | Hospital | Author | Date |
|---|---|---|---|

**Background**

What is the history of this project? Why have you decided to focus on it? How does it link to the organisation's goals and North Star?

**Current Condition**

Does current performance meet the required standard?
Is there a gap?
Did we go to Gemba, observe and speak to those doing the work?
How do we currently monitor adherence to the standard?
What is the current pattern of work?
What metrics will we use to measure the Current Condition?

**Target Condition**

What is the goal, the ideal condition?
What is the desired pattern of work and what are its outcomes?
How does this relate back to the North Star?

**Analysis**

What obstacles lie between the Current and Target Conditions?
Did you uncover meaningful information to support the analysis?
Were you able to isolate the main components of this gap?
Were you able to extract the root cause/s we need to focus on?

Man | Machine / Equipment / System | Method

Material /Information | Environment

problem or effect

**Improvement Recommendations**

| OBJECTIVE | COUNTERMEASURE | CURRENT CONDITION | TARGET CONDITION | ACTUAL RESULT |
|---|---|---|---|---|

What is the thought process around eliminating root causes of obstacles?
How do we plan to meet the Target Condition?
What countermeasures do you propose?
Have all reasonable countermeasures been explored?
Have possible countermeasures been agreed to by those doing the work?
How will we proceed in implementing the countermeasures?

**Plan**

| NO. | ACTION | WHO | WHEN | PDCA |
|---|---|---|---|---|

What activities will be done, by whom and when?
What indicators will be used to test progress?
What will we do once the test is complete—the next steps?

PDCA

**Follow-up**

How and when will we check that we are getting the desired results?
If countermeasures were implemented, which achieved the desired results and which were ineffective and in need of revision?
How will those that were successful be managed going forward?
What remaining obstacles can we expect?
How will we capture and share our learning?

◄ **Figure 7.24**: A suggestion of questions a coach can ask of a learner to prompt critical thinking—in a Socratic way

## PRACTICAL ACTIVITY: Initiate Breakthrough Change

Planning adequately ahead of the RPIW ensures the Kaizen event kicks off and runs smoothly, ultimately deriving value for the facility, employees and patients. A person specifically trained in conducting an exercise of this sort should facilitate the RPIW and the agenda provided in Part III may be used for this purpose.

Before the RPIW, ensure the following:
▸ Have the model areas that will participate been identified and the staff members who will form part of the improvement team selected? The model areas would have been chosen as part of the change planning activities described in Chapter 5.
▸ Are the leaders aware of the events planned and clear on the role they play in supporting them?
▸ Do the leaders understand how the workshop will benefit their teams and influence the goals for improvement?
▸ Have employees been encouraged to participate and give input and feedback?
▸ Has the model area's staff been prepared for the event?
▸ Have a 5-day agenda and supporting material been prepared?
▸ Has the event been scheduled at a convenient time to limit the impact on patient service?

After the RPIW, ensure the following:
▸ Participants must be held accountable for what they have learned and how to apply it.
▸ Measurement systems and feedback must be sufficient to track new behaviours. Is A3 reporting in place? Has the Daily Management System been initiated (see Chapter 8)?
▸ Leaders coach the learners towards the Target Conditions set (with the support of a Sensei such as an external consultant or experienced internal consultant).
▸ A plan sets out how, and when, to bring additional model areas on board the change effort. Before rolling out the changes to other areas, ensure reasonable stability in the initial pilot sites (refer to the Vision for Change described in Chapter 5).

What do patients visiting your facility value most?

Visitor

They want excellent, efficient service that is provided within a reasonable time frame.

Host

How do you measure the service provided?

Visitor

We measure patient waiting times.

Host

These were some of the questions and answers captured when LIA facilitators and representatives of the Gauteng Health MEC's office visited one of the Cohort 1 hospitals for the first time. The visitors had arrived to warm introductions and refreshments and following a brief overview of the visit's intended purpose, were given a tour of the facility. The walkabout, led by the hospital's CEO, brought visitors together with key members of the executive team—directors and their deputies in clinical services, nursing, pharmacy and patient affairs. The group followed the path an out-patient takes from arrival and registration through to the out-patient clinic until the pharmacy where patients get their medication before leaving (Figure 8.1). This meant that visitors had privileged access to key indicators of the level of care in any public healthcare facility: the quality and speed of the patient journey.

Hospital staff graciously took the visitors through each department's daily workings and openly discussed areas of concern that they hoped the Lean initiative (the GDOH Service Delivery Improvement Initiative) would be able to address. Obliging staff offered candid feedback and shared experiences and patent expertise in response to visitors' poignant questions about processes witnessed. What became more apparent with each new question was the complexity of achieving and maintaining excellence in the patient journey.

▲ Figure 8.1: During a first-time visit to a Cohort 1 hospital, visitors join management to experience the patient journey

The visitors continued down the path of the out-patient journey, listening rather than speaking, but soaking up the opportunities at every turn. Further excerpts from the dialogue that played out during the first Gemba Walk included:

How long is your current patient waiting time?

I would need to check the exact time for you. I believe it is anything from two and a half to three and a half hours. But, remember that the provincial benchmark is currently three hours.

Could you show me how you measure patient waiting time?

We capture details around every patient's visit—from arrival through to making an appointment for their next visit before leaving. This includes data on how long they waited at each stage in the process. This information is provided to our Quality Department who collate the overall waiting times.

What can you tell us about your patients' waiting times? What makes their waiting times even longer than the three-hour provincial benchmark?

We have many defaulters who miss their appointments. They do not show up for their allotted appointments and then arrive unexpectedly on another day, swelling the queues. Our booking system is also poorly managed. Clerks in the ward book patients for their out-patient clinic visit but do not capture the information on the system. They frequently book more than the 110 patients per day that we can cope with—often we are not aware of the numbers to expect and just have to deal with them as they arrive. It is also a problem that doctors start their shifts later than we would like.

We can appreciate your frustration. How many defaulters and unexpected bookings are we talking about? What times are doctors arriving for their shifts?

I do not know offhand but we can work out the numbers from the data captured. We do not measure doctor starting-times but they are usually in from 11 o'clock in the morning onwards. They come in to our clinic in the late morning as they first complete ward rounds.

How often does the nursing staff meet with doctors to discuss problems exacerbating patient waiting times and how these might be addressed?

We have a good relationship with the doctors. One of them visits us every two weeks for discussion of any issues we might have. She, in turn, gives us feedback from doctors and passes the information we provide on to the attending units. She is very helpful and we appreciate her support. But we do not actively problem-solve as a team.

This information is certainly encouraging and offers an excellent starting point on which to build improvement efforts. We hope to show you how to set up systems that bring problems to the surface as soon as they manifest and that allow teams to solve them in a relatively short time frame. We want problem-solving to be something that everyone does every day, really adding value to things that matter to the patient.

This sort of dialogue reveals a hospitals' Current Condition. Here we have a facility making a good start. Not only are this hospital's teams already gathering critical information, but the doctors are also initiating a degree of problem-solving in a manner that suits everyone's schedules as far as possible. Recognising current good practice is a key tenet of Lean Thinking. In this case, LIA facilitators were able to reinforce the positive work already underway and offer guidance that would take it to the next level:

o   One of the first things to consider is a switch from a register containing raw data and no summaries to tools that visually portray information gathered, making it easy for everyone to see the trends at play.

o   Next, the team should agree on key factors influencing waiting times. What are the chronic events that erode performance over time? What are the sharp spikes or 'one-hit-wonder' problems that send the graph off on a tangent? The spikes represent brilliant opportunities for daily problem-solving and the chronic issues are best tackled through a Kaizen event that targets longer-term trends and long-standing problems.

o   With abnormalities eroding performance and lengthening the waiting time made more transparent, teams can launch into daily, evidence-based, data-driven problem-solving.

Chapter 6 introduced us to the three-phase Improvement Cycle (Figure 8.2). Remember that the process begins with MEASUREMENT that captures daily performance and exposes any abnormal states of *Muda*, *Mura* and *Muri*.

The visit referred to above exposed abnormal waiting times that exceeded provincial norms. Can you imagine needing medical care and having to wait up to three and a half hours to be attended to in just one of the departments? In this hospital's case non-conformance to service standards, erratic starting times on the part of doctors and the number of defaulting and unbooked patients add fuel to the abnormality fire. If we are measuring performance, we must ensure ways to use the data derived. Referring back to the Improvement Cycle (Figure 8.2), the first step to correct these issues is expanding the concertinaed accordion playing out the discordant melody of the Current Condition. In this way, we reveal every individual seam in need of a tune-up and every input measure and clarify each contributing factor. Then we can prioritise the order in which we tackle each challenge identified.

Steady progress results from running the Improvement Cycle repeatedly:

o   Stage 1: Graph and compare *exposed abnormalities* against desired benchmarks—the Target Condition.

o   Stage 2: Reflect on the challenges faced and *problem-solving* needed to address them.

o   Stage 3: *Take action* and run your countermeasures through the PDCA cycle to rectify, improve and stabilise performance.

o   Return to Stage 1 and *repeat* the cycle.

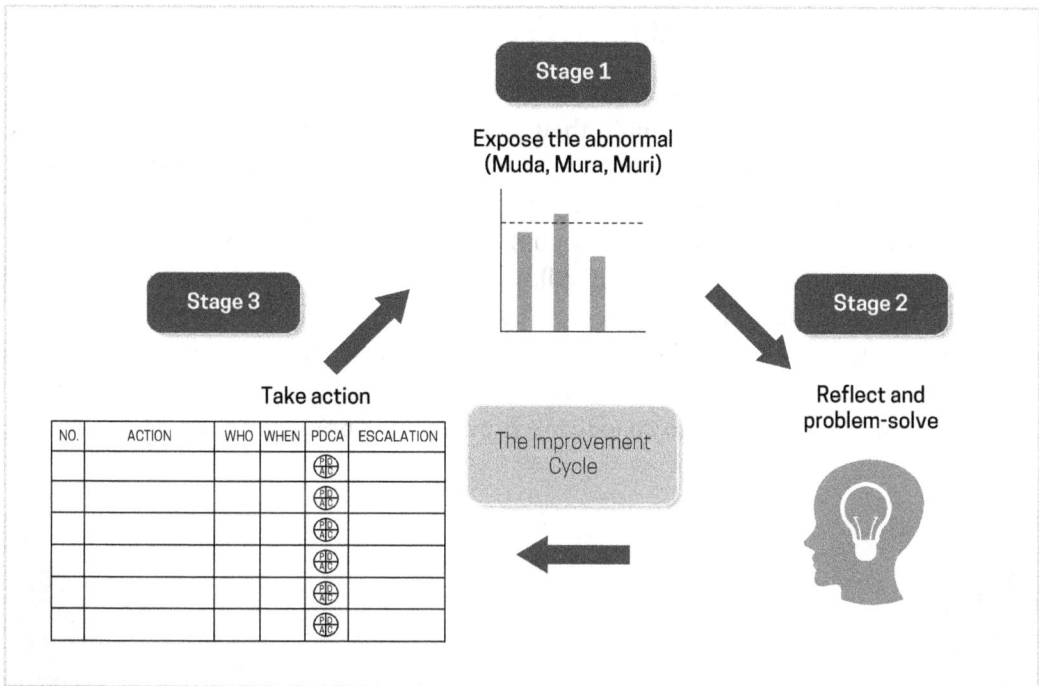

**Stage 1**

Expose the abnormal
(Muda, Mura, Muri)

**Stage 3**

**Stage 2**

Take action

Reflect and
problem-solve

| NO. | ACTION | WHO | WHEN | PDCA | ESCALATION |
|-----|--------|-----|------|------|------------|
|     |        |     |      | ⊕    |            |
|     |        |     |      | ⊕    |            |
|     |        |     |      | ⊕    |            |
|     |        |     |      | ⊕    |            |
|     |        |     |      | ⊕    |            |
|     |        |     |      | ⊕    |            |

The Improvement
Cycle

▲ Figure 8.2: The three-stage Improvement Cycle begins with a *measuring* of abnormalities to direct later stages of *reflection/problem-solving* and *taking action*

The Improvement Cycle is big and bold. It guides our overarching strategy and improvement approach. So, how do we feed it from one moment to the next? How does improvement play out every day on the frontline? We need a system that constantly flags the diamond-in-the-rough problems that hide the real gems of improvement opportunities. We need a structure or a solution that allows us to accumulate regular, positive increments in performance and teaches us to problem-solve as obstacles appear—while hot off the press.

> We need a system that constantly flags the diamond-in-the-rough problems that hide the real gems.

We briefly encountered the solution in Chapter 6. Now we really get our hands dirty. Let us investigate the texture and gritty detail of the *Daily Management System* and deliberate routines that support it.

> Remember that a Daily Measurement board is just a tool. The Daily Management System goes beyond the tool and incorporates the behaviours and routines that drive the Improvement Cycle.

# The Daily Management System

Many organisations hope to realise their grand strategies by sending the wood, the nails and other parts needed to assemble their goals and expectations downstream. They hope that lower-level staff and teams will miraculously deliver on the North Star vision and simply send remarkable change back upstream in the form of a beautiful sea-faring vessel. Should we be surprised or disappointed when departments miss targets and a finger-pointing frenzy ensues? Worse still, to compensate for poor results individuals often launch emergency crisis management tactics that invariably destroy value one way or another. As the dust settles the only survivor is the consequence of failure to properly identify root causes of abnormalities and address them with effective countermeasures. Needless to say, this approach to change rarely ends in celebration.

The antidote to this sort of knee-jerk approach and the discouraging and sometimes devastating aftermath is the implementation of a system that helps teams correct deviations daily—ideally as they occur and while they are still fresh in everyone's minds. Installing a Daily Management System (DMS) will move your organisation away from reactive responses towards proactive, value-driven behaviour on the part of every person employed (planet-lean.com, Ferro, 2015).

This chapter will convince you of the power of the DMS to make employees conscious of the problems they face on a daily basis and connect these to the big picture improvement strategy and North Star goals. Leaders need a system to help them to channel the waters of multiple, disconnected streams of focus into fewer more powerful rivers, so directing people to work on areas that really count towards desired change.

Teams are then able to spend their limited time on edging performance forward—slowly and purposefully. The DMS is such a system and fosters a close connection between the employee and the improvement process. When your people have a finger on the pulse of the organisation, they are able to neutralise threats as soon as they appear on the radar and respond to challenges that could negatively affect daily operations with the right pre-emptive strikes.

Though the DMS might seem a relatively simple concept, certain key elements are needed to manifest its true potential:

o *Clear Direction*: How have you defined your North Star? Which improvement areas will your DMS focus on? Ultimately any successful change effort will be the sum of its parts—the contribution from and quality of each team's bespoke DMS. Think of each hospital unit involved in the change effort as one of the vessels in a flotilla of ships collectively navigating towards the North Star vision

o *Input and output measures*: Define both your input and output measures (refer to Chapter 3). What makes the improvement process tick? How is performance in key improvement areas measured? Which factors contribute most to change?

o *Measurement system*: With the input and output measures defined, ensure the existence of a robust system for gathering and synthesizing data into visual props— charts, diagrams, documents, graphs, photographs and so on—that catalyse problem-solving (refer to Chapter 3).

o *Triggers*: What is the Target Condition for performance? What elements trigger problem-solving? To keep teams motivated and interested ensure improvement targets are both challenging and attainable.

o *Display board*: Where will you display the Daily Management board? Remember that the location should coincide with the area in which daily meetings take place. In some cases, teams are fortunate enough to have a dedicated meeting area where the DMS board takes pride of place. Ensure that you choose a practical location, close to the action. Ideally you should source a whiteboard, felt board or notice board on which to display the DMS but hand-made boards consisting of flipchart or brown paper will do just as well.

o *Standard headings*: Decide on the notice board's headings and focus areas and include the following:
  - Team name
  - North Star vision
  - Target Condition (could be included on the visuals or separately)
  - Current Condition (graphs and visuals that depict the way things are at present)
  - Obstacles (include a Fishbone Diagram to capture obstacles)
  - Experiments (the Action Plan: which countermeasures will be experimented with?)
  - A3 report (Breakthrough Changes and ongoing reporting)
  - Leader Standard Work

- o *PDCA*: Build PDCA cycles into the DMS design. Have teams check off each stage of the PDCA every time they experiment with countermeasures.
- o *Accountability*: Who will update the board? Neglect is to a DMS, what drought is to crops. An overlooked DMS begins to wither and information captured becomes meaningless. Decide who will update the board every day, prior to the Daily Accountability Meeting (see next section). With time and as confidence builds, encourage other team members to share in this responsibility.
- o *Focus*: Too much detail makes teams lose focus. Strike the right balance and ensure that all information displayed is concise enough to make performance transparent, but not so vague as to prevent teams from extracting the most relevant issues. When designing the visuals to display under the Current Condition, limit yourself to three or four indicators and a maximum of seven. Although the Fishbone containing the obstacles will be heavily populated (and this is a good thing), it is important that the team only tackles one obstacle at a time. There is a two-fold advantage to this approach:
  - It restricts overloading the team with problems to solve.
  - The team is able to test one countermeasure at a time. This makes it easier to see which actions are in need of adjustment or discard and which have brought about desired impacts that can be standardised.

To help you get started on designing a Daily Management board refer to Figure 8.3. Once up and running it is only a matter of time before teams refine behaviours and routines that drive the DMS. The board allows employees to very easily follow specific routines to complete and repeat an Improvement Cycle. These behaviours include grasping the current situation, identifying obstacles, running experiments and reflecting on the evidence. In this way, any new heights of performance reached can be stabilised. We use an exercise called *Kata* to establish these Best Practice routines. More on *Kata* further on in this chapter.

# MOPD CLINIC DAILY MANAGEMENT SYSTEM

## NORTH STAR

## TARGET CONDITION

Waiting Time: 90min by end Sep 2016
Clinic start time: 0700 by 15 Aug 2016
Defaulters: <5% by end Nov 2016

## CURRENT CONDITION

Waiting Time: 110min
Clinic start time: 0815
Defaulters: 10%

WAITING TIME

CLINIC START TIME

## OBSTACLES

OBSTACLE

LIST POSSIBLE CAUSES OBSERVED

WORK ON MOST LIKELY

USE 5WHY IF NEEDED

ALWAYS CHECK FOR EVIDENCE

Man

Machine / Equip / System

Method

Material / Information

Environment

## EXPERIMENTS

| # | 3M OR OBSTACLE | POSSIBLE CAUSES | COUNTERMEASURES | EXPECTED IMPACT ON TARGET CONDITION | WHO | WHEN | PDCA | ACTUAL RESULT |
|---|---|---|---|---|---|---|---|---|
| | | | | | | | P D A C | |
| | | | | | | | P D A C | |
| | | | | | | | P D A C | |
| | | | | | | | P D A C | |
| | | | | | | | P D A C | |

## A3 REPORT

Title
Hospital
Author
Date

Background

Current Condition

Target Condition

Analysis

Improvement Recommendations

Plan

Follow-up

## LEADER STANDARD WORK

---

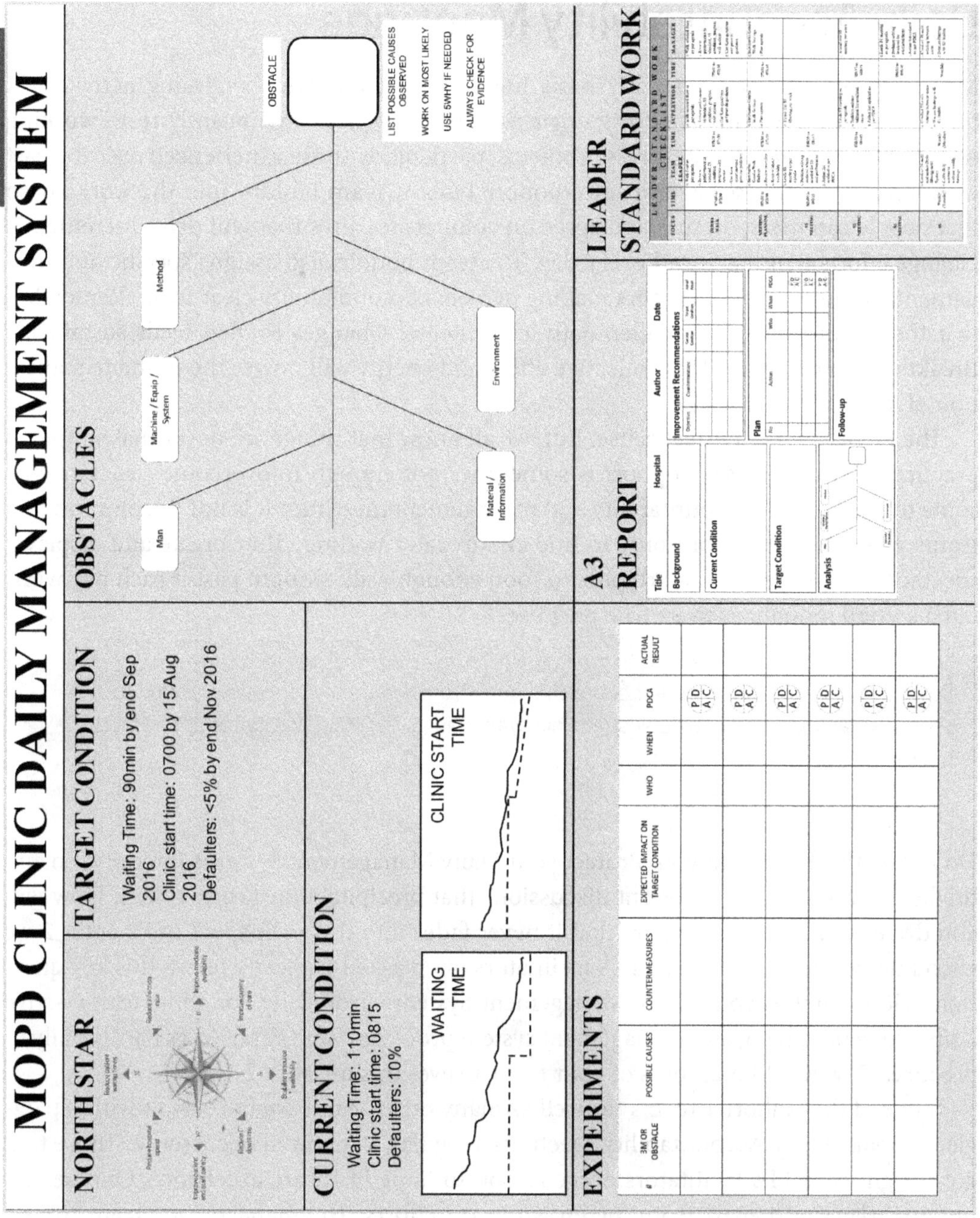

▲ Figure 8.3: Example of a richly populated Daily Management board that lifts a Daily Management System out of one-dimensional theory and into multi-dimensional, visual practice

# Daily Accountability Meetings

Managing operations on a daily basis literally means actively analysing activities at the coalface of performance *every single day*. Teams benefit significantly from working together to solve hot-off-the-press problems, particularly those experienced over the past 24 hours. To set this behaviour into motion, build a 'team huddle' into the workday so that people can meet, discuss and agree on countermeasures that will drive Incremental Change efforts that day—and every day. The team huddle also assigns specific and fundamental tasks to team members making personal accountability clear to all. Remember that the accumulation of smaller, daily Incremental Changes is what feeds sustainable Breakthrough Changes. This collective effort and energy will power the ultimate realisation of the North Star vision.

The theory makes perfect sense. But, we all know that things are never that simple in practice. Even significant support is sometimes not enough to overcome reluctance by some to ensure daily accountability and management meetings. It is not uncommon that teams give their all upfront only to find energy later waning. They create and display a spectacular management board only to soon enough walk straight past it each day without a second thought as to its true purpose.

> Beware of the Daily Management board that goes from being a respected watchdog to a toothless lapdog—pretty to look at and always on display but hardly capable of any sort of bite.

Do not let this happen to you. Protect your Daily Management System's integrity. Ensure the board leads to daily, relevant discussions that precipitate on-target action. How will you drive your system to ensure that it never fades into the wallpaper? In Chapter 2 we encountered the way in which LIA facilitators often asked Cohort 1 teams this key question: 'How 'daily' is your Daily Management System?' Ironically, for some teams active *daily* problem-solving and management system processes were exposed as hardly daily in practice. How would members of your team answer this question?

Some of the Cohort 1 teams (as well as many other teams we have dealt with) struggled to make Daily Accountability Meetings a regular, structured occurrence. Those that got it right gave LIA facilitators every reason to hope in future excellence. One person in particular stood apart from the crowd in his efforts. The manager of a team from a patient registration area in one of the hospitals designed an agenda (Figure 8.4) which he displayed on the Daily Management board making it visual and accessible to everyone ahead of the Daily Management meeting.

**Meeting**

Lean: Daily Management System

Time: 14h45 Date: 2015/11/04

Venue: Registration Area (Booking and Registration)

Present: A .L Mofokeng, T. Tshabalala, T. Zungu, K. Mukheli, S. N Thoko and H. Rahube

Agenda

| Items | details |
|---|---|
| 1. | Welcome |
| 2. | Issues of the day encounter/ Current conditions |
| 3. | Current obstacles and causes of action |
| 4. | Plan for tomorrow/ way forward |
| 5. | Closure |

▲ Figure 8.4: Example of a Daily Accountability Meeting agenda

Though it was the first time he was conducting a meeting of this nature he facilitated the session with enthusiasm and dedication. Well-prepared, he did not deviate from the agenda and listened to team comments with open-mindedness and genuine interest, all the while expertly guiding his people through the agenda points (Figure 8.5).

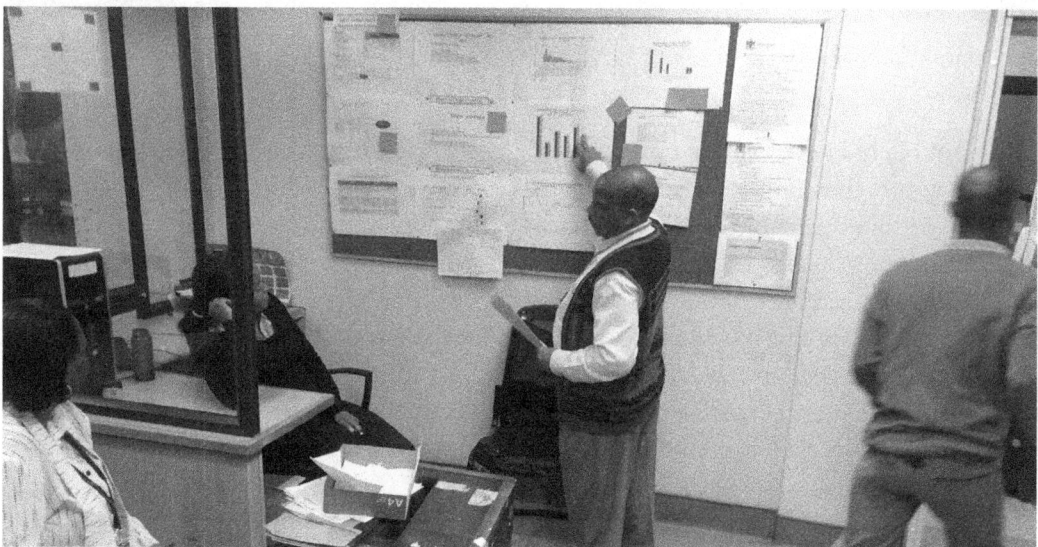

▲ Figure 8.5: A patient registration area manager discusses the Current Condition with the team during the Daily Accountability Meeting

He constructively directed the conversation towards obstacles that might hinder service on the day in question. To trigger the team to offer creative solutions he refreshed their insight into the meaning of Lean. Using an effective analogy—that of rocks blocking the flow of a river—he encouraged identification of registration area 'rocks' or waste that hindered the flow of service. He went so far as to use his laptop to share extracts from the Lean training he had undergone to trigger further discussion (Figure 8.6).

▲ Figure 8.6: The patient registration area manager takes the team through slides from his Lean training

The team offered detail on the obstacles they observed during the day. The manager was able to capture these onto the Fishbone Diagram in Figure 8.7 which ensured each would be dealt with in due course. The team then focused on a particular obstacle, in this case relating to the standard of the queue marshal's work. This made it easier to develop an action plan to address deviations from a desired standard and the visual plan was updated on the board. This also made the team realise that the queue marshal should have been part of the meeting and needed to be included in future meetings. The team had been coached by the manager, obstacles discussed and a countermeasure to improve on the queue marshal's duties, agreed on. All in all a very successful first meeting that lasted a total of 15 minutes!

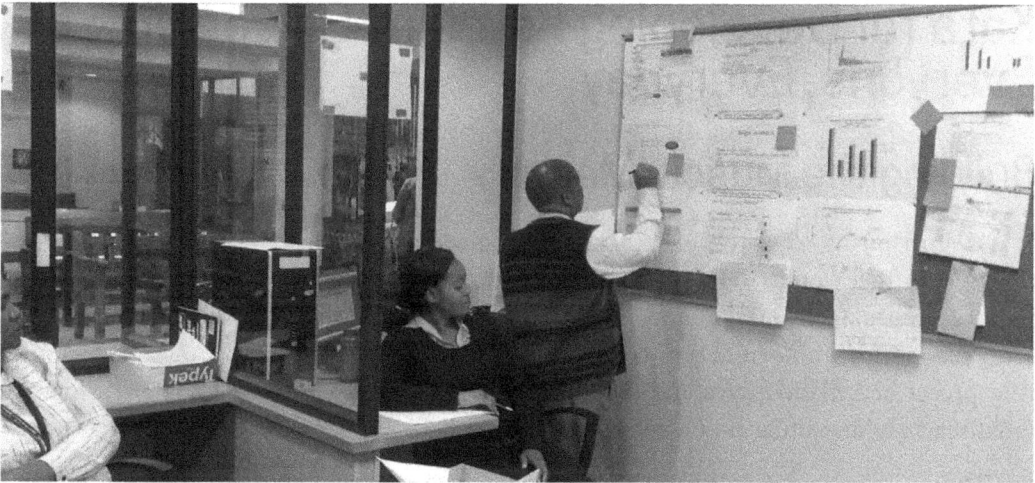

▲ Figure 8.7: The patient registration area manager captures the obstacles discussed prior to determining the course of action to be taken

Held regularly, these sorts of meetings encourage improvement discussions that become second nature among staff. Positive change is slowly and deliberately realised, one day at a time.

An effective Daily Accountability Meeting exhibits the following characteristics:

o It takes place at the same time each day—either before shift start or at shift end.
o A structured agenda guides the discussion and maintains efficient use of time.
o It starts and finishes on time.
o The meeting is long enough to allow for discussion but not so long as to interfere with patient service or workload (15 minutes is a good guideline).
o The meeting is well-attended. Poor attendance is properly dealt with.
o The meeting takes place with the team huddled around the Daily Management board.
o Though the meeting is chaired by a team leader or manager, the team actively participates in the discussions. Participants ask more questions than they are given answers (in the Socratic way). Over time, team members can even rotate this responsibility.
o The meeting is focused on matters directly affecting performance. Distinct effort is made to ensure that irrelevant or more general matters are discussed in other forums.
o Countermeasures and solutions generated through the discussion are immediately captured, and one person is made responsible for trialling the action (with team assistance where needed).
o A specific date is decided on for implementation of each countermeasure and includes time for a run through the PDCA cycle.
o Problems that cannot be solved in the meeting are escalated or assigned to a special session dedicated to tackling those particular challenges.
o The team is coached to focus on the process rather than the person carrying out the process.

# Kata for Developing Problem-Solvers in Everyone, Everyday

## Building the Muscle Memory

It is awe-inspiring to watch perfectly synchronised athletes carry out martial arts routines. From Taekwondo to Judo, Karate or Kickboxing, perfecting a martial arts discipline requires hours of dedication and practice. Those athletes willing to give it their all are soon set apart from normal trainees. Think about the precision with which they administer prescribed manoeuvres and the automatic responses with which a trained martial artist reacts to any situation or threat encountered. This is Kata.

More specifically, Kata is the choreographed set of movements typical of martial arts. It is the pattern of learned reactions that allows an athlete to defend against attack. When a student of the martial arts follows the pattern repeatedly, the relentless practice embeds the prescribed routines into muscle memory and changes them from conscious movements to automatic responses. Of course, when a student stops practicing, their ability to react automatically degenerates and they have to work hard to build their expertise up again.

Similarly, in achieving organisational Operational Excellence, learners use routine practices to build the muscle memory that eventually produce the automatic habits defined as Best Practice. As discussed in Chapter 2, when everyone follows the routines the sum of their habits creates the overall culture needed for change.

A Kata culture energises people to bravely block and deflect attacks of variation, obstacles and problems every day, in a sustainable way. To achieve this we need to implement the key new routines that feed this sort of improvement culture and turn our people into fearless, scientific problem-solvers. The routines that drive the Improvement Cycle feature two major components (Rother, 2011):

- o *Improvement Kata*
- o *Coaching Kata*

This formidable Kata combo develops mental agility, adaptability and strength in the same way as hours of blood, sweat and tears will condition a fighter's physical body ahead of attack. The Kata combination teaches employees tactics to protect themselves in times of battle to achieve the ultimate victory: the Target Condition. The combination of Improvement and Coaching Kata allows for the development and sharing of problem-solving skills and so strengthens people both individually and in teams.

# Building a Community of Scientists

Daniel Kahneman won the 2002 Nobel Prize in Economic Sciences. In his book *Thinking Fast and Slow* he describes how our brain works through both *fast* and *slow* thinking systems. The *fast* system is automatic, intuitive and often biased. It can therefore result in a dangerous overconfidence in certain facts, tricking us into believing we already have the answer. When this system kicks in it increases the risk of jumping to conclusions. On the other hand, the *slow* system allows for a more deliberate, analytical and conscious thought process, perfect for seeking out the facts before generating alternative opinions. By consciously choosing one of the systems we can approach a problem with less bias and more insight. Yet, they do not always operate separately. Sometimes when we engage the *slow* thinking system, a bump in the road might send us off into the *fast* thinking lane. Simple awareness of both systems helps us to adjust our behaviour while problem-solving. If you fall into the trap of jumping to conclusions, you are able to stop, reflect, and override the *fast* thinking system. How? Through scientific thinking.

Scientific thinking—a *slow* thinking system—is a wonderfully fulfilling, purposeful and knowledge-seeking approach that enhances learning. It intentionally aligns theory (what we think we will happen) and evidence (what actually happens) and allows

> The scientific mindset puts truth before knee-jerk and flawed conclusions.

for learning from the difference (Rother, 2011). We know that the PDCA cycle also follows this sort of deliberate *scientific* approach: we make a prediction, test it and, based on the results, adjust.

*Slow* thinking is vital to achieving both Incremental and Breakthrough Changes. Yet, scientific thinking is not something that always comes naturally. Rather, it is a skill anyone can learn and apply by using routines that rewire our old, ingrained and biased thinking patterns. It implies that we do not know everything and that, as knowledge-seekers, we have already understood that there is something new to discover. That is a fantastic point of departure for problem-solving. If you are tackling a new problem and feel you already have an answer before you have examined the evidence, you are likely heading down a dangerous *fast thinking* path. Imagine a doctor taking one look at a patient and prescribing a drug automatically and before examining a patient's symptoms. The scientific mindset puts truth before knee-jerk and flawed conclusions. It uses a cycle of experiments that iterate towards the Target Condition. Problems are more effectively solved and with less chance of recurrence. Every step of the way offers a chance at improved knowledge of the process.

Scientific thinking is social in nature. Where a group of people are working together and using a scientific mindset to achieve a common goal we start to see a *community of scientists* take form. In this way, everyone collectively solves problems every day in a scientific manner that is aligned to the North Star. Kata routines extend problem-solving capabilities across an organisation. They equip each person with the right way of thinking to drive the right reactions to challenges faced.

# Challenging the Threshold of Knowledge

> How much do you really learn when everything always works out as expected? And how realistic is that expectation anyway?

It is not easy to overcome a fear of failure. Many of us learn at an early age that failure is bad. So we put tremendous pressure on ourselves to get things right the first time we try them out. But how much do you really learn when everything always works out as expected? And how realistic is that expectation anyway? Let us neither aspire towards instant success nor catastrophic failure. In the context of Operational Excellence, our aim is to run controlled experiments where safety, quality and service are preserved, but where small failures provide a precious platform for learning. A good coach keeps a learner safe from disastrous consequences while encouraging frequent, quick turn-around, safe experiments that push boundaries and challenge norms while driving toward the Target Condition.

> Run controlled experiments where safety, quality and service are preserved, but where small failures provide a precious platform for learning.

What we currently know represents our Threshold of Knowledge. As we run experiments and apply principles of scientific thinking, we invariably learn something about a process we did not know before. Having extended what we know, we reach a new Threshold of Knowledge. When a leader or coach sets a new Target Condition they trigger a new cycle of experimentation geared at problem-solving. The learner now has a brand new opportunity to shift the Threshold of Knowledge to new heights. Figure 8.8 (adapted from Rother, 2011) illustrates the learning path undertaken. This cycle of aspirant and continuous learning develops *scientists* or Thinking People.

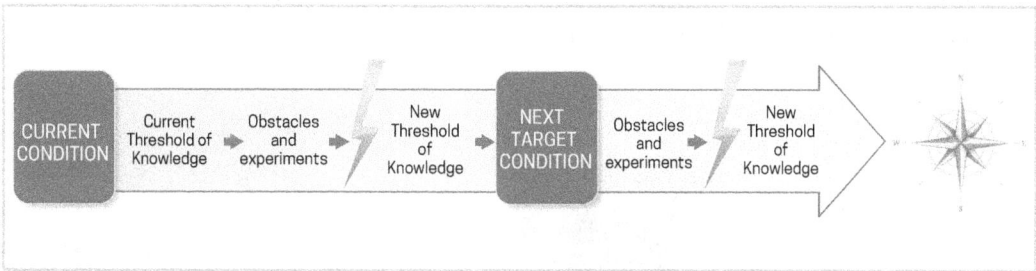

▲ Figure 8.8: Our Threshold of Knowledge shifts as we experiment, fail, learn, experiment again and so drive towards a Target Condition

To hit the ceiling of a Threshold of Knowledge is to arrive at the door of opportunity. Instead of accepting that what we know is all there is to know (and listening to the dictates of our *fast* thinking system), we climb atop the threshold and find a vantage point from which to see the rising sun of new levels of learning on the horizon. We then design an experiment that will provide fresh and valuable evidence from which to draw new conclusions (through our *slow* thinking system).

Let us first ask:

o What do we currently know?

o And, what do we still need to discover to take the next step towards the Target Condition?

Do not stagnate in the pool of comfort. Allowing a belief that what we know is sufficient will breed complacency. Be brave and propel yourself into unknown territory. Break through comfort zones and enhance your knowledge for your own benefit as well as that of the patient.

# Backwards Bicycles and Plastic Brains

Most of us learnt to ride a bicycle at an early age. We might have started out with training wheels and, as confidence built, bravely hopped onto an unsupported two-wheel bicycle. Notwithstanding a few bumps and scratches we then learnt to balance and fearlessly ride with the wind in our hair. Can you remember that feeling?

At first, a child has to concentrate hard on using practiced routines to stay on the bike. But eventually the skill is developed and riding a bike becomes second nature for life! The child has essentially created and reinforced a neural pathway in the brain that is forever unlocked and that makes riding a bicycle, well...as easy as riding a bicycle!

Destin Sandlin is an American engineer known for his online educational video series and successful YouTube channel *Smarter Every Day* (smartereveryday.com). One of his videos tells the story of the way in which a friend called Barney—a welder who liked to play jokes on engineers—challenged him to ride a bicycle he had modified. It operated in reverse to what one would expect. A normal bicycle turns left when you steer left and right when you steer right. This one was welded so that a left-turn of the handlebars turned the bicycle right, and vice versa. Destin was both utterly confounded and fascinated by what this trick-bike meant for rewiring the adult brain to unlearn a biased form of behaviour.

He decided on an experiment: was it was possible to carry out an activity that the brain recognised as learned and automatic—riding a bicycle—but with the added challenge of the new steering method? Could the brain be rewired to ride a bicycle in a completely counterintuitive way? At first Destin found riding the new bike impossible. He was unable to get his brain to direct his body to reverse the normal pattern of actions and practiced routines he had learnt as a child and could not ride this backwards bike without falling sideways. After many tumbles he came close to concluding that riding this bicycle was simply impossible. Then one day, after eight months of steadfast trying, he quite suddenly could ride it! The switch was profound.

He had over 8 months managed to carve out the new neural pathway needed to unlock the potential to perform this new skill. Yet, interestingly enough, the slightest distraction would cause him to forget how to ride the backwards bicycle and regress to old habits. And, once he had learned to ride the new bicycle in the new way, he was unable to automatically ride a normal bicycle in the old way. When he tried to do so, on the streets of Amsterdam, it took him 20 minutes to remember how to ride a normal bicycle—much to the amusement of bystanders! His brain needed time to unlock the old neural pathway that he had put away for months while he learnt to ride the backwards bike. With a little effort his memory of riding a normal bicycle—learnt at the age of six—returned!

He had set out to prove that he could free his brain from cognitive bias—the bias that says there is only one way to ride a bicycle. His adult brain was flexible enough to allow him to learn both methods with success and, once learned, access both neural pathways. Yet, he also showed that his brain could only cope with one bicycle-riding thought pathway at a time.

How do we apply this to Operational Excellence?

Do you agree that Destin's experiment represents an interesting manipulation of mental muscle memory? Do you see the potential of this research for changing old habits? If our brains prefer to prioritise one particular neural pathway or one way of carrying out an activity, how do we ensure we are channelling all of our efforts into the thought path that manifests our very best habit and behaviour?

Neuroscience has developed significantly over the past decade. Science no longer believes that the brain and our ways of thinking and consequent habits cannot change as we age. Research shows that our brains are in fact malleable, like plastic. Scientists call this phenomenon *neuroplasticity*. Given the right new routines, we can change the way we think—at any point of life. Although we may have firmly established patterns of thinking that might seem impossible to change, we can carve out new pathways in the brain through simply repeating new mental and physical exercises or routines.

Think about school children crushing grass underfoot in the same place and direction every day as they traverse a field to get to class. The repeated behaviour wears out a walking path where there once was none. Were they suddenly to walk a different part of the field, new paths would form there and the old path would fade until accessed again. The children walk one path at a time depending on their needs. In the same way, continually walking the path of a new way of thinking, new behaviours and the routines that result, in turn breed new habits.

We may have become accustomed to a specific way of thinking about problems, our work or our lives. Regardless of how things have always been done, we can use tools such as Improvement and Coaching Kata to introduce new and better routines and transform our employees into mentally powerful, problem-solving, plastic-brained, *slow* Thinking People.

# The Routines Underpinning the Improvement Cycle

Which habits and routines do we need to introduce to create new neural pathways in the brain to drive new improvement behaviours on the ground?

*Improvement Kata* and *Coaching Kata* are two distinct routines that run in parallel and set an Improvement Cycle into motion. Both routines begin with the coach (or leader) providing Clear Direction to the learner and targeting problem-solving to meet North Star expectations. Guided by the coach, the learner can grasp the Current Condition, define the next Target Condition, and iterate towards daily improved performance. This deliberate pattern of thinking forms the backbone of the Daily Management System and drives the Improvement Cycle.

A similar thought process underpins both The Improvement Cycle and A3 Thinking. Remember that A3 is based on the principles of PDCA and relies on a coach helping a learner to think through a problem in the *Socratic* way *before* attempting to solve a problem. The Improvement Cycle also relies on the guidance of a good coach. At each stage of the learning process, the coach helps the learner to develop key new routines that will drive new ways of thinking and acting. This cycle is distinct in that it occurs more frequently than the A3 cycle. It also plays out at process-level to deliver on Situational-tier (or S3-level) changes (refer to Chapter 5's 3S Model to refresh your memory on S1, S2 and S3).

Figure 8.9 describes the relationship between coach and learner, and the role played by each (adapted from Rother, 2011) during the Improvement Cycle.

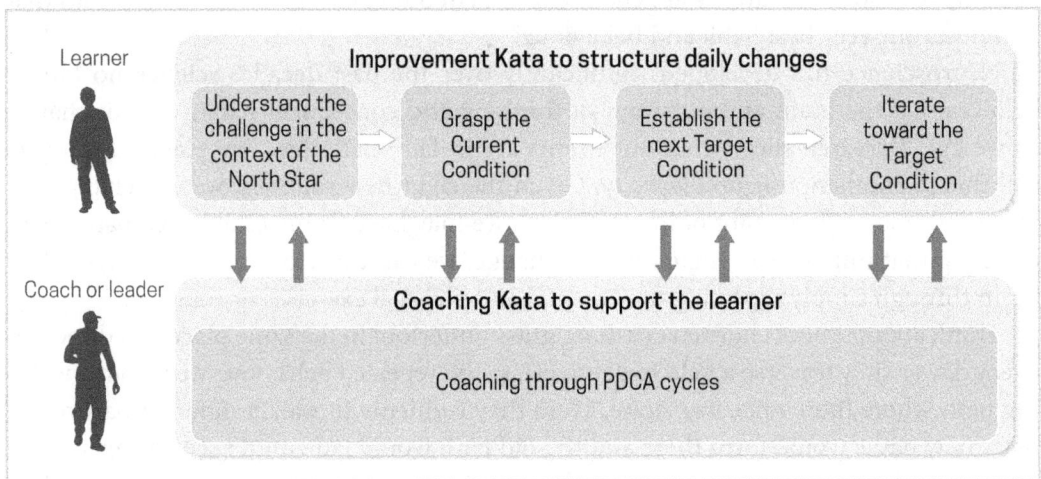

▲ Figure 8.9: The interaction between the coach and learner during an Improvement Cycle

A learner's problem-solving skills evolve through a coupling of scientific thinking and Kata (Figure 8.10) and relentless practice of new routines. This alliance significantly strengthens the Daily Management System.

| Scientific thinking | + | Kata routines | = | Effective problem-solving |

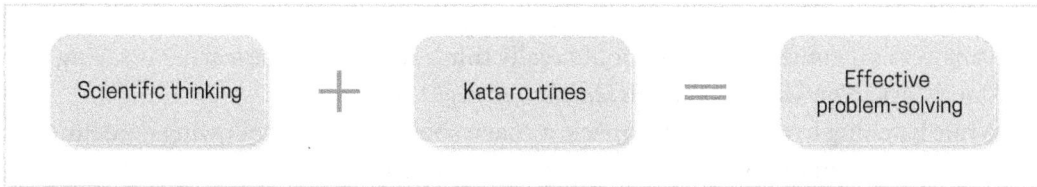

▲ Figure 8.10: A powerful equation for effective problem-solving

Chapter 6 introduced us to two approaches to coaching:

  o *A3 Thinking* to support Breakthrough Change (a Systemic or S2 focus) using the A3 reporting tool to structure the conversation.
  o *Coaching Kata* to support Incremental Change (a Situational or S3 focus) using the Coaching Kata card to structure the conversation.

The Coaching Kata card (Figure 8.11) illustrates the key questions a leader or coach follows to structure the conversation with the learner. But Coaching Kata is about so much more than just a card with a few questions on it. The coach must really pay attention to a learner's answers to ensure that their thinking flows correctly and follows the principles of scientific thinking.

**COACHING KATA**

**FIVE KEY QUESTIONS**

① What is the Target Condition?
② What is the Current Condition?

---turn card over if you have implemented an action---

③ What are the current obstacles preventing you from reaching the Target Condition? Which *one* are you working on?
④ What is the next action or next experiment to be tested? What results do you expect?
⑤ When can we 'go-see' the change and what we have learned?

**COACHING KATA**

**REFLECTION**

✓ What was your last action?

✓ What did you expect to happen?

✓ What actually happened? Did it work? If not, why not?

✓ What did you learn from taking this step?

---turn card over and go on with question 3---

▲ Figure 8.11: The Coaching Kata card

Instead of the coach just following the Coaching Kata card mechanically and accepting each answer as it comes, he or she should really think about what the learner is saying and constantly ask: *How can I define this learner's thought-pattern*?

While listening to a learner's feedback, a coach should keep the following guidelines in mind and use them to polish their follow-up questions (Adapted from Rosenthal, 2016):

o Can the learner articulate the Target Condition in relation to the North Star? How does their understanding influence patient satisfaction? Is there a clear link between what they are working on and the North Star strategy for change?

o Has a time frame or deadline been assigned to meeting the Target Condition? Is this period reasonable? It often takes achieving several interim Target Conditions to reach the ultimate North Star goal. Help the learner structure these interim achievements.

o Is the learner comparing apples with apples? Is the way the Target Condition is measured similar to the way in which the Current Condition was measured? If both are evaluated using the same indicators, then the process is relatively straightforward. If the Target Condition is not distinctly measureable but rather a pattern of work to be observed, more creative ways of comparing conditions may be required.

o How will a learner undertaking PDCA know that a target has been reached? How will the learner CHECK this? How will they know when they have reached a point where the outcome achieved is the outcome sought?

o A coach must ensure all ideas raised are heard and that learners feel respected while also maintaining focus on what matters in the present. Remember that this is a brainstorming process. Allow the learner to document as many obstacles as they wish. However, be sure to carefully scrutinise whichever obstacle a learner or team chooses to tackle at each learning stage. Can you see a clear relationship between overcoming this obstacle and reaching the Target Condition? Ensure an unambiguous link between obstacles tackled and the Target Condition. Novice learners will include obstacles that may have merit in their own right but that may not have the desired impact on the Target Condition once solved. Prioritise the obstacles that need immediate address and park the rest for another day.

o To get to the Target Condition, the learner will need to grasp the Current Condition. Getting to grips with possible causes of the current state often requires plenty of investigation and digging. Check that the learner has enough grit under their nails. Have they made sufficient effort to understand and dissect the Current Condition (without going so far as to risk *analysis paralysis*)?

o Ask the learner what they expected before trialling a countermeasure already implemented. What did they hope to learn from taking this step? Then go into the results. Help the learner to compare expected with actual results and identify how the learning process expands their experience beyond the current Threshold of Knowledge.

o Sometimes a coach's probing makes it apparent that a learner has used a ten-pound hammer on a two-pound job and planned unnecessarily large or complex steps to tackle a relatively small obstacle. A coach should probe the countermeasure with the right questions and simplify the process to accelerate interim wins.

The coach takes on the responsibility of engaging the learner and providing a level of support that slowly shifts the Threshold of Knowledge into new frontiers. Constantly raising the threshold adds momentum and energy to the Improvement Cycle and so brings the Daily Management System to life—over and over again.

> If the learner has not learned, then the teacher has not taught.

## Following Kata during the Gemba Walk

Regular Gemba Walks form part of the Leader Standard Work and is the perfect time to review the Improvement Kata and offer the Coaching Kata. Any Gemba Walk becomes that much more effective when guided by the Kata routines. Together these help a leader to standardise the improvement conversation and ensure everyone is learning the same continuous improvement language. Even on days when visitors approach the area to learn from what has been achieved the feedback is easily delivered and already prepared. Impromptu visits are no longer a challenge since leaders and teams already have their fingers on the pulse and can provide accurate feedback in a heartbeat.

One of the most inspiring Gemba Walks to be observed at a Cohort 1 hospital saw a team member use the Coaching Kata card (Figure 8.12) to structure the conversation that took place at an out-patient clinic (Figure 8.13). The feedback was well-prepared, results-driven and elicited positive comments from those present who could see first-hand the progress achieved. Everyone could relate to the common language spoken. Teams from the four Cohort 1 hospitals were easily able to collaborate on learning.

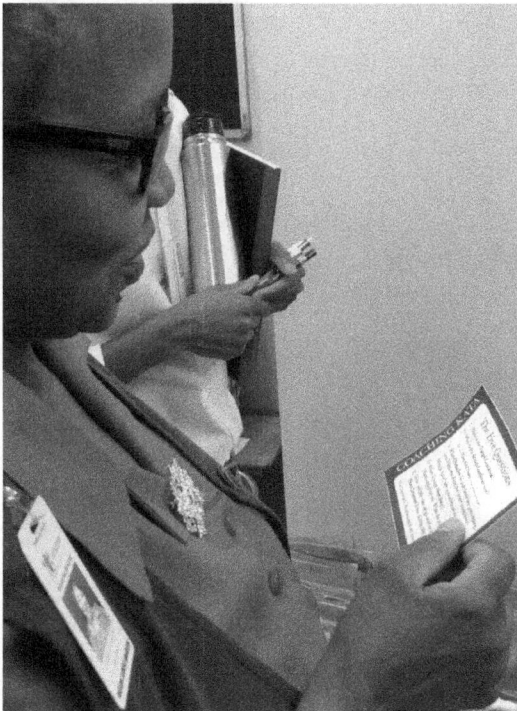

No matter the hospital, the card's questions were followed to the letter. At another hospital the team huddled around the Daily Management board where visual elements of the Daily Management System could be referred to while feedback was given. The discussion was evidence-based and focused on achieving an improvement in the management of capacity and inputs that affected patient waiting times (Figure 8.14). In Figure 8.15 the team from the Patient Affairs department explains the Target Condition defined for their area—again following the Coaching Kata card's questions.

◀ Figure 8.12: The structure of the Coaching Kata card gives teams confidence to proceed through a learning conversation

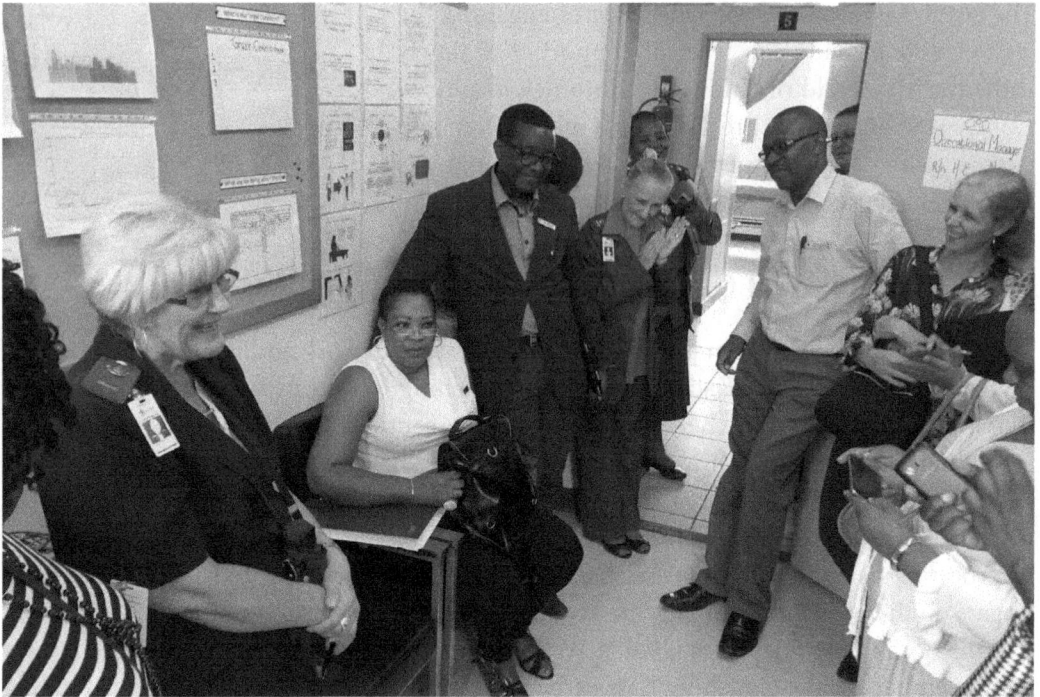

▲ **Figure 8.13:** The Gemba Walk was structured, focused and the Cohort 1 visitors were utterly engaged by the feedback prepared

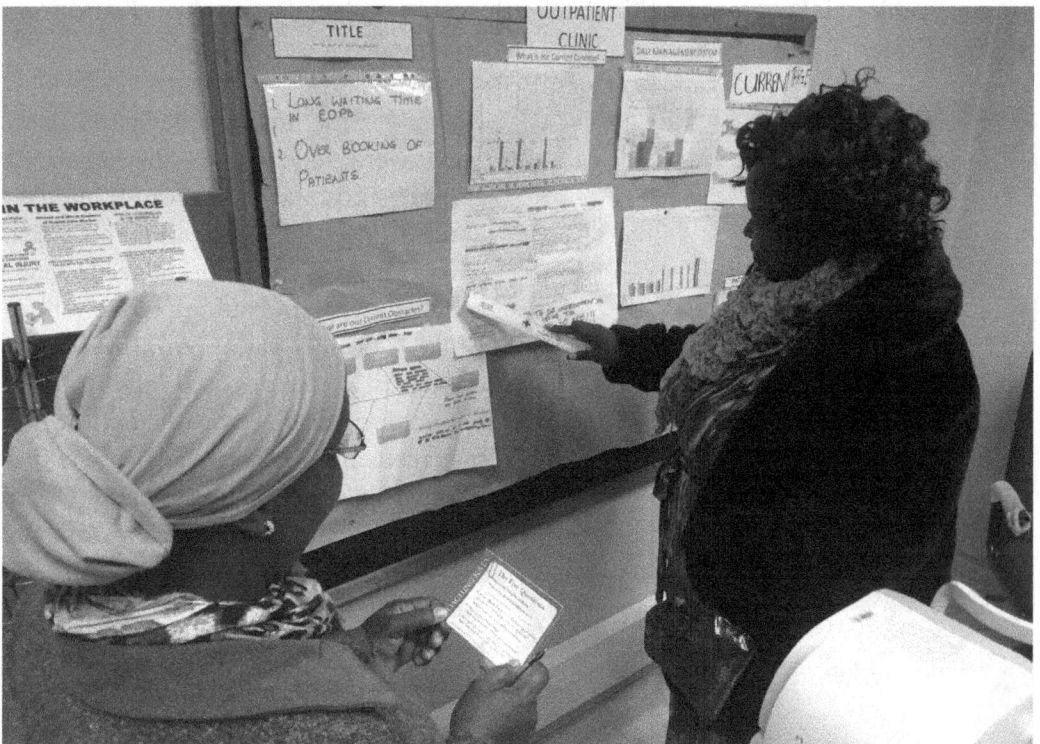

▲ **Figure 8.14:** A review of the Coaching Kata questions during a Gemba Walk to an EOPD Clinic

▲ **Figure 8.15**: A Gemba Walk to the registration and payment area leading with a Target Condition discussion

Gemba Walk participants visited the MOPD Clinic team and followed the Coaching Kata questions. They listened to the analysis of the Current Condition as defined by average patient waiting time, clinic start times and number of patients seen. Visitors were impressed by the layout and content of the Daily Management System which had been purposefully designed to suit the area (Figure 8.16). Thereafter the participants walked to the pharmacy to follow the same process of questioning. Here the area manager explains the challenges they face in accurately measuring patient waiting times (Figure 8.17) while visitors offer their input. The visits are effective, informative and stimulate cross-learning.

▲ Figure 8.16: The MOPD Clinic presents the Current Condition

▲ Figure 8.17: The pharmacy manager answers the Coaching Kata questions

# Preserving the Fundamentals

Imagine that you are creating a work of art. Kata is the mould, the protective and form-defining shell that surrounds delicate new routines and thought-processes when they are fragile and taking shape. But once new patterns have been internalised into people's behaviours and habits, the Kata mould can be gently removed to reveal the hard-wired new habit that has set solidly, deep inside—now made to last. And, though the Kata mould's support is no longer needed it remains important to care for our work of art. Just as we polish a valuable sculpture and protect it from harm, so too do we pay attention to the principles guiding new improvement routines achieved to ensure they stay intact and able to function.

The PDCA cycle is a die-hard principle of utmost importance. As mentioned in Chapter 6, there are many ways to solve a problem. Different methods call for different tools and there are many good tools on hand from which to choose. Be conscious of selecting the right tools. Allow your teams to be guided by a knowledge-seeking approach and thought process based on hard evidence. Be sure to experiment with the countermeasures developed and repeatedly test them against the Target Condition desired. Do all you can to mitigate against the risk of superficial problem-solving which invites the same problems back time and again and threatens to derail your organisation's improvement efforts and chance at excellence.

Chapter 6 introduced us to the principles that underpin Standard Work—we first perform the work to the desired standard and then improve on our processes and standardise them anew. Improvement and Coaching Kata follow the same pattern. It is recommended you follow the theory behind Kata very precisely at the beginning of an improvement process. Only once new neural pathways and new routines have stabilised is it safe to make adjustments to the Kata combo to suit your specific organisational needs.

It may take several months for your Daily Management System to stabilise and perform to the expected standard. Encourage faith in the process and support the new routines employed and your scientists, your teams of Thinking People. Allow them the space to learn from mistakes made and, with each new attempt at change, gaze boldly forward towards the twinkling North Star vision. Trust that, given a little time, the system will deliver value for your organisation, your patients and employees—one meaningful day at a time.

## PRACTICAL ACTIVITY: Achieving Daily Incremental Change

Allow for several attempts at getting the Daily Management System working optimally. Start with optimising the Daily Management display board and ensure it is updated routinely. This board will inform the correct approach to new 'Thinking' routines and practices. Ensure that you:

▸ Select a suitable area for displaying the Daily Management board.

▸ Decide on and source the material needed to make the board and any particular display areas it will feature. Decide on what you will use to attach any documents, images or information to the board.

▸ Together with your team, develop a mock-up of the display. Agree on key focus areas and designate each a portion of the board. What will be displayed under each? How will it be displayed?

▸ Set up the board according to the design agreed on by the team and hang it in the chosen area.

▸ Agree on accountability. Who will update each area of the board? What information is required for the updates? How often will updates happen? Provide the team with training so that all understand the purpose of the board and how it supports the Daily Management System in achieving daily Incremental Change. Encourage everyone to get involved.

▸ Agree on the timing of Daily Accountability Meetings and design an agenda through which to structure the meetings (refer to the template provided in Part III).

▸ Initiate Daily Accountability Meetings that follow the agenda. Allow the team time to internalise all new routines that support the Daily Management System.

▸ Encourage the team to follow the Improvement Kata and initiate the Improvement Cycle.

▸ During Gemba Walks, feedback or coaching sessions, follow the Coaching Kata card's questions and encourage the team's learners to prepare ahead of time and respond in a structured, *slow thinking* and scientific way. Ensure that day-to-day changes achieve the team's goals and align with the department or organisation's North Star expectations.

# 9 THE DIFFERENCE

Think about the philosophies, concepts, tools and techniques presented in this book. Do they really make a difference? Yes! If you commit to breaking apart the fences that surround your comfort zones you will experience significant reward for your efforts. Trust that tangible and intangible benefits are yours for the taking—if you are bold enough to reach for them.

## Will You Grow?

Allow yourself the space to think for a moment. Did you enjoy the learning journey taken while reading this book? Have you considered the new dimensions of thinking suggested? Have you gained new ways of approaching complex situations? Have you plotted unchartered routes to new destinations? Have you identified new ways of approaching the storms faced by your organisation? Have you put plans in place to support the processes needed to transport you from the Current Condition to the prosperous waters of the Target Condition? So many questions, but if you answered 'yes' to any of them, then you are not the same person that you were when you first took hold of this book. Keep going.

## Will Your People Grow?

The final GDOH Service Delivery Improvement Kaizen event is the stuff of which memories are made. Pride and unity suffused the atmosphere. In Figure 9.1 teams gathered together to reflect as one for the last time, surprising guests with a remarkable and spontaneous rendition of Bill Withers' timeless song *Lean On Me*. Rich voices proclaimed *You just call on me brother, when you need a hand. We all need somebody to lean on. I just might have a problem that you'll understand. We all need somebody to lean on.* A collective consciousness sang loud and clear that everyone had gained—both personally and professionally—from

▲ Figure 9.1: The team sings 'Lean on Me' with their own variations on lyrics

being a part of the GDOH initiative and that their hearts were in it for the long run. Imagine your people feeling the same way. Not only will you improve service delivery but also the lives of your colleagues, staff and team members—the people whose efforts give your healthcare facility its very oxygen.

# Eye-Witness to Change

A profound transformation in people who travelled the GDOH Initiative journey with the LIA team was observed. At first, no one knew what was expected of them or what lay ahead. Together we overcame the fear of the unknown as we led people, held their hands and lifted them up and over initial obstacles. Sometimes people dug in their heels. Coaching (and coaxing) encouraged even non-believers, reluctant participants or apprehensive team members to give us the benefit of the doubt, and follow. Then—the shift that makes a Lean coach's work worthwhile.

When people experience the benefits of Lean Management's tools and processes and the changes in their ways of thinking and acting, they willingly succumb to growth. We start with a push system, in

> It all starts with a push system which evolves into a pull system. Employees begin to ask for more.

which employees are coerced into taking part in improvement. It shifts into a pull system that sees employees ask for more and seek support to feed their improvement aspirations. People begin themselves to ask a key question: 'Where to from here?'

# How Did Patients Benefit?

Did the GDOH Initiative make a difference to patient service? Waiting times were slashed in every model area. Granted, some teams are still fighting to stabilise their targets, but all improved. The results illustrated in Table 9.1 are evidence of these tangible benefits.

Did the patients notice? In early 2016 and in true 'go-see' style, I sat among patients at one of the Cohort 1 hospitals quietly observing and later chatting to people in the queue. A few of them had not noticed any real change and explained their stance giving me wonderful input for future change efforts. But a number of the patients who spent time with me explained how they visited the hospital every few weeks and testified that waiting times were much reduced. They emphasised a definite improvement. No voice sings a healthcare facility's praises as truly as a The Voice of the Patient.

Those working in public healthcare should never tire of gathering data directly from those served. Use the Voice of the Patient as a way to give weekly feedback to employees. On occasion, compliments received by Cohort 1 teams were shown to me by elated model area managers (Figure 9.2). The Compliment Form depicted here is true cause for celebration. It is also the ultimate proof that Lean Management has much to offer in improving public healthcare.

**WAITING TIME RESULTS**

| HEALTHCARE FACILITY | MODEL AREA | CURRENT CONDITION BEFORE RPIW (min) | TARGET CONDITION FOR END OF RPIW | ACTUAL CONDITION AT THE END OF RPIW (min) | % IMPROVEMENT AFTER RPIW | TARGET CONDITION ACHIEVED? | LAST RESULTS CAPTURED (min) (UP TO 15 MONTHS AFTER RPIW) | TARGET CONDITION FOR 12 MONTHS | TOTAL % CHANGE AT LAST RESULT CAPTURED | TARGET CONDITION ACHIEVED? | COMMENTS |
|---|---|---|---|---|---|---|---|---|---|---|---|
| HOSPITAL 1 | REGISTRATION | 276 | 10% | 102 | 63% | YES | 38 | 30% | 86% | YES | Registration and MOPD have made marked improvement which is now stable and presents the opportunity to revise the Target Condition. Pharmacy stabilised to under 30min but this has escalated again in 2016. Investigations into Patient Demand Patterns are in progress and plans to reduce waiting times are underway – the teams require concerted effort to sustain previous improvements made. |
| | CLINIC | 211 | 10% | 183 | 13% | YES | 115 | 20% | 45% | YES | |
| | PHARMACY | 79 | 25% | 61 | 23% | NO - 2% SHORT | 54 | 50% | 32% | NO - 18% SHORT | |
| HOSPITAL 2 | REGISTRATION | 143 | 10% | 43 | 70% | YES | 59 | 30% | 59% | YES | Patient waiting time stabilised in registration despite an increase in the patient numbers. Significant doctor availability improvements in the clinic and excellent progress in the pharmacy, but ongoing improvement remains a challenge and a focus. |
| | CLINIC | 112 | 10% | 74 | 34% | YES | 96 | 20% | 14% | NO - 6% SHORT | |
| | PHARMACY | 40 | 25% | 13 | 68% | YES | 24 | 50% | 40% | NO - 10% SHORT | |
| HOSPITAL 3 | REGISTRATION | 77 | 10% | 55 | 29% | YES | 61 | 30% | 21% | NO - 9% SHORT | Registration has been unstable but steadily improving overall. The clinic has been stable for a few months and they are ready for new Target Conditions. The pharmacy was stable for a time, but after relocating to a new facility processes destabilised and they are actively working at bringing them back under control. |
| | CLINIC | 112 | 10% | 83 | 26% | YES | 87 | 20% | 22% | YES | |
| | PHARMACY | 15 | 25% | 5 | 67% | YES | 15 | 50% | 0% | NO - 50% SHORT | |
| HOSPITAL 4 | REGISTRATION | 137 | 10% | 86 | 37% | YES | 37 | 30% | 73% | YES | Registration is ready for revised Target Conditions. The clinic Current Condition was measured on a quiet day, whereas the Actual Results were established on a busy day. Shortage of doctors at the time of the results measurement led to longer waiting times. Increase in patient numbers and improvements in Patient Admin processes compounded the pressure downstream. Therefore the overall result was an actual improvement although the results reflect the opposite. |
| | CLINIC | 45 | 10% | 21 | 53% | YES | 50 | 20% | -11% | NO - 31% SHORT | |
| | PHARMACY | 64 | 25% | 41 | 36% | YES | 42 | 50% | 34% | NO - 16% SHORT | |

*Different methods were employed in the measurement of waiting time at the facilities. Results can therefore not be compared at an inter-hospital level.

◄ **Table 9.1**: Results and comments captured for the GDOH Service Delivery Improvement Initiative

**health and**
**social development**
Department: Health and Social Development
GAUTENG PROVINCE

CHRIS HANI BARAGWANATH ACADEMIC HOSPITAL
Quality management department
New building , first floor
Tel: 011 933 8925/933/741
Fax: 011 933 8906
Share cell: 0840 002 721

COMPLIMENT FORM

Name: ......................................................................

Address: ...................................................................

Telephone number: ......................................................

Age: ........................................................................

Sex: ........................................................................

Ward: ......................................................................

File number: ..............................................................

Date: .......................................................................

What an excellent Service. Quicker
than I expected.
KEEP UP WITH THE GOOD WORK!!
HALALA Chris Baragwanath
Halala!!

Thank you

▲ Figure 9.2: A compliment received for outstanding service

# Your Big Picture

Even the smallest difference will add substance to the bigger, North Star picture we are building. Always remember how substantial Lean Thinking's collective efforts really are and the butterfly effect at work (Figure 9.3):

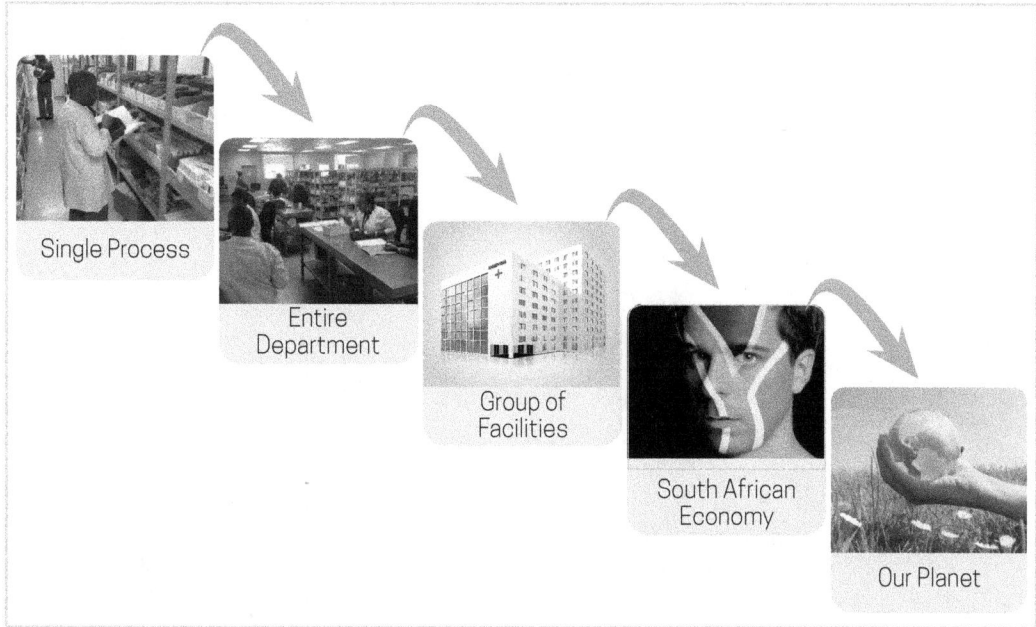

▲ Figure 9.3: The butterfly effect at work when you make a difference

| You may have just begun. |
| You may only be improving one small process. |
| You may only be improving one department. |
| You may only be improving one facility. |
| You may only be improving one group of facilities. |

Wherever your focus and no matter how small you think your efforts are, remember that you are not only making a difference to your area of control but also to your patients, the society that surrounds your facility and your country as a whole. You are setting new benchmarks for future generations to improve upon, one process at a time.

Now, this is Purpose worth spending time on. Go ahead and *make a difference.*

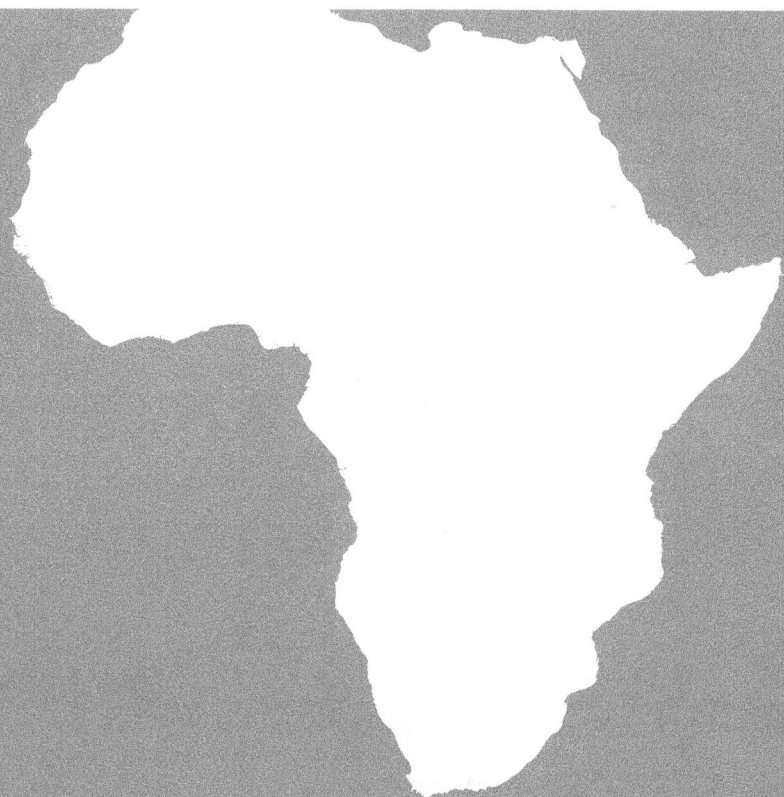

# PART III

EXAMPLES AND TEMPLATES

## FACILITY-LEVEL
### Monthly Steering Committee Agenda

**FREQUENCY**: 3rd Tuesday of every month at 2pm
**LOCATION**: Start in Patient Affairs Registration Area
**DURATION**: 2 hours
**CHAIRPERSON**: Dr. B. Maluleke (CEO)
**ATTENDEES**: Mr. B. Hlongwane (Patient Affairs); Ms. J. Mecer (Quality); Dr. S. Vilakazi (Clinical Services); Mr. C. Mhlangu (Pharmacy); Ms. E. Jackson (Human Resources); Dr. D. Moloi (Clinical Services); Ms. E. Khumalo (Nursing)

**PURPOSE**: Evaluate progress
Guide and define next steps
Remove obstacles

| NO. | AGENDA ITEM | DURATION | RESPONSIBLE |
|---|---|---|---|
| 1 | Welcome and attendance | 3 min | BM |
| 2 | Patient Affairs Gemba Walk<br>• Kata questions (DMS)<br>• A3 feedback (Kaizen)<br>• Obstacles and escalations | 20 min | BH |
| 3 | OPD Clinic Gemba Walk<br>• Kata questions (DMS)<br>• A3 feedback (Kaizen)<br>• Obstacles and escalations | 20 min | SV |
| 4 | Pharmacy Gemba Walk<br>• Kata questions (DMS)<br>• A3 feedback (Kaizen)<br>• Obstacles and escalations | 20 min | CM |
| 5 | Actions from last meeting | 30 min | BM |
| 6 | Target Condition to Current Condition review: North Star indicators | 10 min | BM |
| 7 | New risks and escalations | 8 min | ALL |
| 8 | Update new actions | 8 min | BM |
| 9 | Next meeting and close | 1 min | |

▲ **Appendix 1:** Facility-Level Monthly Steering Committee Agenda

## DEPARTMENT-LEVEL

## Weekly Meeting Agenda

**FREQUENCY:** Every Tuesday at 9am

**LOCATION:** Patient Affairs Daily Management Board

**DURATION:** 1 hour

**CHAIRPERSON:** Mr. B. Hlongwane (Patient Affairs Manager)

**ATTENDEES:** Mr. J. Ndlovu (File Storage Leader); Mr. A. Ledwaba (Registration Leader); Mr. P. Molape (Cashier Leader)

**PURPOSE:** Evaluate progress
Guide and define next steps
Remove obstacles

| NO. | AGENDA ITEM | DURATION | RESPONSIBLE |
|-----|-------------|----------|-------------|
| 1 | Welcome and attendance | 1 min | BH |
| 2 | File Storage Gemba Walk<br>• Kata questions (DMS)<br>• Obstacles and escalations | 10 min | JN |
| 3 | Registration Gemba Walk<br>• Kata questions (DMS)<br>• Obstacles and escalations | 10 min | AL |
| 4 | Cashier Gemba Walk<br>• Kata questions (DMS)<br>• Obstacles and escalations | 10 min | PM |
| 5 | Actions from last meeting | 10 min | BH |
| 6 | A3 feedback for Patient Affairs | 10 min | BH |
| 7 | Update new actions | 8 min | BH |
| 8 | Next meeting and close | 1 min | |

▲ **Appendix 2:** Weekly Accountability Meeting Agenda

| | TEAM-LEVEL<br>Daily Meeting Agenda | | |
|---|---|---|---|

**FREQUENCY**: Every day at 7am
**LOCATION**: Registration Daily Management Board
**DURATION**: 15 minutes
**CHAIRPERSON**: Mr. A. Ledwaba (Registration Leader)
**ATTENDEES**: Mr. F. Sejake (Clerk); Ms. T. Mhlapho (Clerk); Ms. J. James (Clerk); Mr. N. Mzimba (Queue Marshal)
**PURPOSE**: To manage daily operations and solve problems as a team

| NO. | AGENDA ITEM | DURATION | RESPONSIBLE |
|---|---|---|---|
| 1 | Welcome and attendance | 1 min | AL |
| 2 | Kata questions<br>• Target Condition<br>• Current Condition<br>• Reflection<br>• Current Obstacles<br>• Experiments<br>• Escalations | 8 min | AL; FS; TM; JJ; NM |
| 3 | Update new actions | 4 min | FS |
| 4 | Plan for the next 24 hours | 2 min | AL |
| 5 | Close | | |

▲ **Appendix 3**: Daily Accountability Meeting Agenda

## BASIC 5S AUDIT SHEET

| 5S STAGE | NO. | AUDIT CHECK | IMPROVEMENT AREAS | SCORE | | |
|---|---|---|---|---|---|---|
| | | | | 1 | 2 | 3 |
| SORT | 1 | All equipment, consumables and items necessary to service patients are clearly located and easily accessed. | | | | |
| | 2 | Items of secondary importance are allocated to a holding area or archive. Responsibility has been allocated to ensure its maintenance and upkeep. | | | | |
| | 3 | A clear policy guides the regular discard of unnecessary items. | | | | |
| | 4 | The area is audited weekly for SORT OUT opportunities and these are added to a clearly visible action board. | | | | |
| SHINE | 5 | Necessary items are clean and fit for purpose. | | | | |
| | 6 | Cleaning schedules follow regular routines. | | | | |
| | 7 | The floor area is clean and free of dust and litter. Cupboards, storage areas, drawers, keyboard and mouse sets, desks etc. are clean. Walls, windows, lights are clean and in good condition. Tea rooms, rest areas, meeting areas are clean and hygienic. Cables are properly bundled and free of dust. | | | | |
| | 8 | The area is audited weekly for SHINE opportunities and these are added to a visible action board. | | | | |
| SET IN ORDER | 9 | All essential items are:<br>• Located according to frequency of use<br>• Labelled for ease of retrieval<br>• Laid out so as to reduced motion and time waste<br>• Inventory monitored to ensure min and max levels are maintained | | | | |
| | 10 | Working areas are properly demarcated and labelled. | | | | |
| | 11 | There are well-marked storage areas for all items e.g. files, medicines, consumables, archives, waste, kitchen containers etc. The manner of marking chosen highlights a missing item's absence. | | | | |
| | 12 | Regular-use items are kept close to where they are needed. All documentation, standards and procedures are located close to the working area and are clearly demarcated. | | | | |
| | 13 | Containers are safely stacked. | | | | |
| | 14 | Waste containers are clearly marked, stored and segregated. | | | | |
| | 15 | The area is audited weekly for SET IN ORDER opportunities and these are added to a visible action board. | | | | |

**TOTAL SCORE OUT OF 45 AND %**

▲ **Template 1**: Basic 5S Audit Sheet

| NO. | AUDIT CHECK | IMPROVEMENT AREAS | 1<br>Not in place | 2<br>Partially in place | 3<br>In place |
|---|---|---|---|---|---|
| 1 | North Star goals are clear and cascade through leadership levels to guide all team goals. Teams can see how their individual goals contribute to the bigger picture strategy. | | | | |
| 2 | The area is audited weekly for 5S opportunities. These are updated on Daily Management System visuals and action plans. 5S consistently improves with time. | | | | |
| 3 | Input and output measures are defined and visually depicted on the Daily Management board. Both the Current Condition and Target Condition are clearly defined and updated. | | | | |
| 4 | Current obstacles and root causes are illustrated through Fishbone Diagrams and answers to 5 Why questions. Obstacles dealt with are removed from the list and fresh obstacles added for attention. | | | | |
| 5 | Countermeasures to address obstacles that hinder the achievement of the Target Condition are clear and tracked using PDCA. There is clarity on actions to standardise and actions to remove or revise. | | | | |
| 6 | Action plans define who will do what and by when. These plans are updated daily. Actions that do not achieve the desired outcomes trigger coaching by team leaders. Escalation and feedback loops are evident. | | | | |
| 7 | Leader Standard Work is visual and up to date in each area. The leader follows standard practices and regular routines are evident. Process-level Standard Work is visual and up-to-date. Leaders and employees are able to compare the Current Condition to the latest standard with ease. | | | | |
| 8 | The visuals illustrate a focus on both short-term (Incremental Change) and long-term (Breakthrough Change) tracking. | | | | |
| 9 | The Improvement Cycle allows for at-a-glance analysis of Current Condition metrics, daily problem-solving activities, countermeasures employed, the thought-process that follows PDCA and the resultant change in performance that results from these efforts. | | | | |
| 10 | Daily Accountability Meetings take place according to the agenda displayed on the Daily Management board. | | | | |
| TOTAL SCORE OUT OF 30 AND % | | | | | |

▲ Template 2: Visual Management Checklist

| Time | DAY 1 | Time | DAY 2 | Time | DAY 3 | Time | DAY 4 | Time | DAY 5 |
|---|---|---|---|---|---|---|---|---|---|
| 08h00 to 10h00 | Overview and preparation. Identify team leader and time keeper. | 08h00 to 10h00 | Define Current Condition through Value Stream Map, Spaghetti Diagram, data-gathering, current patterns of work, bottlenecks and obstacles. | 08h00 to 10h00 | Identify key obstacles affecting patient waiting times Identify causes. Discuss possible countermeasures. | 08h00 to 10h00 | Implement countermeasures, conduct experiments, evaluate progress (using PDCA) and adjust where necessary. | 08h00 to 10h00 | Finalise experimenting with any additional countermeasures agreed on at the end of from Day 4. Complete storyboard and put up on walls. |
| 10h00 to 10h20 | Tea | 10h00 to 10h20 | Tea | 10h00 to 10h20 | Tea | 10h00 to 10h20 | Tea | 10h00 to 10h20 | Tea |
| 10h20 to 10h45 | Introduce team to staff in the focus area and brief staff. | 10h20 to 12h30 | Continue to develop Current Condition | 10h20 to 12h30 | Continue with analysis. | 10h20 to 12h30 | Continue with PDCA-experiment cycles. | 10h20 to 10h40 | Prepare for presentation. |
| 10h45 to 12h30 | Go-see and ask questions (always with respect). Start Value Stream Map. | | | | | | | 10h40 to 12h30 | Conduct mock presentations. |
| 12h30 to 13h15 | Lunch | 12h30 to 13h15 | Lunch | 12h30 to 13h15 | Lunch | 12h30 to 13h15 | Lunch | 12h30 to 13h15 | Lunch |
| 13h15 to 15h00 | Go-see, ask questions (always with respect). Develop Value Stream Map. Develop plan for Day 2. | 13h15 to 14h30 | Continue to develop Current Condition | 13h15 to 15h00 | Develop action plan for Day 4 and prepare for staff briefing. | 13h15 to 14h30 | Continue with PDCA-experiment cycles. | 13h15 to 13h30 | Final preparations and 5S of the room. |
| | | 14h30 to 15h15 | Consolidate the day's findings. Make findings visual and plan a briefing session with focus area staff. Develop a plan for Day 3. | | | 14h30 to 15h00 | Review results of the experiments and update the storyboard | 13h30 to 13h40 | Master Facilitator to introduce teams and welcome guests. |
| | | | | 15h00 to 15h30 | Brief model area staff and discuss proposed countermeasures to be implemented on Day 4. Allow 15min for questions. | 15h00 to 15h30 | Gather input from staff: • what worked well? • what did not work? • possible countermeasures to try on Day 5? | 13h40 to 14h00 | Team 1 feedback. |
| 15h00 to 16h00 | Meet in boardroom to debrief and explain your plans for Day 2 (who will do what?). Confirm Day 2 agenda. | 15h15 to 15h30 | Brief model area staff. | | | | | 14h00 to 14h20 | Team 2 feedback. |
| | | 15h30 to 16h00 | Meet in boardroom to debrief and explain your plans for Day 3 (who will do what?). Confirm Day 3 agenda. | 15h30 to 16h00 | Meet in boardroom to debrief and explain your plans for Day 4 (who will do what?). Confirm Day 4 agenda. | 15h30 to 16h00 | Meet in boardroom to debrief and explain your plans for Day 5 (who will do what?). Confirm Day 5 agenda. | 14h20 to 14h40 | Team 3 feedback. |
| | | | | | | | | 14h40 to 15h00 | Questions and Master Facilitator's closing. |
| | | | | | | | | 15h00 to 1530 | Way forward, questionnaires and certificates. |
| 16h00 | Close | 16h00 | Close | 16h00 | Close | 16h00 | Close | 15h30 | Close |

▲ **Template 3:** RPIW Pocket Agenda

| Title | Facility | Author | Date |
|---|---|---|---|
| **Background** | | **Improvement Recommendations** | |
| **Current Condition** | | | |
| **Target Condition** | | **Plan** | |
| **Analysis** | | **Follow-up** | |

▲ Template 4: A3 Report

INSERT GRAPH TITLE

INSERT MONTH

| | | 31 |
| --- | --- | 30 |
| | | 29 |
| | | 28 |
| | | 27 |
| | | 26 |
| | | 25 |
| | | 24 |
| | | 23 |
| | | 22 |
| | | 21 |
| | | 20 |
| | | 19 |
| | | 18 |
| | | 17 |
| | | 16 |
| | | 15 |
| | | 14 |
| | | 13 |
| | | 12 |
| | | 11 |
| | | 10 |
| | | 9 |
| | | 8 |
| | | 7 |
| | | 6 |
| | | 5 |
| | | 4 |
| | | 3 |
| | | 2 |
| | | 1 |

INSERT UNIT OF MEASURE

▲ **Template 5:** Daily Graph

INSERT GRAPH TITLE

INSERT UNIT OF MEASURE

| | WEEK 1 | WEEK 2 | WEEK 3 | WEEK 4 | WEEK 5 | WEEK 6 | WEEK 7 | WEEK 8 | WEEK 9 | WEEK 10 | WEEK 11 | WEEK 12 | WEEK 13 | WEEK 14 | WEEK 15 | WEEK 16 | WEEK 17 | WEEK 18 | WEEK 19 | WEEK 20 | WEEK 21 | WEEK 22 | WEEK 23 | WEEK 24 |
|---|---|---|---|---|---|---|---|---|---|---|---|---|---|---|---|---|---|---|---|---|---|---|---|---|

INSERT PERIOD

▲ **Template 6**: Weekly Graph

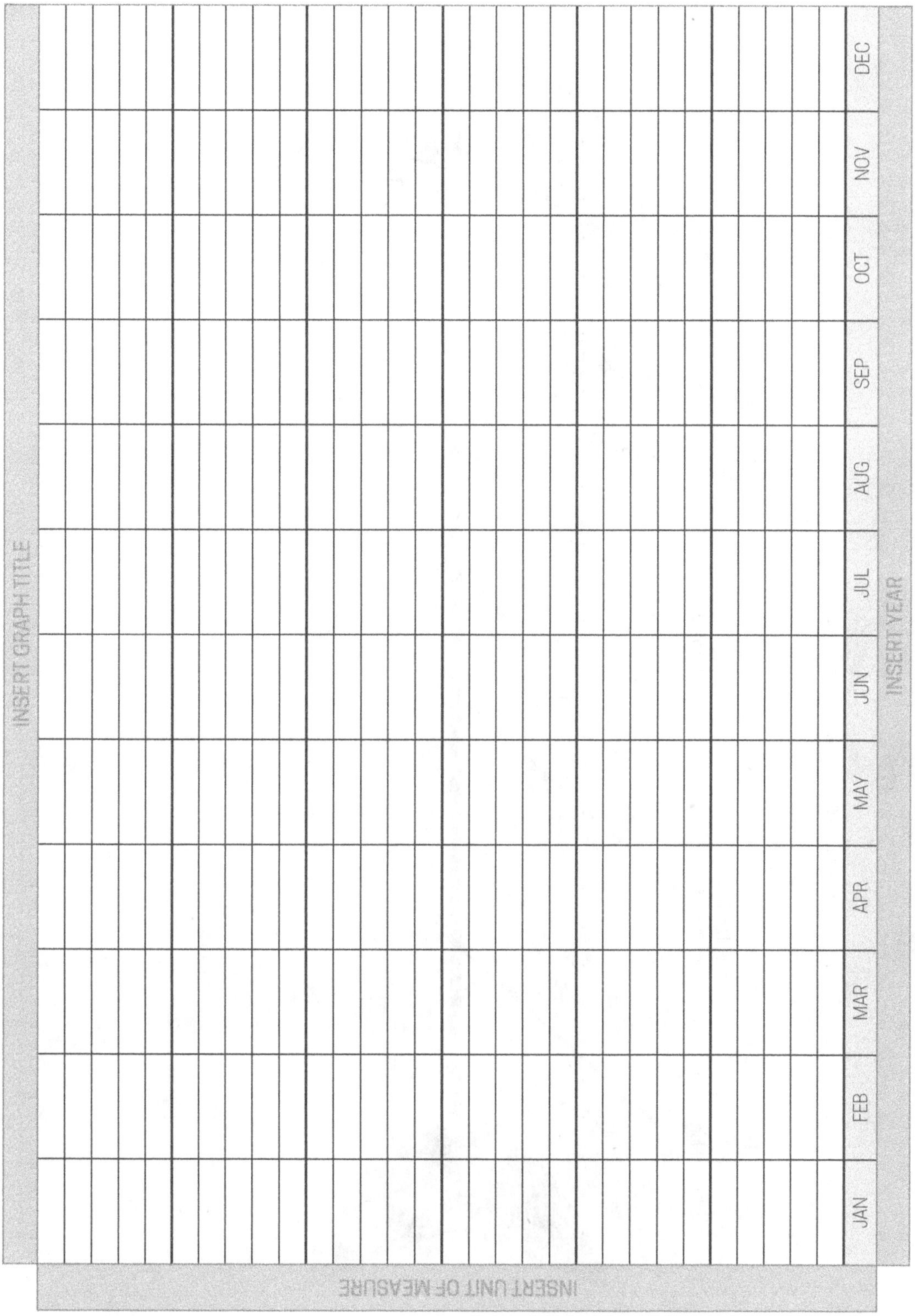

INSERT GRAPH TITLE

INSERT YEAR

| JAN | FEB | MAR | APR | MAY | JUN | JUL | AUG | SEP | OCT | NOV | DEC |
|-----|-----|-----|-----|-----|-----|-----|-----|-----|-----|-----|-----|

INSERT UNIT OF MEASURE

▲ **Template 7**: Annual Graph

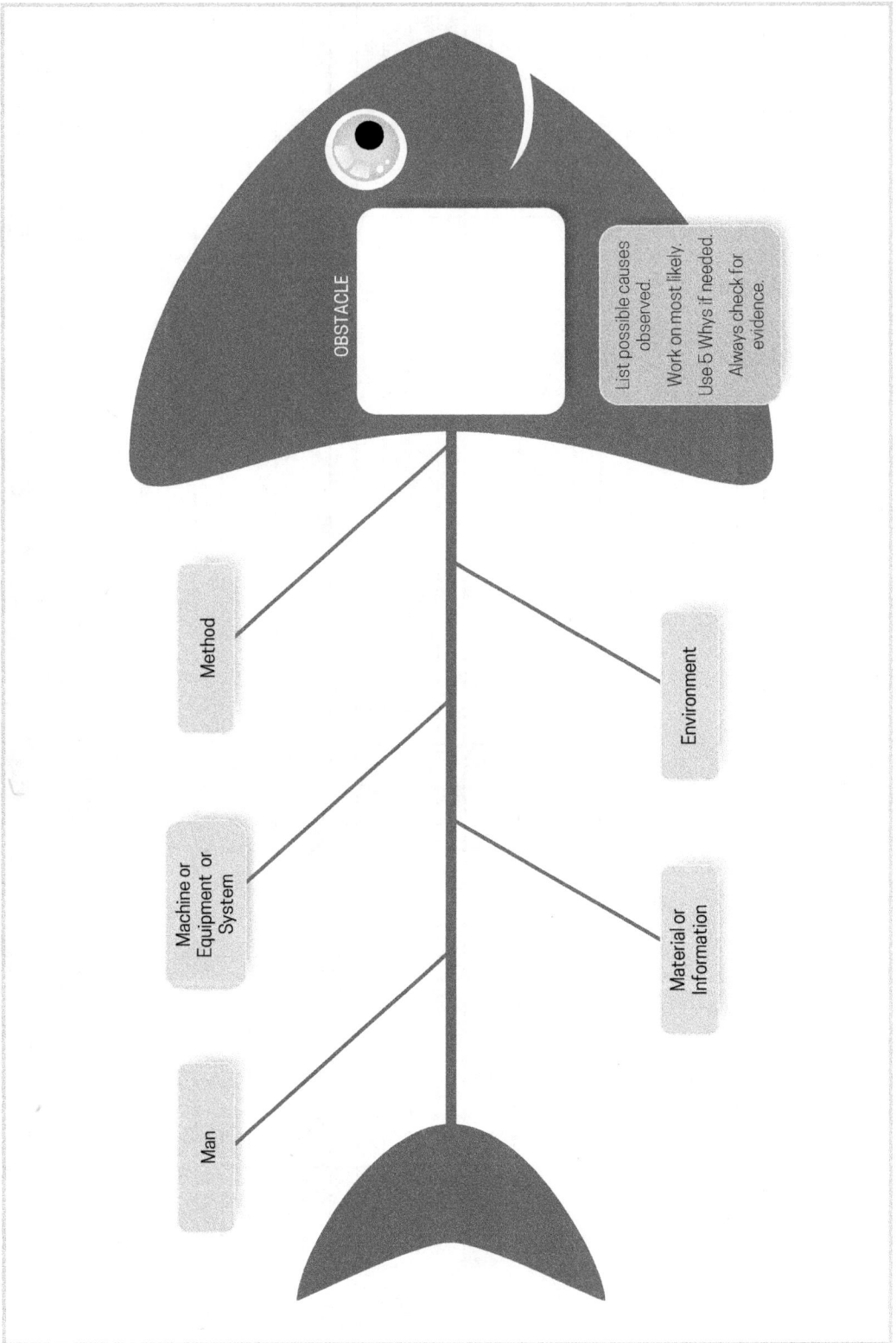

OBSTACLE

List possible causes observed.
Work on most likely.
Use 5 Whys if needed.
Always check for evidence.

Method

Machine or Equipment or System

Man

Environment

Material or Information

▲ **Template 8:** Fishbone Diagram

| OBSTACLE: | WHY? | WHY? | WHY? | WHY? | WHY? | POSSIBLE COUNTERMEASURE: |
|---|---|---|---|---|---|---|
| | | | | | | |

▲ Template 9: 5 Whys

| ACTUAL RESULT | TARGET CONDITION | CURRENT CONDITION | COUNTERMEASURE | OBJECTIVE |
|---|---|---|---|---|
| | | | | |
| | | | | |
| | | | | |

▲ **Template 10:** Countermeasures

| NO. | ACTION | WHO | WHEN | PDCA | ESCALATION |
|-----|--------|-----|------|------|------------|
|     |        |     |      | P D A C |            |
|     |        |     |      | P D A C |            |
|     |        |     |      | P D A C |            |

▲ **Template 11:** Plan

## COACHING KATA

### FIVE KEY QUESTIONS

1. What is the Target Condition?
2. What is the Current Condition?

---turn card over if you have implemented an action---

3. What are the current obstacles preventing you from reaching the Target Condition? Which *one* are you working on?
4. What is the next action or next experiment to be tested? What results do you expect?
5. When can we 'go-see' the change and what we have learned?

## COACHING KATA

### REFLECTION

✓ What was your last action?

✓ What did you expect to happen?

✓ What actually happened? Did it work? If not, why not?

✓ What did you learn from taking this step?

---turn card over and go on with question 3---

▲ **Template 12:** Coaching Kata Cards (Adapted from Rother, 2011)

# WAY FORWARD

Congratulations! You have come a long way. Though you are at the finish line of this book, you are just starting a thrilling new journey. Be brave, dig deep and look ahead knowing that your preparations will stand you in good stead.

Having followed the guidelines set out in *Making a Difference* you now have a good idea of how to map the course of your unique route to Operational Excellence. You have articulated Purpose, established your interim Target Conditions and your North Star. You have perhaps sampled the tools provided and experimented with the processes described, triggering cycles of PDCA. You and your teams may already have crossed a Threshold of Knowledge and achieved a milestone worthy of celebration. Now is a good time to reflect on the progress you have made and to ask the following questions:

- o What will our next challenge be?
- o How will we move forward into a new, potentially uncomfortable, learning zone? A place where patients are better served and resources are better utilised?
- o What obstacles lie between us and the next interim Target Condition?
- o How will we remove the obstacles and make change happen, all the while engaging the minds and hearts of those involved?
- o How will we ensure we stay focused on the North Star—even in challenging times?

If you continue to stay the improvement course and use the information and advice provided in this book to nurture your efforts, you will be rewarded with benefits such as those described in the final chapter. Enjoy the journey and all the best with your own personal growth.

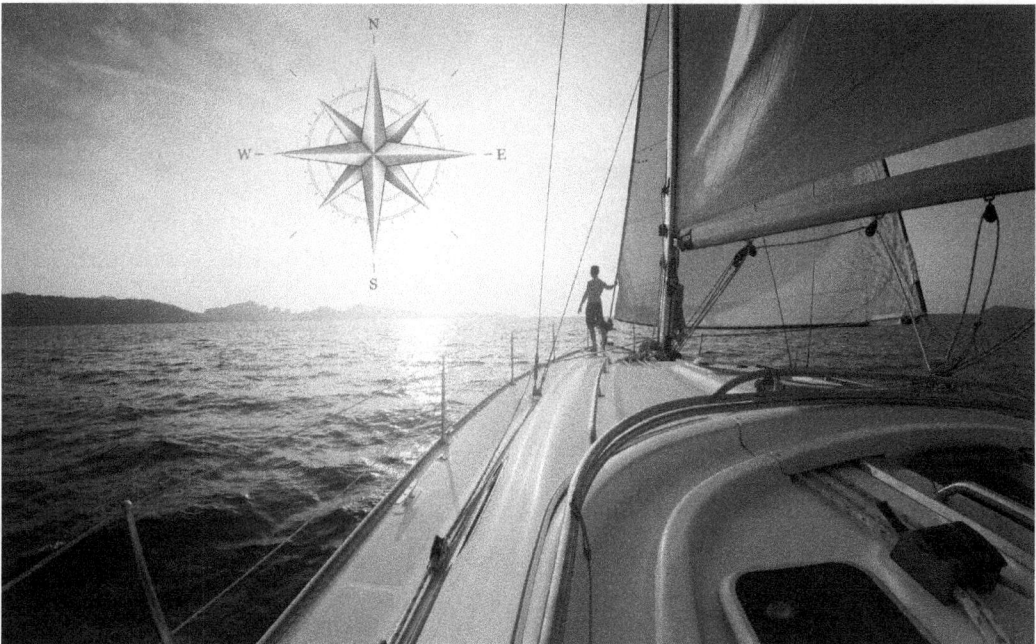

# BIBLIOGRAPHY AND FURTHER READING

Balle, M. & Balle, F. (2009) *The Lean Manager*. Cambridge MA, The Lean Enterprise Institute

Balle, M. & Balle, F. (2014) *Lead with Respect*. Cambridge MA, The Lean Enterprise Institute

Barnas, K. (2014) *Beyond Heroes*. Appleton WI, ThedaCare Center for Healthcare Value

Bicheno, J. (2004) *The New Lean Toolbox*. Buckingham, PICSIE Books

Bicheno, J. & Catherwood, P. (2005) *Six Sigma and the Quality Toolbox*. Buckingham, PICSIE Books

Bossidy, L. & Charan, R. (2002) *Execution The Discipline of Getting Things Done*. London, Random House Business Books

Bragg, S. (2010) *Cost Reduction Analysis*. New Jersey, John Wiley & Sons Inc.

Brinkerhof, R. (2010) *L&D: Business Partner, not Order Taker*. Michigan, BTS

Dennis, P. (2009) *Getting the Right Things Done*. Cambridge MA, The Lean Enterprise Institute

Evans, J. & Lindsay, W. (1996) *The Management and Control of Quality*. New York, West Publishing Company

Faull, N. (1998) *Competitive Capabilities: A novel strategy for re-engineering*. Cape Town, Juta

Ford, D. (1999) *Bottom-Line Training*. Houston, Gulf Publishing Company

Glenday, I. (2007) *Breaking through to Flow*. Ross-on-Wye, Lean Enterprise Academy

Goldratt, E. & Cox, J. (2004) *The Goal*. Great Barrington, The North River Press Publishing Corporation

Grütter, A. (2010) *Introduction to Operations Management*. Cape Town, Pearsons

Harvard Business Review (2008) *Manufacturing Excellence at Toyota*. Boston, Harvard Business School Publishing

Hopp, W. & Spearman, W. (2000) *Factory Physics (2nd Edition)*. New York, McGraw-Hill

Jacob, D., Bergland, S. & Cox, J. (2010) *Velocity*. New York, Free Press

Kotter, J. (2002) *The Heart of Change*. Boston, Harvard Business School Publishing

Liker, J. & Meier, D. (2006) *The Toyota Way Fieldbook*. New York, McGraw-Hill

Liker, J. & Hoseus, M. (2008) *Toyota Culture*. New York, McGraw-Hill

Mann, D. (2005) *Creating a Lean Culture*. New York, Productivity Press

Ohno, T. (1988) *Beyond Large Scale Production*. Portland, Productivity Inc.

Rother, M. & Shook, J. (1999) *Learning to See*. Cambridge MA, The Lean Enterprise Institute

Rother, M. (2010) *Toyota Kata*. New York, McGraw-Hill

Shook, J. (2009) *Managing to Learn*. Cambridge MA, The Lean Enterprise Institute

Sobek, D. & Smalley, A. (2008) *Understanding A3 Thinking*. Boca Raton, Productivity Press

Toussaint, J. (2015) *Management on the Mend*. Appleton WI, ThedaCare Center for Healthcare Value

Worth, J. et al (2012) *Perfecting Patient Journeys*. Cambridge MA, The Lean Enterprise Institute

# INDEX

www.ingramcontent.com/pod-product-compliance
Lightning Source LLC
Chambersburg PA
CBHW061402210326
41598CB00035B/6071